FRANCIS CHADWICK

THE WINDING ROAD OF FAITH

A journey through life, belief and humanity

Arrived Sat. 18 March 2023.
God Led. Exodus. 13:18.

FRANCIS CHADWICK

THE WINDING ROAD OF FAITH

A journey through life, belief and humanity

MEREO
Cirencester

Mereo Books

1A The Wool Market Dyer Street Cirencester Gloucestershire GL7 2PR
An imprint of Memoirs Publishing www.mereobooks.com

The Winding Road of Faith: 978-1-86151-876-7

First published in Great Britain in 2018
by Mereo Books, an imprint of Memoirs Publishing

The address for Memoirs Publishing Group Limited can be found at
www.memoirspublishing.com

The Memoirs Publishing Group Ltd Reg. No. 7834348

The Memoirs Publishing Group supports both The Forest Stewardship Council®
(FSC®) and the PEFC® leading international forest-certification organisations. Our
books carrying both the FSC label and the PEFC® and are printed on FSC®-certified
paper. FSC® is the only forest-certification scheme supported by the leading
environmental organisations including Greenpeace. Our paper procurement policy
can be found at www.memoirspublishing.com/environment

Typeset in 12/18pt Century Schoolbook
by Wiltshire Associates Publisher Services Ltd. Printed and bound in Great Britain
by Printondemand-Worldwide, Peterborough PE2 6XD

DEDICATION

St. Boniface College Warminster was founded by The Rev. James Philipps in 1897. A permanent missionary college was later completed in 1901. From 1948 until its eventual closure in 1969 it served as a postgraduate facility for theological students from King's College London, and has since become part of Warminster School. In 2015 I attended the annual Conference and Retreat for former students in thankfulness for sixty years of ordained ministry.

We had all noticed some of the present Warminster students walking around the College in bright yellow T shirts boldly emblazoned 'Embassy'. Late one evening two of them greeted me and asked if I was one of the 'old monks'; they had heard that a lot of old monks were going to invade their school swimming pool the next day! I told them that this old monk had a wife and asked why they were wearing Embassy T shirts. They explained that Embassy organised English language study centres worldwide and they were busy preparing to welcome some overseas students to their school. They then asked what we old monks were doing. I explained who we were and why we were all there and that

I had been a student in the college from 1954-5. "Wow" one replied, and asked if I had a message for them.

I thought for a moment before answering and told them that this old monk believed that Jesus had come into this world to teach us about the love that God has for each one of us and for all mankind, and that we should all do our best to share that love with one another. It was his reply that impressed me: "That's a lovely message, it's so simple."

I have no idea who those students were, but this book is dedicated to those two young people, and to all who are searching for a faith that can restore meaning and a sense of purpose to our lives, and bring hope to those striving to help free this world from some of the injustice, evil and pain that we human beings seem so capable of inflicting on one another.

ACKNOWLEDGEMENTS

I own an enormous debt to my wife. Together we have achieved far more than either of us could ever have done on our own. I am also especially grateful to the team at Mereo Books for all their hard work and their very thorough attention to detail during their handling of the whole editorial process. I pay tribute to the hundreds of witnesses to Faith who have guided me along my life's journey; my parents and family, my teachers in Wensleydale and Durham, King's College London, and the people of all the parishes in which I have served both at home and abroad. I owe a special tribute to Bishop Jackson and his wife Dorothy, who enabled us to visit churches all over the Diocese of South Rwenzori; also to many local clergy in Tanzania and Rwanda and around our Anglican communities across the world, as well as all our friends in Eastern Europe. Together they have helped weave a rich tapestry of Faith from among the events of our everyday lives, a faith that Jesus himself came to share with the whole of humanity based upon his revelation of God's overflowing love, compassion and mercy for his whole Creation, and for each one of us.

CONTENTS

PART TWO

FOREWORD

In 1991 Francis and Jill entertained Andrew and Naome Nghima in their parish of Stockbridge. Eleven years later they paid their first visit to Africa, and my wife Dorothy and I welcomed them into our own home. That first visit was followed by seven more, during which we developed close contacts with parishes all over the Diocese of South Rwenzori.

FIPHAI (Fighting Poverty with Hands On Initiative) is the project we founded to build the Bishop Jackson School for orphans and poor children in Kasese, which Francis and Jill, with the help of their friends in Devizes, have supported from the outset. They continue to make a big contribution to the building of the potential of children in Africa, and have further contributed to the planting and growing of the Church in Uganda, as well as in Rwanda and Tanzania. It is amazing to hear people talk about Francis preaching and work in Kasese. Over three thousand members of the Church of Uganda, Kitabu Parish, count him as one of their Parish Priests because of his huge pastoral ministry to them and the support they have received over the years.

At the Bishop Jackson Nzerebende Primary School, the presence of Francis and Jill speaks for itself and will do so for very many years to come. It is a visible, living, tangible legacy they have left on the continent of Africa.

The Winding Road of Faith is based upon real life and experience and the need for us to help each other to grow in Faith, and to share God's love as we all travel the road of life together.

(South Rwenzori Diocese)

INTRODUCTION

Life's Journey

Hardly a single cloud darkened the horizon as I stood outside my garden door one hot sultry summer's day. The sky was intensely blue. Two Birmingham Council workmen were busily painting the windows of the flats overlooking our home. Suddenly the heavens delivered a single almighty clap of thunder. As the thunderbolt struck, one of the workmen all but dropped his paintbrush and from the top of his ladder raised both hands in the air and exclaimed, "I believe, Lord!" That was probably the nearest he had ever been to praising the Lord with uplifted arms!

In 1978, somewhere beyond Sochi in the former Soviet Union, my wife and I met a group of Russian Baptists travelling in a minibus. Like us they had stopped to buy roadside honey. Soon we were sharing mugs of coffee brewed over our old camping stove. It was cool, damp and misty in those hills high above the Black Sea coast. My wife, pointing to the sky, tried to explain that it also rained in England; their leader then promptly pulled a Bible from his pocket, and gesturing with folded hands he exclaimed that he also believed in God! The contrast has always remained in my mind, the council workman with no religious background and the believing Russian Baptist, both proclaiming their belief in God.

Montserrat is a famous Spanish monastery built high among the eastern slopes of the Pyrenees. Most tourists make their way by coach, but in the early nineteen-fifties eleven foolhardy students began their assault on foot from the almost inaccessible southern approaches. The last section involved chimney work; searching for a handhold above before looking downwards to search for the next toehold. The view of the near thousand-foot vertical drop to the valley below was daunting. Going back was no option. It was a case of hanging on until one reached the summit. Through life we all need some sort of faith to lead us on our way. We need vision and determination to survive the challenges repeatedly thrown in the path of our human existence. We also need humour and courage and the ability to reflect, but above all the capacity to hang on when the going is tough, something deeper than just saying "I believe Lord" when under assault.

Every human life is a journey, and in mapping my journey I want to share with you the faith that has worked for me. An ordained priest for over sixty years, I have often found that faith challenged both by personal tragedy, but also by the unsuspecting ways in which nearly all the Christian churches seem at times to have clouded the passionate vision that drove Jesus in his attempts to re-unite us with the eternal purpose of our human destiny. Of course there are also occasions in all our lives when our own personal shortcomings have much the same effect, sometimes creating a great deal of haze, and perhaps just once in a while even dense fog.

Travelling has held me in thrall ever since first venturing to

Spain in 1953, and has led me to many Christian communities across the world. All travellers need a map of some sort. 'Roadmaps' are all the current jargon at the moment. We have the somewhat moribund roadmap for peace in the Middle East. We have roadmaps for the Health Service, for education and for nearly every Government department. Why roadmaps, I wonder? Presumably because they are meant to be leading us to where we want to go.

Each one of our lives comes with a roadmap. The starting point is the moment we are born and our destination is death. On that journey we travel along the M1 of all our lives. There are also trunk roads to help us get around, side roads to lead us to where we think we want to go; though sometimes these can turn into loops and bring us back to where we began! There are also roads that are dead ends and roads that carry the sign 'No Entry'.

Roads are very important in all our lives. A former Bishop of Guildford, David Brown, had travelled extensively in the Middle East. He often described himself as a 'Theologian of the Road,' by which he meant the road of life. That road had taken him across the desert. Camel trains crossing the desert are led by a guide who has the roadmap of the sand stored in his memory. Despite the shifting sands, the only way that the next generation can safely cross the desert is if that map is carefully passed on.

Most ordinary people have no great knowledge of theology, nor do many who attend church either! But all people share one thing in common; we are all walking the road of life together. We too need a roadmap stored in our memory to guide us through the sand dunes of life. I believe that God has sent us just such a guide who speaks to ordinary folk in the only sort of language we can all understand; the language of our humanity. Christianity is all about Jesus tramping the road of life beside us, living the life of a human *being* so that he can restore a sense of purposefulness to all our lives' journeys. Beyond all ambition, beyond all our hopes and fears, successes and failures, the one thing we all need to learn in life is how to BE.

Many people today share a sense of the meaninglessness of so much of modern existence, and have an awareness that between the apparent boundaries of birth and death much of life does not seem to make sense. In the pages that follow I want to share with you some of the road that I have trodden, and how the experiences of day-to-day life have led me to a closer awareness of God's purpose in our lives. This awareness has come about not so much through religion or theology but through faith, and more particularly from among the thousands of people who have walked beside me as the roadmap of my life has been etched upon the atlas of my own personal journey. Like most of you this has included doubt, pain, sadness, anguish and frustration; but also wonder, joy, faith and hope.

I begin my story in my own mythical Garden of Eden. Like the first chapters of the book of Genesis it is not written as a factual account; some is imaginative, some written with hindsight, but much more does happen to be true. My dawning awareness of the world was coloured by the extreme beauty of the garden in which I first awoke to life and I have remained an enthusiastic gardener all my life long. This is where my story begins, in the Garden of Eden! But just like Adam and Eve, the day would come when I would have to leave that garden and travel through the gate that led to the rest of the world.

CHAPTER ONE

FAITH IN THE MAKING

The Garden of Eden

I was born in the Garden of Eden – at the age of three! Over the centuries, theologians and philosophers have struggled to find the exact location of the Garden of Eden. I know exactly where it is. It surrounds an old Georgian vicarage in the village of Bilton on the outskirts of the city of Kingston-upon-Hull. That is where the particular roadmap of my life began. My very first childhood memories were those of a wonderful, wonderful garden that happened to have a house in it! *(See Note 1, author's birthplace)*

An inborn sense of reverence for the beauty by which I was surrounded led me to a childish awareness of God's presence. As those early years passed me by I came to believe that it was God who had given me my life, a reality I still affirm; after all it says so in one of the Psalms: 'It is God who has made us and not we ourselves.' The idea that my parents might have played any significant part in it never entered my head! I was also deeply aware of being surrounded by a great deal of love.

There were no rivers bordering the garden like the rivers talked about in the Bible, the ones with those complicated and almost unpronounceable names – Hiddekel, Psion, Gihon and Euphrates. Instead to the north and west there were monstrously high hedges of holly and yew which were trimmed every year at Christmas time. Even after three years when I reached the age of six, they still excluded all sight of the rest of the world. I found it easy to believe in miracles in those days. They were happening all around me. I knew instinctively that I had been born in the Garden of Eden because there were lots of pleasant trees where God could walk in the cool of the day!

To the east of the garden stood a large orchard where the chickens lived. On the southern boundary there was a hawthorn hedge that covered most of a rusting white painted metal fence; rather like those that belonged to my toy farmyard used to prevent the leaden bulls and sheep from straying too far from where they lived beneath the sideboard in the sitting room. Through the gaps one could just catch a glimpse of field upon field stretching interminably towards the horizon.

I also knew exactly where God lived. He lived in Hedon! At night time from my bedroom window in the rambling Georgian vicarage that stood in the middle of the garden I looked with the wonder of a child at the twinkling lights of

Hedon aerodrome as they rushed towards me across the plain of Holderness. I knew that was where God lived because it said so in the Lord's Prayer which I was struggling to learn, 'Our Father who art in Hedon'. I used to think that if I were to walk far enough in that direction I would eventually get to 'Hedon', but it would have taken an eternity for my three-year-old legs to have made it that far, even had I had the courage to climb over the fence in one of those places where the hawthorn had run out. It was the sole barrier between me and the Kingdom of Heaven!

I also knew that 'Our Father' must be God. After all, everybody said so in their prayers in church, most of which seemed to begin 'O God, our Father.' But sometimes you heard people saying, 'Oh God I don't know what I shall do, or My God, or By God or Good God, or By Christ' and other such things. Even my father did occasionally! I was nowhere near so trusting when it came to the 'daily bread bit'; that was delivered twice a week to the back door in a bright red van which bore the name Jackson's of Hull. The van had a long red nose, with lamps stuck on long stalks on either side, by today's standards a most unaerodynamic vehicle (a word I could not then pronounce, nor which had any meaning for me at that moment in time. I don't think I had even heard of it!)

The 'Stop Me and Buy One' man on his tricycle used to come to the back door selling iced lollies wrapped in brightly-coloured triangular packaging. He came every day just after I had had my tonsils removed! That was done by first putting a mat over my face, soaked in ether, or was it chloroform? How life has changed. The 'Wallsy Man' carried all sorts of other delights in the boot of that wonderful machine. I was beginning to think that the Garden of Eden was a bit like Paradise, another big word that I did not then really understand. It wasn't even mentioned in the Lord's Prayer. I had however very quickly grasped what 'temptation' meant – a much more meaningful expression to a child than some of the modern equivalents with which supposedly wise theologians once sought to replace it, like being brought to 'a time of trial'. I used to pronounce it 'twemptation'. By the age of six I thought I knew all there was to know about twemptation, though later years were to prove that I still had much more to learn!

Jackson's and the Stop Me and Buy One man reached the vicarage by the long winding lane that passed between another high hedge and a small beech copse that in springtime was carpeted with bluebells. Earlier in the year it was bordered by large drifts of snowdrops and 'Antinaconites', as I called them. It was the only way to the outside world, and because I was only three the gate at the end was always kept firmly closed. It was an iron gate, painted a fading green with blisters here and there. I would often peer between its bars.

By the time I was six I had discovered which tree in the garden was the tree of the Knowledge of Good and Evil. It stood in the centre of the orchard and took the form of a stately pear tree. In my father's study was a carefully positioned mirror that enabled him to see all that was happening in the orchard. This was long before the days of closed-circuit television, but it served exactly the same purpose and was entirely maintenance free! In the autumn, as the apples and pears began to ripen, my father displayed an extra vigilance in the attention paid to that mirror. Its only purpose, beyond providing surveillance of the chickens, was the expectation of catching any wretched urchins bold enough to scrump fruit from the orchard. The village children never entered the garden from the 'lane that led to the rest of the world'. They were far too worldly wise to do that. They crept through a hole in the holly hedge on the north side of the house!

The pear tree was the easiest of all the trees to climb, and that's where they were most often caught. It was perfectly obvious to me that this was the tree of the knowledge of Good and Evil. The pears, especially at the top of the tree, were very good, the boys who were scrumping them were obviously quite evil. It couldn't possibly have been any other tree! I was by no means so certain of the whereabouts of the Tree of Life, but I eventually settled for a large tree quite near the house and right opposite my bedroom window. That it happened to be dead didn't really matter. It stood like a gigantic lofty scarecrow, festooned with ivy from which six bare branches protruded at most awkward angles.

Two owls spent all their time there guarding that tree both by day and by night. One was adorned by what appeared to be a mortar-board, which lent him an air of grave dignity. He was of all owls the very personification of ultimate wisdom. They guarded the tree rather sleepily during the daylight hours, often hiding among the ivy. But at night-time they flew constantly round and round the tree, making ghostly hooting sounds, successfully deterring anyone who might have been so brave as to approach it. To my mind they were more than a sufficient substitute for the Cherubim and Seraphim described in the book of Genesis, though they didn't possess any flaming swords! Gradually there became no doubt that this was most certainly the Tree of Life. After all, was it not guarded both by day and by night? As the son of the local vicar I was eventually to discover where Hell was located. Beyond the path that led to the church there was a little 'wicked gate' let into the churchyard wall. It looked quite wide to me at that time, though in fact it was very narrow, like the one that is supposed to lead to the Kingdom of Heaven. The path to the 'wicked gate' ran beside another holly hedge in front of which there were large clumps of Montbretia and some giant Astilbes. Once you had passed through the wicket gate it was only a very short distance to the church, which stood just outside the garden, but was still quite a long way from the rest of the world.

I once got very angry with my father, very, very, very angry! I can't now remember why, but I was so angry that I wanted to tell him to 'go to Hell'. I hadn't yet discovered that word, though the idea was firmly implanted not only in my subconscious but in my above conscious as well! In my anger I can still hear myself saying, "Go to.... go to.... go to.... go to church!" That satisfied my anger for the moment, and seemed to me to be the most plausible way of describing Hell of which my six-year-old mind was capable. After all, that was exactly where I wanted my father to go – right out of my sight! The church was the place where I was taken on Sundays to be bored, so it seemed to me at the age of six that it would serve very well indeed as a substitute for the word Hell!

I went to 'Hell' every Sunday, each time walking along the little path that ran beside the hedge, the clumps of

Montbretia and the giant Astilbes. The name 'wicked gate' seemed quite an appropriate description of the way to 'Hell'. I always went with the best of intentions, though the path that led to the wicked gate was paved only with crunchy gravel!

There were two sorts of 'Hell'. Sunday School was the lesser of the two evils. You were given nice coloured attendance stamps, portraying the most unlikely-looking people. Some even had wings. These were called Angels. You used to stick these stamps in a book and if you collected enough you were given a prize at the end of the year at the Sunday School party where you played pass the parcel, musical chairs and a hunting we will go, and chatted up the girls. There were no girls in the Garden of Eden! They came from the rest of the world.

I was already beginning to develop a sort of childish theology. I was learning about God fast and really felt I was beginning to get to know Him, which is what theology is meant to be all about. I knew he existed and that He lived in Hedon, which was across the plains of Holderness where the bright twinkling lights were – everyone knew that there were bright twinkling lights in Heaven. I knew that he was kept company by Angels. The Bible says so, hundreds of them Cherubim and Seraphim, and Archangels too. I think it was David Frost who once called this celestial class distinction! I had discovered 'Hell' (on earth, where it most often is!) I wasn't at all sure that it existed anywhere else, an opinion I still hold. I had learned something too about the Church. I had located the tree of the knowledge of good and evil, and the tree of life. I was beginning to learn about Jesus too, and that he bade me to shine just like the lights that I could see twinkling on the horizon from my bedroom window. By the time I was six I had begun to explore what lay beyond the 'Gate that led to the rest of the World'. Like Alice, I had slipped past it from time to time.

I had also begun to learn a little bit about pain and evil. One Good Friday, coming back from the 'church', as I now called Hell, I remember feeling very strange. It was a beautiful, sunny spring afternoon; the sky was a piercingly bright blue, invaded from time to time by large fluffy white clouds. The garden was full of spring flowers. God was good at creating things, and especially at planting Forget-me-nots and Siberian wallflowers beside the Montbretia and the Astilbes along the path that led from the wicket gate to the back door of our home; they were of course delivered by wheelbarrow, from which I passed them to my father.

The Cross seemed such an outrage to my childish mind. It was all wrong. How could anybody ever think of doing such a thing? And I remember wondering whether there were big fluffy white clouds scudding by on the day that Jesus was crucified. How could anybody be so cruel? But I had already begun to learn just a bit about pain. Running down the path that led to the rest of the world I once fell on the crunchy gravel and cut my lip, which began to bleed profusely. Back in the kitchen my mother promptly fainted! It also hurt quite a bit. Things in life often do hurt quite a bit and we don't always know what to do with pain, either our own or someone else's.

Any sort of faith that doesn't take account of pain is a bit of a travesty, a word added in hindsight. Hindsight is often very useful. However there was one thing that still perplexed me, the whereabouts of Adam and Eve. Nor had

I ever come across snakes in the Garden either, and if I had I wouldn't have expected them to talk, though there were plenty of hedgehogs snuffling among the forget-me-nots and wallflowers. Unlike most children I had a rather literal turn of mind. Abstract thought doesn't readily occur in the early years of childhood, but I possessed a vivid imagination.

I took a menagerie of soft toys to bed with me each night – we often held conversations. Among them was Wilfrid, a rather fetching monkey with a long tail. Somehow he has survived into as old an age as have I, though in the mid nineteen-sixties he was transformed by the addition of a long sleeved black jersey with a clerical collar attached, a pair of grey trousers and a smart little black beret, the work of my mother-in-law. For a while he became a companion for our two young sons, and somehow survived that trauma with the loss of only half an ear. Now in his old age he lives in my wardrobe. Perhaps there's a story hiding there – 'The Monkey, the Bear and the Wardrobe', in which Wilfrid could be introduced to Archibald Ormesby-Gore (Archie) and Jumbo the Elephant, the two soft toys that stayed with John Betjeman to the very end of his life.

I had one very, very close playmate named John. We combined our Hornby clockwork trains and made the most complicated layouts in what was called the Nursery. We transported all our farm animals on open flat trucks and delivered imaginary mail to all the stations. We would play there for hours. One Christmas we left the adults to their own devices and set about oiling the engines and the wheels of all the carriages, the hand-operated points and all the signals with three-in-one oil. We really copped it for nearly ruining the playroom carpet! We also played endless games of Monopoly, and pushed each other up and down the long drive that led to the rest of the world in a wonderful old banger pedal car. Our lives have always come back together; John was best man at our wedding in 1956 and made another speech at our golden wedding. Sadly in later years he developed severe dementia. Because of our shared childhood memories I possessed a unique facility for reawakening the memories of his early days. *(See Note 2, John Naylor)*

I often helped my mother to dust. Much of the furniture was mahogany; I couldn't quite get my tongue round 'mahogany' and I would walk around the house saying 'Mind mummy's best hogany'. My younger brother, nine years my junior, would later stab the mahogany dining table with the handle of his fork; the marks are there to this day. Whenever my father was working in the garden I would be beside him. My fingers very soon turned green, or more accurately rather grubby, with soil more or less permanently lodged behind my fingernails, a condition that still persists! By the age of seven or eight I could recognise many plants from their first true pair of seedling leaves, or by their smell; wallflower, marigold and nasturtium leaves and many more exude a different sweetness all of their own long before they reach maturity. In my dreams I used to sleep in a bed of Geraniums red and Delphiniums blue, curled up like the dormouse. Is it a coincidence that in later years I have filled all my gardens with magnificent Delphiniums, whereas Chrysanthemums have hardly ever had a look in?

At, the age of three plus five, I still had no real idea where I had come from. I thought God had provided my parents especially to look after ME. My mother could not possibly be equated with Eve. For one thing she could never have climbed any of the apple trees in the garden, let alone the tree of the knowledge of Good and Evil! Up to that time life in the Garden of Eden continued to be one full of almost uninterrupted bliss and theological certainty. In adulthood I still believe that God has as much a hand in giving us life as we do. As parents we are only the agents of creation. We only pass on the gift of life which we ourselves have also received from God. The birth process is the moment when we become poised between time and eternity as William Wordsworth illustrates so perfectly in his Ode on the Intimations of Immortality.

INTIMATIONS OF IMMORTALITY

Our birth is but a sleep
and a forgetting.
The soul that rises with us,
our life's star,
hath had elsewhere its setting,
and cometh from afar;
Not in entire forgetfulness
and not in utter nakedness,
But trailing clouds
do we come.

(From the *Ode on the Intimations of Immortality – William Wordsworth*)

There are many who come nearer to God's heart in a garden

than anywhere else on earth, or perhaps when listening to some wonderful music – or reading poetry, but Wordsworth was not blind to the suffering of humanity. Elsewhere he writes:

The budding twigs of May
spread out their fan
to catch the breezy air
and I must think, do all I can
that there was pleasure there.
If this belief from heaven be sent,
if such be nature's holy plan,
have I not reason to lament
what man has made of man?

(*From Lines written in early Spring – William Wordsworth*)

I have often wondered where I would have begun my life's story had I been born in a block of concrete flats, or in a Birmingham slum, or amid the war-torn streets of Berlin or a refugee camp on the borders of Syria. Soon after the start of the Second World War I remember watching the news in our local cinema showing some Nazi soldiers shooting Norwegian civilians; a black patch of blood slowly began staining the white snow and my eyes immediately turned it into bright crimson. I came home as horrified as I had been when the Crucifixion story first hit me on that lovely spring day in the garden.

I have never doubted the truth of my awareness of God's presence in the beauty of my Garden of Eden; I grew up with the privilege of seeing how the world can be when one is aware of God's love and when we share it with one another. I was also learning to take account of all the pain and suffering that seems to have been so much a part of the life of our world from its earliest history. It is only as we begin to grasp the depth of God's love revealed by Jesus' suffering on the Cross that we can begin to make any sense of all the world's pains and sorrows. We can indeed become very near to God's heart in a garden, as I know only too well, but if we fail to find God's heart of love on the Cross and amid all the pain and the suffering of this world we have only discovered half the truth. (More hindsight!) But for now life for me was to continue in my own personal paradise.

I was also beginning to make progress in human relationships. I christened my favourite aunt Auntie Bluebell. She was a regular visitor to the garden and we often picked bluebells together; her real name was Vera and her father manufactured boiled sweets in the town of Elland in the industrial West Riding of Yorkshire. He made me toffee walking sticks and toffee pipes stuffed with coconut tobacco; he also fed me from an enormous seven-pound tin of McVities' assorted chocolate biscuits, of the kind they don't make any longer. My aunt supplied me with ice cream from the luxury of her fridge in the days when fridges were still a novelty, gave me lemonade to drink instead of water, and made me very special 'butterfly buns'; Auntie Bluebell was without doubt my favourite aunt.

One day when she was taking tea with my parents in the garden I said to my father, "Daddy, how old was Auntie Vee when you married Mummy?" I forget now what answer I was given, but my next question was made with very serious intent "Daddy, why didn't you marry Auntie Vee instead of Mummy?" I can still hear myself asking that very impertinent question in my young childish voice. Mothers make you go to bed, scrub your knees, wash your neck and swallow cod liver oil, and spoon medicine down your throat while nipping your nose. To my mind he had made a ghastly mistake!

My father tried to protect me from the outside world and for a whole year he struggled to teach me at home, but with little success; I thought fathers were for playing with and telling stories! I was much more interested in planting seeds than arithmetic. I finally entered Bilton Elementary School just before my sixth birthday. I well remember my first days there and among them the moment in which I disgraced the whole class, and more especially my father. It was when Miss Broadbent invited us all to recite a favourite poem. My thrusting hand went up among a forest of others and was finally selected. I began to declaim the following little ditty.

There was a little man
And he had a little gun
And he shot his little mummy
In her bum, bum, bum!

Horror, convulsions, consternation and a ghastly puce complexion seized the Headmistress amid the chaos of unbridled childish laughter that invaded the whole classroom. Miss Broadbent, flushed and shocked to the core, demanded who had taught me such a rude rhyme. "Please Miss" I said, "My dad taught it me." My dad happened to be the local vicar and Chairman of the School Governors! That was not the only time I caused my parents embarrassment.

Just before the outbreak of the Second World War we left the Garden of Eden. We weren't ejected. We just left. Beforehand I recall my father and his closest friend, my playmate John's father, pacing up and down among the trees of the garden with deep anxiety written all over their faces. Both had served in the First World War, the war to end all wars, a phrase much on our lips as we observed the centenary of its outbreak in 2014. The last time I moved through the gate that led to the rest of the world was in May 1939 in a taxi headed for the Yorkshire Dales. My father had been appointed the vicar of Coverdale.

The Yorkshire Dales

Coverdale is one of the most beautiful of all the Yorkshire dales. In 1939 the narrow winding tarmac road from Middleham only reached as far as the little hamlet of Woodale nestled at the foot of Great Whernside; there it turned into a rough mountain track frequented by Highland cattle. It was still very isolated; no electricity, no mains drainage, no buses and few telephones. However the calm of our first night was shattered by a loud procession of motor bikes engaged in a rally that led them to the head of the dale before descending to Kettlewell via Park Rash, a steep hill with a one in four gradient and two fiercely steep double bends. I was to walk that road many a time; then it was a rough track, now it is tarmac all the way.

My younger brother was born three months after our arrival, the first child to be born in Coverham Vicarage for sixty years. My mother was attended by Nurse Shepherd, the local midwife, who 'shepherded' him safely into the world just after midday on August 2nd. It was then that I finally realised how I myself had been born!

Coverdale is real James Herriot country and he may well have visited some of the farmers in my father's Parish. One farmer, Dawson Yeoman could well have appeared in 'All creatures Great and Small'; he always wore a felt hat shaped by the grease of untold years spent in both the cowshed but also as an accompaniment to his Sunday best! He was Churchwarden of the little church of St. Botolph, Horsehouse. St. Botolph is a little-known patron saint of travellers, and Horsehouse was once on the main packhorse routes from the south of England to Northumbria. It lies at the foot of Deadman's Hill, where highwaymen lay in wait to seize and sometimes kill unwary travellers. One Sunday Dawson mislaid his collecting bowl. Being a good Yorkshireman he decided he must get the 'brass' in somehow; what better than his old felt hat? My father turned to face him as he came up the aisle and had no alternative but to receive the greasy hat, raise it for a blessing, and place it on the altar.

In the countryside the Harvest produce was often auctioned and the money given to a local hospital. This had always taken place in the school, but during the war years the church was the only public building which was 'blacked out' other than the pub. Dawson looked around the church, solemnly removed the old Bible and began hammering the lectern soundly as he sold the apples and cabbages. Half way through the proceedings he called for a break; he left the church, and came back a few moments later with a lamb. Who says church can't be entertaining? This sort of thing still takes place in African villages to this day, where chickens sometimes stray around the feet of the choir, and the odd goat is occasionally brought into church to be auctioned.

During the war country families were encouraged to keep pigs; the two we shared with a neighbour inhabited a fenced-off section of the garage, a stable in bygone days. They could be fed on almost anything. No one breathing down your neck from Brussels in those days. Jim Dawson, the local 'pig sticker', was our next door neighbour; his only problem was that he was only allowed to kill half a pig at a time!

My mother was a very quiet unassuming lady-like soul and it sometimes fell to her lot to feed the pigs when my father was away in London. She had been struggling for half an hour trying to persuade James and John (the sons of Boanerges) to remove their trotters from the fence so she could tip their swill into their trough. But would they move? It was then that the local butcher appeared on the scene delivering the weekly meat ration. "Oh, Mr Pickersgill" my mother said plaintively, "Can you help me? I've been trying to feed these pigs for the last half hour and can't get anywhere near them."

"A think a can do summat about that, give me t'bucket," said Mr Pickersgill. Then, swearing like a trooper, he growled, "Gr'up you silly old bastards!" The pigs rushed to the end of their run. He tipped the swill over the fence into their trough and then turned to my mother and said in his best Oxford English, "There Mrs Chadwick, you'll know how to do it next time won't you!"

Despite the war there was a certain romance about life in the Dales. Coverdale had no mains drainage; after the war, when that all became a memory, Jos Watson complained that his rhubarb had never been the same since! There was only one phone housed in the local Post Office and village shop; everyone knew everyone else's business. When my father lay dying in January 1949 I would phone our nearest relatives from that shop. You dialled '0' for what were called trunk calls, but before being connected the local operator would first ask how my father was. Calls lasted three minutes. How life has changed. A mobile phone wasn't even science fiction in those far-off days. Tommy Handley drove the one and only bus, which went twice a week to Leyburn, once on a Friday to the market, and on Saturday evening to the local cinema. I think it was Pathe News who showed that report of Nazis shooting those innocent Norwegian civilians as they tried to escape. Before Christmas we went carol singing; such was the stillness of the dale that from the village of Carlton we could sometimes hear the chapel singers in the little hamlet of West Scrafton the other side of the river Cover, over a mile away. We always finished with mince pies and green ginger wine at Agglethorpe Hall.

Coverdale was a place where you could roam the hills in total freedom, your feet free to follow charted or uncharted paths through the bracken and heather; all the while the haunting cry of the Curlew and the Peewit floated above you, or a startled grouse would shout *'grrback, grrback'* as it flew away. So far I had grown up without the chatter of much accumulated theology and philosophy, and in the hills you can welcome thoughts as uncharted as your footsteps, just as they burst into your mind. That is a freedom that was to prompt subsequent travels across Europe, and in later years around the globe, and it also helped develop a rather enquiring mind.

My close friend John often came to Coverdale to escape the bombing in Hull. We walked all over those hills together, and to this day I could still find all the tracks we used to follow, though some of today's sheep will have made many new paths by now. Hill sheep are interesting creatures. They pass on their knowledge of the hills to their offspring, just as the camel drivers pass on the 'map of the sand' to the next generation of camel drivers.

John and I often played at trying to dam one of the small tributaries of the river Cover by building a barrier of stones, twigs and small branches of dead wood, and whatever turfy stuff we could lay our hands on. Diverting the flow to one side we built quite a well-engineered barrier, only blocking the final section at the last minute to create a sizeable reservoir. Of course the flow of the stream finally prevailed, but we would succeed for a while.

In later life I have often used this childhood memory as a parable. We sometimes resist, and on occasion even block the paths of the Holy Spirit by which God tries to surround us with his love, causing us to lose our way along the path of our life's journey. The Church has also at times erected barriers; events like the Crusades and the appetite for prestige and power which overcame some of the Mediaeval Popes, all blocking Jesus' vision of the Kingdom of God. But just as my friend John and I tried to dam that little stream on its way to the river Cover and never quite succeeded, the Holy Spirit is never thwarted. The water in that stream always found a way to continue, sometimes creeping round the side, sometimes underneath, but mostly by going over the top. So does the Holy Spirit when we get in his way.

The local schoolmaster, Mr Wilson, was not one to be crossed. He maintained a strong discipline in the elementary school of which he was Head. He stood no nonsense, and the ruler was always at hand. Any attempts to flout his authority met the same fate as our attempts to block that little stream. At the age of eleven I won a scholarship to Yorebridge Grammar School in Wensleydale, a distance of some fifteen miles from my home.

Every Monday three of us boarded the 'Wensleydale Express' from Wensley to Askrigg and for three years during term time I lived in Hardraw Vicarage with the vicar and his wife and ten-year-old daughter. From there I still had to walk one and a half miles to the market town of Hawes to catch a number 26 United Bus to Askrigg. Half way to Hawes I used to meet two evacuee girls from Sunderland who were much more to my liking than the vicar's daughter, a rather mousy girl, who only began to attend the grammar school a year later. I walked with her that first day, but afterwards I strode ahead to meet the twins!

The girls did domestic science on Thursdays, so the return journey to Hawes was brightened by sampling their culinary efforts. The boys learned woodwork skills from Mr Winsby, a master carpenter, who taught us how to stroke a piece of wood to discover the flow of the grain; he showed us all the mysteries of furniture making, dovetail and mortise joints, and how to make glue in an old cast iron glue pot. He left with me a love of wood and trees which has remained ever since. Mr Shorter, the Headmaster, was just as much a disciplinarian as Mr Wilson, but we did all learn to work. School dinners were very basic because of the war, but very balanced and healthy, and we all had milk in the morning.

After fifty-eight years one member of the form that assembled for the first time at Yorebridge in 1941 arranged a reunion. It's quite a challenge trying to recognise former classmates whom you haven't seen for nearly sixty years, but you somehow take up just where you left off. I even met the twins! I conducted a short service in Askrigg parish church. Yorebridge has now become a local primary school. We continued to meet for several years until overtaken by old age.

Durham

After three years at Yorebridge I began a new life at Durham School, where the Headmaster was a tall, lanky clergyman by the name of Canon H.K. Luce. He stood a full six foot three inches, his back was somewhat arched and he possessed large protruding front teeth. Wretched boys that we were, we indecorously christened him 'Teeth, Tool and Trousers', the middle epithet deriving from his somewhat Darwinian attempts to inform us about the facts and the origins of life, and how to look after ourselves in that particular department. For his sins he was also the Examining Chaplain to the Bishop of Birmingham, Ernest Barnes. With what extraordinary titles the Church of England dignifies some of its clergy. I mean just how do you examine a Bishop? He had certainly examined Bishop Barnes' controversial book *The Rise of Christianity*, which had so shocked the orthodox wings of the conservative church by doubting the Resurrection and denying miracles and the existence of Angels. *(See Note 3, Bishop Barnes)*

Part of my education in the history Sixth Form was a monthly visit with three other senior boys to the historic deanery of Durham Cathedral. The then Dean, Cyril Argentine Allington, a former headmaster of Malvern and Eton, used to welcome us into the large deanery drawing room by throwing peppermints at us. The Dean was a very keen cricketer, and should you fail to catch them you were in deep disgrace. In the early months of the year it was heavily scented by two enormous bowls of hyacinths, each containing some twenty or more blooms. Ostensibly our business was to learn more history, but beside his history of Europe the Dean was also a prolific writer of detective stories and poetry. On most occasions we were treated to excerpts from his latest novel and once were given the task of reviewing some poems. Only after we had expressed our very honest opinions did he inform us that he was responsible for all of them. The best history lesson I ever received was when my classmates were all sick; the Dean gave me a personal tour of the whole cathedral from the depths of the crypt to the clerestories high above the nave.

On one visit we had copies of Dante's Inferno thrust into our hands, most of them in the original Italian. I was invited to read, my friend Michael to translate. And then there followed a discussion on Angels. Each of us was asked in turn whether or not we believed in their existence. Our answers were far reaching; from denial to acceptance to fence sitting. I think by then I had only one leg over the fence. The following Sunday in Durham Cathedral our discussion on angels was the subject of the Dean's sermon addressed to all the two hundred Durham School boys who used to attend 'Abbey' once a month.

Another Sunday we were treated to high drama. The retired Bishop of Gloucester, Bishop Headlam, was preaching. After only moments in the pulpit he coughed out his false teeth! The pulpit stood a full twelve feet above the nave; fortunately for the bishop, his dentures bounced off the pulpit rail back into the pulpit. For nearly two minutes one bishop disappeared entirely from sight, during which time two hundred Durham School boys were convulsed by uncontrollable laughter. We were laughing so hard that we were in pain. Our masters were marching up and down the aisle trying to restrain us, but inwardly they were struggling to control the pain in their own stomachs. Eventually the Bishop reappeared, his teeth sorted, and blandly began to read from the paragraph where he had stopped with no acknowledgement of the debacle that had overtaken him. Had he only made a joke he could have had our rapt attention for the rest of his sermon.

Many years later in the 1970s I heard this tale being recounted as an after-dinner story. The speaker, whom I knew well, had no idea that it had really happened. I said to him: "Archie, that's no story. I was there." I gave him a more complete account than the one with which he was now familiar. I have always felt that this is a perfect illustration of how the Gospels came into being. At first all the events of Jesus' life were passed on by word of mouth as stories. In the telling some of the details were no doubt lost, while others that never took place may have been added to enforce the writer's purpose in the telling; but hidden behind every story lies an important specific event that triggered the writers of the Gospel to record them in the first place.

In a fascinating book about how the North Sea trading

routes affected the development of northern Europe Michael Pye tells the story of the 'Gospel according to Heliand', which means Saviour. It describes how all four Gospels moved away from the Mediterranean to a colder northern world, where years were measured in winters. It likens Jesus' disciples to the band of men chosen by a chieftain who assembled his warriors with the expectation of personal loyalty. They were enrolled to stand by their Lord and die with him if necessary. Zacharias brings up John the Baptist as a 'warrior companion' for Jesus; Mary becomes a woman of the nobility and Joseph the equivalent of a noble chief. After the Crucifixion Jesus rises from a barrow, like those at Stonehenge, not a rock-hewn tomb. The Saxon world and the Gospel story begin to merge to meet the needs of their contemporary world. The purpose of doing so was to assist the chieftain in the conversion of the pagan world around him by using parables they would understand, related to the way that their own world was then ordered. Much later in Celtic Britain St. Cuthbert, preaching to the inhabitants of Northumbria, won their hearts by adopting the same principle; in contrast, when Paulinus was sent by the Pope to Canterbury he met stiff local opposition in his attempts to impose the worship of the Western church.

I have led worship at Heddington Church near Calne for over twelve years. At their Carol Service in 2017 I first heard the Huron Carol. Like the 'Gospel according to Heliand' it was used to spread the Christmas story in the native language of the local Indians living around the shores of Lake Huron where my wife and I visited a Canadian priest and his wife in 1992. *(See Note 4, Michael Pye)*

Our English master at Durham was one Major Le

Fleming. He introduced us to the wonders of Edmund Spencer and Geoffrey Chaucer but in a very personal way. Camel Kershaw (hump backed of course) and myself were the most senior members of the English Sixth. One of our tasks was to select readers from among our classmates. Some stanzas of Edmund Spencer's Faerie Queene represented what then just about passed as pornography for adolescent boys. We saw one such stanza looming on the horizon and duly deputed a younger member of the class who possessed the squeakiest breaking voice to read the following passage. It was a verse from the *Bower of Bliss* and describes how Sir Guyan, an unsuspecting Knight, stumbles upon maidens bathing in the nude. The voice, already sounding extremely embarrassed and agitated, began to croak even more effectively when the following stanza arrived.

The wanton Maidens him espying stood
Gazing at his unwonted guise;
Then th'one her selfe low ducked in the flood,
Abasht, that her a stranger did a vise,
But th'other rather higher did arise
And her two lily paps aloft displayed,
The rest hid underneath him more desirous made!

The Headmaster kept chickens and ducks on the palace green below the Chapel. Among them was his pet guinea fowl. It frequently used to make its rather raucous and continuous honk just outside our classroom door. One day it died, and the major produced a parody on Wordsworth which has stayed with me all my life long, and has given that bird an air of immortality.

> *ELEGY TO A DEPARTED GUINEA FOWL*
> *She dwelt outside my classroom door*
> *beneath the Chapel Hill,*
> *a fowl I really did abhor*
> *and often wished to kill*
> *A saw's unceasing tuneless whirr,*
> *a wheel in need of oil*
> *were melody compared to her*
> *incessant loud turmoil.*
> *But now that wretched fowl is dead,*
> *the earth is once more free*
> *of piercing call and fateful tread*
> *And oh! The difference to me!*

So I left Durham School in 1949 with a passion for history, a knowledge of the English classics, and some slight poetic ability; all acquired against the background of chapel and cathedral worship, and accompanied by a radical questioning of Christian truth fostered by the examining chaplain to the Bishop of Birmingham, and with a now rather ambivalent opinion of the angels in which I had once firmly believed.

The Industrial West Riding

We often travel through life without giving much thought to God. Some of us are born with an innate consciousness of his presence, but in our youth all sorts of other thoughts chase across one's mind. We sometimes need a jolt to rediscover that presence. I suffered just such a jolt with the sudden and entirely unexpected death of my father at the age of 51. Life was suddenly transmuted from the beauty of the Yorkshire Dales to the then smoky grime of the industrial town of Elland in the West Riding of Yorkshire, where my uncle, like his father and grandfather before him, had manufactured Joseph Dobson's boiled sweets.

Later that year I would be called to begin life as a National Serviceman in the King's Royal Rifles, another steep learning curve and a rather formative step along the roadmap of my life. A vicarage is a tied house and has to be vacated within three months. It fell to my lot to deal with my father's estate, the taxman and the insurance policies and to organise our removal to a flat beside the sweet works in Elland, as well as completing my studies in preparation for Higher School Certificate (the equivalent of today's A levels). No way could my mother have been left on her own in what was then still a very remote part of the Yorkshire Dales.

My father had always been full of fun, sometimes embarrassingly so. In front of other boys he would call me his 'darling son', causing me considerable distress. On my returning home from school he would fly the Union Jack out of the bathroom window for the entire village to observe. He could be forgiven for this perhaps, as his own mother had established that particular tradition. He was an enthusiastic gardener and we enjoyed tramping the hills together.

When he died, my first thought was to care for my mother and younger brother, but I do remember shedding a tear or two when I went to complete the pruning of the raspberry bed on which we had both been working before he left to conduct a funeral service on a bitterly cold January morning in 1949. He collapsed at the graveside and suffered a severe cerebral haemorrhage before even completing the committal. I had been hand-pumping the bellows of the old pipe organ beforehand and someone came to the vestry to warn me of what had happened. This was not only a severe shock to us all but caused the bereaved family equal distress. It was a full hour before the local Methodist minister arrived to complete the interment. My father died four days later.

The rector of Spennithorne, Joe Jory, my father's closest friend, made my brother welcome in his own home until after the funeral. During that time he built him a wonderful toy garage. When Tony eventually returned home I remember my mother telling him he didn't look very well and asking if he had been sick. He whispered very meaningfully, "You know why I look like I do." We must never underestimate young children's emotions; they are quite comparable to our own, but our mother was in a state of extreme stress.

My first encounter with death came very early in life and in a very personal way. My immediate response was to carry on living with the same sense of fun with which my father had approached life. Somehow, once faith has helped you come to terms with death, you become more free to live your remaining life to the full. I had sat through many of my father's church services and listened to a fair number of his sermons as well. There is not much that I remember, except for two very significant remarks. The first: 'There wouldn't be a decent novel worth reading if there were no sin in the world.' No Sherlock Holmes, Poirot or Foyle's War. Just think about that. But the second is much more profound: 'No one can take all the world's problems upon their own shoulders; there is only one person who can do that.' That is something we all need to take to heart when all the troubles of the world bear down upon us.

My time in Elland was brief. There was much to be done in our new home; putting up the old-fashioned metal curtain rails that I had already removed from the vicarage, and considerable painting and decorating. My DIY skills increased by leaps and bounds aided by my carpentry skills learned at Yorebridge. There was no garden, so I took over the one adjoining All Saints church. Throughout this time I continued my studies from home. Durham School sent me a study programme which included submitting essays by post. I returned to Durham for the last two weeks before taking my exams. Despite all these difficulties I passed with credit in English and History, but failed my French subsidiary paper by only a narrow margin on only one paper. In those days this debarred you from receiving the Higher School Certificate itself, but I was sent the details of the marks for all my papers, which were sufficient to present for University entrance.

Life was not easy in the Industrial West Riding, which was still very black and grimy from all the mill chimneys, a far cry from the Garden of Eden. I joined the church choir in the parish where my father had been a curate, and the local youth club, a branch of the Anglican Young People's Association (AYPA), which was eventually to play a very formative part in my early life. Within six months of our arrival I was to journey to Winchester to begin my National Service.

National Service

On the 20th day of October 1949 an eighteen-year-old youth boarded a train for London embarrassingly clad in a grey school blazer trimmed with bright green piping, the breast pocket emblazoned by a bright Durham School badge. Slung over his arm was a navy blue belted gabardine raincoat. What few belongings he possessed were stuffed into a small old-fashioned leather suitcase of the sort now mostly exhibited in Museums. After the Yorkshire Dales, travelling on the London underground was like trying to solve a gigantic cryptic crossword, but kind people guided me to Waterloo Station. After boarding a train bound for Winchester hauled by a Western Class steam locomotive, later that evening, together with four other new recruits, I was bundled into the back of a 15cwt Army truck and delivered to a barrack room at Bushfield Camp, a mile or so along the Southampton road.

I shall never forget that first night. Half of those meeting for the first time in that barrack room were Saaf Londoners, barrow boys and the like; the other half were from grammar or public schools, there to do their basic training before being posted to the Royal Army Education Corps. Both groups were embarrassed, neither daring to make the first move to go to bed; we because we had brought pyjamas, they because they had not! I had mostly up to that time been in the habit of saying a few prayers beside my bed last thing at night. At school in Durham the prefect in charge of the junior dormitories used to ball 'Pray!' like a military command. We all knelt by our beds; I doubt God heard many prayers. But you certainly don't kneel by your bed in an army barrack room at the age of eighteen among total strangers; instead my prayers were said silently between the sheets.

The next day I became 22189049 Rifleman Chadwick, Sir! That's a number I remember to this day. In the morning the Commanding Officer of 'C' Company, Major Martin Charteris, came to address us. In 1952 Princess Elizabeth appointed him her private secretary and after her accession to the throne he continued as assistant secretary until becoming her permanent Private Secretary in 1972. After his address we were all marched to the Regimental barber.

Among our company was a certain Rifleman Day whose hair when combed forward reached to his navel. The barber, a wickedly gleeful expression creasing his face, seized his largest pair of 'shears' and snipped it off right to his temple. Never did you hear anything like the barrage of F words that rang out of that mouth; they remind me of a young girl who once came into the local Oxfam shop in Devizes where my wife works as a volunteer. The girl's boyfriend rang her mobile asking where she was to which she responded, "I'm in the effing Oxfam Shop and I effing well don't know what to effing well buy." Only the word was not just effing. The shop was reduced to silence. The lady dowagers of Devizes present raised their eyebrows in utter horror, their faces assuming the inimitable variety of expressions that so often crease the wrinkles of the Duchess of Downton Abbey when she raises hers.

My time in the Army brought me up with a bump

against another world that I had not really encountered before; four-letter words (and longer) which had never been part of my own personal vocabulary; dirty stories, some of which were just plain funny, some uncompromisingly filthy, and much much more. I can still hear our platoon corporal, Corporal Scott, saying as he taught us how to strip down a machine gun: "Now lads, first of all you remove the body-locking pin, more commonly known as 'ladies delight'. Then…" It wasn't long before we had the Bren reduced to all its constituent parts. I rather suspect that modern weaponry has changed beyond all recognition, though perhaps not the platoon corporal.

Winchester was to play a formative roll in my younger pilgrimage. It was then a much more restful city than it is today, full of churches that had not yet been amalgamated. I tried them all, looking for the one with the best youth club and the prettiest girls! This at the time turned out to be the rather Anglo-Catholic church of Holy Trinity. After three months square-bashing at Bushfield Camp (now returned to field and pasture), half our company was posted to Walker Lines Camp in Bodmin in Cornwall to be trained for the Education Corps. I wasn't really cut out to be a sergeant at that time, so after another three months I found myself back once more in the city of Winchester.

Five of us arrived at Winchester station one brisk March morning. Fired by youthful enthusiasm, we had boarded the overnight milk train and arrived a day early. We decided to spend an unofficial night in the YMCA. The following morning we were still ahead of schedule, but at that time Red Caps patrolled the city streets. Knowing that fatigues were the most likely outcome of our reporting before 1400 hrs, we decided to lose ourselves. Where better place than the Cathedral? Surely we would be free from the arm of the law amid its graceful columns. Throughout history many people have sought sanctuary in cathedrals and churches.

Winchester Cathedral is one of the largest in Europe with a long history, and is dedicated to St. Swithun, whom Thomas Hood describes in his Ode to St Swithun as a 'Sloppy Saint'. Trying to look interested in the stained glass windows and artifacts, we were approached by the Head Verger, a robust middle-aged man with a handlebar moustache. "H'a knows what you lads h'ar on" he says "Until six months hago h'a was Har. S.M. of t'Ampshires and I as this 'ere Cathedral hon parade every morning wiv all t' chairs standing to attention in fwees! Good luck to you mates. I won't split on yer." The Hampshire regiment were the deadly rivals of the Green Jackets and shared the adjoining barracks.

Back once more in a barrack room of the old historic Winchester Depot, I plucked up my courage and knelt beside my bed to pray for a few minutes. There were guffaws at first, but after that my every action was subject to close scrutiny. It had already become public knowledge that I attended one of the local churches in the city, what's more getting up at 7.00 on a Sunday when they all had a lie in. After a week or two, all was accepted. I played ball and only took two or three minutes, during which time everyone was silent. Anyone speaking during those three minutes might have run the risk of being thrown out of the barrack room window; had I been half an hour it would have been me who would have ended up on the Parade Ground.

Quite early on, a barrow boy from Saaf London with no

church background whatever came up to me and said "Ere, you goes ter church, tell me, what's gonna 'appen ter me when I dies?" I forget now just what answer I gave all those years ago to the question that we all ask at some moment in our lives. I wasn't a vicar then, nor at that particular moment did I have any intention of becoming one. But that young man and his question have lived with me all my life long. As a teenager I had perforce on occasion to make up a foursome at Mothers Union whist drives in my father's country vicarage. Having become rather skilled in the art of bridge I not infrequently won the first prize. That more often than not consisted of a jar of my parents' home-bottled gooseberries that I had helped both pick and top and tail. No way would I ever become a vicar! But I did, and largely because of my time in the Army.

The Christian faith above all else is God's message given by Jesus concerning life and death and all that happens to us on the road between the cradle and the grave. Every single human being shares this experience, and we all have to learn how to handle the time between these two momentous events. We may never fully understand all that happens along the way any more than we are able to explain how God is God, or why the Universe is as it is, even though our knowledge of its structure is increasing by leaps and bounds. But we are often given glimpses.

Travelling by steam train in the earlier part of the twentieth century possessed an air of romance all of its own; we have never quite fallen out of love with the steam engine. The departure and arrival times of trains in the Bradshaw's railway timetable of those days, so beloved by Michael Portillo, were always prefixed by the letters DV (Deo

Volente – God willing) a precaution that those granted the franchise of running our modern timetables could well take to heart. As you looked out of the window you could often see evidence of the engine pulling you along in the form of smoke and steam. Just occasionally if you let down the leather strap and popped your head out, you might even glimpse the engine in full majesty as it rounded a steep curve. Modern travellers are denied that luxury.

In a blinding moment of certainty some people are occasionally confronted by the 'Engine Driver' of all our lives. St. Paul experienced just such a moment on the road to Damascus; I have twice shared a similar sort of experience. As time goes by the immediacy of such moments is dulled and you remain woefully human as you continue your struggle with all life's challenges. But the memory of them remains and comes back to haunt you. Like everyone else you have to content yourself with the gleanings of what is left behind, but recalling such moments continually strengthens you as you pursue your life's journey.

Army life soon adopted a rather civilian pattern. I dumbfounded my fellow soldiers by planting marigolds and cornflowers along a strip of land adjoining the barrack room. My gardening instinct was not to be defeated by such unlikely surroundings! Having decided I lacked any military ambitions whatsoever, the Army in its wisdom found me a job in the Orderly Room; I was employed as the documents clerk and learned to type fast and furiously with two fingers and was placed in charge of the large messy Gestetner machine. No computers or word processors in those days. One of my duties was to complete a new recruit's record, Army form B2562, I think. Almost the first questions asked was, Religion? Most answered C of E; one young recruit, however, misheard his predecessor and answered H of E. I made a mental note: Hell or elsewhere!

My presence in the orderly room must have had some effect. In the winter months it was heated by an old coke stove and became rather stuffy, with a mixture of coke fumes married to cigarette smoke and the vapour of strong language. One winter's day the ORQMS, Sergeant McCue, turned round and said "Let's have half an hour without swearing now for old Chad".

*****

It was then I met my first serious partner, as one would call them these days, in the church Youth Club of course, another branch of the AYPA. Being of a more serious nature at that time I found this to be an almost religious experience. I believed that the struggle against one of the 'sins' listed in my confirmation prayer manual, and often attributed to single sex education would now be over! Of course other temptations took its place. "How's she in bed, mate?" I was asked. My new-found army friends just couldn't understand my not having slept with her. Who says modern youth is more promiscuous?

This experience was all mingled with a growing sense of the Divine; I thought Zoe was also divine! With ordination now in mind I had begun to study New Testament Greek. Zoe is in fact a Greek name and comes from their word for life. For me, life had finally begun! There is nothing quite like the first kiss, in this case one of four, each bolder than the last. I kept the lipstick on my clean handkerchief for over a week. The kisses were given, and more importantly, received, beneath the gloomy light of a lamp post that stood some distance from number 23 West End Terrace. It was too dangerous for Zoe to be escorted to her door by a soldier!

Though she was 19, her father had placed her in the care of the two maiden ladies who had earlier run the little private school from that address, at which Zoe herself had been a pupil. She was chaperoned with extreme vigilance. Later we became more emboldened and hid beneath the garden wall that adjoined the garage, where the farewell kisses soon became canoodles. By some grapevine or other the Misses Warren and Layton were apprised that their charge had a boyfriend, and not just an ordinary boyfriend, but a soldier to boot from the Barracks, a short distance down the Romsey Road. The riot act was read out and we were forbidden to meet. But the ultimatum was not really capable of enforcement. Zoe was not banned from the Youth Club on Fridays, nor from attending the church on Sundays. Young love being as it is, we also met behind the shelves of the public library on other evenings.

Recognising defeat, the two spinsters then adopted a scorched earth policy, inviting me to breakfast, lunch and supper at weekends, where we could be safely supervised. The front page of the voluminous *Sunday Times*, its cover page in those days covered in plain text adverts, provided adequate camouflage while Sunday lunch was being prepared; a squeaking floorboard acting as an alarm signal to return our attention to the crossword as they entered the sitting room. The time came when we were permitted to go for an afternoon walk, accompanied by two other chaperones in the persons of William (a black Scotty dog) and Ginger (some sort of terrier). Maybe Zoe's guardians were extremely innocent or ignorant, or both. They never realised how simple it is to tether a dog's lead around a small sapling! It is hard to imagine such a scenario taking place in our modern world.

One Sunday afternoon Miss Layton suddenly announced that it was high time that I met her father; her mother had died of cancer some time earlier. We were both bundled into her old baby Austin and driven to Alton without any means of preparing ourselves for the occasion. All this time I was leading a semi-civilian life in the Army, putting on my 'Civvies' after 5 pm, singing in the church choir, and for a performance of Hiawatha with the Winchester City Choir and tending the church garden on the weekends when Zoe went home.

This blissful life was to cease when I was demobbed in the August of 1951 to attend King's College London the following October. My time in the Army had brought me up with a bump against another world, a world that I had not encountered before. The contrast certainly helped focus my early Christian experience, and was formative in my decision to seek ordination, despite that bottle of my parent's home-bottled gooseberries won at a Mother's Union whist drive!

CHAPTER TWO

KINGS COLLEGE LONDON

At the beginning of the academic year, students from all faculties were invited to share in the opening of term service in the college chapel. I well remember the first lesson taken from the book of Ecclesiastes and read by the Chaplain, Dr Frank Coventry; it closed with these words: 'Of the making of books there is no end and too much study is a weariness to the flesh.' That was real encouragement to those just about to begin their studies! So in the autumn of 1951 I was welcomed by a family in South Norwood and began to study Theology, travelling to the college each weekday on a 196 London bus.

London is a good place to study Theology. Your time in the lecture room was immediately challenged by walking straight into the hurley burley of the Strand. Dear old

Professor James, our lecturer in philosophy, would try to convince us that the table in front of us only existed because there was a mind to perceive it. That of course is partly true, when you think about it, though most people don't. However this observation left one with little encouragement to walk straight in front of an oncoming London taxi with one's eyes shut.

The former philosophical truth is aptly illustrated in the well-known ditty which he used to recite:

Sir, I find it exceedingly odd
that this sycamore tree
should continue to be
when there's no one about in the quad.
Sir, your amazement is odd,
I am always about in the Quad,
and that's why this tree
will continue to be
as observed by yours faithfully, God!

So far I had lived without what I earlier described as the chatter of accumulated theology and philosophy, spontaneously welcoming uncharted thoughts as they jumped over each other in their arriving. Now I was faced with the dialogue of the recorded history of the church and its catalogue of orthodoxy and persecution. For some reason I always wanted to plead the cause of the heretics, who by and large seemed to be possessed of more open-mindedness and greater human dignity than their persecutors.

As a lay person I had read the Bible sometimes with a little confusion, but perhaps with rather more imagination than that offered by the method known as 'form criticism'. This can involve a certain sort of slavery to the text which can easily cloud the message that is being recounted. I was searching for inspiration and guidance and had never before given the actual text a second's thought. At King's I entered a whole new realm of Old and New Testament studies, Philosophy, Ethics, Psychology, Church History, New Testament Greek, and Eucharistic and Pastoral Theology.

Once a month on what were called 'Fridays at Ten', Lecturers from other faculties spoke about their own disciplines. Professor Coulson, the then Chair of Theoretical Physics at King's, gave one fascinating lecture. With the help of a brilliant lecturer I could always follow the argument all the way, but the moment he sat down I would come back to earth with a big bump.

I soon joined 'The Bio-Theolog' group, a forum for Science students and Theologs. We shared many interesting debates and discussions. In conversation with one young scientist violently opposed to all religion, I recall asking him if he had ever read the Bible. He shook his head. I pointed out that I would not dare to criticise theories of atomic physics without at least having taken the trouble to read a layman's book on the subject. It is so important that we learn to respect one another's knowledge as we set out to explore the meaning of our existence in the world.

Each year we attended a weekend conference at Cumberland Lodge in Windsor Great Park, where we were treated to a wide range of professional lecturers. As residents we also had the privilege of worshipping in the Chapel Royal. One Sunday on leaving the Chapel after Matins, we were treated to a visual audience of the Queen and Prince Philip and other members of the Royal family as they stood chatting on the grass only a few yards away. Not knowing what to do, we talked our way past them.

Having stood in the near presence of royalty, I turn to what theologians call the Doctrine of the Real Presence, discussing at what precise moment Christ became present in the sacramental bread and wine. Was it when the priest laid his hands on them? Also under discussion was the Catholic teaching of Transubstantiation, of how the bread and wine of Communion are transformed into the body and blood of Christ. The bread and wine were often described as 'the elements', which seemed to me to rob the experience of communion with God of all its wonder and sense of mystery. In my late teens I had never ever thought about the sacrament in that sort of way at all.

Somewhat naively perhaps, I would prepare myself for 'Communion' first by thanking God for all the good things I was always receiving at his hand, then telling him what I was sorry for during the past week, and then asking for his help so that I wouldn't have to say sorry for the same things next week as I had last week! That worked for me without bothering to argue just how God was present. Worship however does help to focus one's awareness of that presence, which is also much strengthened by fellowship. I found a great deal of Eucharistic doctrine just plain confusing and still do. I also found it rather sad that throughout history the Communion service has often became a source of division and separation among Christians.

Further study in my eighties led me to discover the Didache – the teaching of the twelve apostles, the manuscript of which was only found as late as 1873 in a monastery in Constantinople. The Didache was a little booklet in circulation in the early second century when local Christian communities were beginning to be more organised. It is divided into two sections; the first part contrasts the Christian and the pagan way of life, the second part outlines the earliest forms of Sunday worship, which it describes as follows:

"In the service of thanksgiving called the Eucharist give thanks thus – first for the cup 'We thank thee, our Father, for the holy vine of David thy child, which thou hast revealed to us through Jesus thy child. Thine is the glory for ever.' Then for the broken bread: 'We thank thee, our Father for the life and knowledge which thou hast revealed to us through Jesus thy child. Thine is the glory for ever. Even as this broken bread was scattered over the mountains and was brought together and made one, so may thy church be brought together from the ends of the earth into thy kingdom. For thine is the glory and the power through Jesus Christ." How sad that this simple form of early worship which was then seen as binding the church together should often have become the focus of so much argument and division.

By some strange chance, a letter of mine to my mother sent from 75 Beulah Hill, Norwood, has found its way into my personal archives. In it I first thank her for a parcel of washing. I then continue, "I haven't quite made up my mind what I think of Kings yet. I am not at all sure how I like what appears to me to be a rather smothering ecclesiastical atmosphere. They seem to be at so much pains to explain things. It may very well be me that is wrong – but the explanations they give seem more like complications than anything else." It seems that I have not changed all that much. A cake would sometimes also arrive wrapped among my clean underwear!

Then there was what some church people label 'churchmanship', another word that had never before been part of my vocabulary, and that would have been meaningless to Jesus. King's College contained a wide variety of 'churchmanship', but on the whole it had a leaning to what is known in the trade as High Church; 'bells and smells' as it is sometimes called. Some of my fellow students of this persuasion regarded the sacrament as celebrated by extreme Evangelicals as *invalid*! Those of a more fundamentalist turn of mind would inform you in no uncertain terms that you were not a 'proper' Christian unless you had experienced the Holy Spirit, been born again, and come to accept Christ as your personal Saviour. I wasn't then quite sure what either group was talking about. The core of my vocation was driven simply by the desire to share God's love.

All this sort of argument seemed to me to be extremely arrogant and totally unrelated to what ministry is all about and nearly prompted me to abandon the whole exercise. After having been accepted for ordination by CACTM (The Central Advisory Council for Training of the Ministry) I had to write a letter to the Dean of King's College, Eric Abbott, stating my reasons for seeking ordination. I still have the carbon copy of that letter, typed on an old army typewriter, saying 'That when you have experienced God's love one feels compelled to share that love with others'. That original prompting has survived, but not without many challenges on the way.

The priestly calling can also run the danger at times of becoming patronising. You've got it – they haven't! My time in the Army had brought me up with a bump against another world that I had not experienced before. It could have been all too easy to write that world off as unchristian and to see one's vocation to make everyone else just like us, forgetting that at the heart of Jesus' own ministry was meeting all people where they are, to listen to them and to help them discover their own faith.

So such faith with which I started my priestly calling was a curious mixture of the 'official teaching of the Church' according to King's College and the Church Fathers, tempered by my recollection of the modernist teaching of Bishop Barnes acquired at Durham and my own spiritual surmisings, all mixed up with the vicissitudes of daily life. One of these vicissitudes was being abandoned by my first girlfriend. That nearly sank my theological studies at a stroke, as the whole experience had been so closely linked in my mind with my initial vocation.

I entered a period of prolonged depression. Those who have never experienced the depths of depression cannot fully understand the trauma that it causes. Depression comes about when a whole variety of pressures hit you from all directions all at once, adding to the normal stresses of everyday life. I have often since compared the experience to that of a spider trapped in a china wash-basin. Despite its frantic attempts to escape its prison, the spider always slides back down to the bottom of the basin, where there is what must seem to a spider to be an enormous gaping black hole waiting to swallow it up. These days we now know all about the black holes in space that swallow up everything that comes their way, acting as gigantic space vacuum cleaners with infinitely more suction power than the most advanced Dyson, as they Hoover the garbage of the universe into a vast black bin-liner!

In Margate, cut deep into the white chalk cliffs, there is a fearsome dungeon into which prisoners were thrown. The walls were greased and the chalk still retains a waxy grey look. At the bottom of the chasm there was also another gaping black hole just wide enough to deliver the prisoner to the raging sea beneath. There was no escape. For the person suffering from depression, the whole point is that there seems to be no way out of one's predicament.

There is a world of difference between severe clinical depression and that caused mostly by the loss of a girlfriend. For a moment the bottom had dropped out of my world. One cold autumn evening a priest somewhere in south London found a rather distressed theological student standing on his doorstep. I had knocked at random on a vicarage door. I joined him in his study, was given a cup of coffee, and before leaving was informed in a kindly but totally uncomprehending manner that God was still in his heaven, that the world was still going round and that everything would be all right. Just at that moment for me there was no God in heaven, my world had stopped going round and everything was all wrong. His words gave me little or no comfort at the time, but they have stood me in good stead in knowing what not to say when dealing with others with the same sort of problems.

It was some weeks later, walking up a slight slope to post a letter to my mother, that the memory of the house runs at Durham came flooding into my mind. The only sport at which I ever vaguely excelled was cross-country running. Two thirds of the way along the course there was a very, very steep hill. By the time you reached this spot your legs wanted to carry you no further. For this reason your schoolmates assembled there and cheered you on and you continued upwards. So the thought came into my mind that if I could get up that hill I could somehow get away from the gaping black hole which had been so much a part of my life for the last four or five months.

It took time, it didn't all happen at once, but slowly the world picked up speed again. God was still there in his heaven and life once more gradually began to be 'all right'. Maybe that had something to do with meeting my future wife, though that didn't happen till well after the world had taken a considerable number of further turns on its axis. We met as members of the Kings College Chorus in the January of 1954. I had two tickets for the Royal Festival Hall burning a hole in my pocket; the young lady supposed to accompany me had stood me down. I invited Jill to accompany me instead. Afterwards, in romantic mood, I took her to Charing Cross station for her journey home. We may have even exchanged a kiss, or two – or four! She had a dimple and was wearing a pair of black furry gloves. By mid-February I had proposed as we sat side by side on a Green Line coach while making our way back to London from a visit to Cambridge. She said Yes!

Girlfriends were only allowed to visit the theological hostel in Vincent Square for a brief two hours on a Friday and a little longer on Sunday afternoons. I pride myself that I married the one with the steadiest hand while wielding a rather blunt bread knife across a very soft fresh white loaf, bought from a lovely old bakery just around the corner in Strutton Ground. After completing my final examinations, I would have got on any train to take me anywhere had it not been for Jill, who scooped me up and took me back to her home in Croydon. Almost the next day in the summer of 1954 we travelled together to the south of France to visit Anne-Marie, her French pen friend. The friendship still flourishes and is now well over sixty years old, a personal *entente cordiale*.

On arrival I was left marooned in a French kitchen, surrounded by Madame Gaudin and a bevy of her young daughters. "Do you like French cooking?" I was asked. What can you say in reply? "Oui" is hardly interesting conversation, and "non" is out of the question! So producing my best schoolboy French, I muttered "Quand je suis en Angleterre je préfère la cuisine anglaise, et quand je suis en espagne je préfère la cuisine espagnol, et quand je suis en France je préfère la cuisine française." So began my skills in diplomacy.

Warminster days

There followed a final year at St. Boniface College, Warminster, studying 'spirituality' and more practical matters, like how to conduct baptisms, weddings and funerals, and how to preach sermons. I remember only one 'sermon practice'. It was given by Gavin Fargus, a rather eccentric young man who enjoyed beagling and also read *The Field* magazine.

"There was once a certain lawyer dressed in a pinstripe suit, carrying his brief-case and a rolled umbrella. As he walked home along the streets of Pimlico he was mugged and left barely conscious in the gutter. It happened that the Bishop of Pimlico was passing that way in his chauffeur-driven car. Seeing the man in the gutter, he muttered to his chauffeur 'Disgusting for a man to be drunk so early in the day!' They drove on. I cannot recall who the second man was, but next on the scene was the leader of the local Communist Party passing by on his bicycle. He all but fell off as he ran over the rolled umbrella, whereupon he spat and cursed all capitalists. Then of course he goes to the man's aid, picks him up and takes him to the nearest pub and buys him a meal."

You don't have to have read the Bible to know that that is the story of the Good Samaritan in modern dress. It doesn't matter whether the man was walking to Jericho, Pimlico or Timbuktu. The truth lies in the story itself. We all instinctively recognise that the man on the bicycle did the right thing.

The Warminster year ran its course. Jill would visit occasionally. We loitered in the bluebell woods at the foot of Cley Hill, which we also climbed a time or two. Many years later, while travelling home late one night, we once clambered to the top of Cley Hill in the moonlight and romantically watched an eclipse of the Moon.

All theological students have to spend Holy Week in 'retreat' – not running away somewhere, but making time to listen to God. Spending time in silence was never a hardship to me, though others may find it quite demanding. However, the clatter of forty pairs of knives and forks attacking forty dinner plates masked by no other sound whatever was a totally new and quite extraordinary experience and my internal laughing was as hard to quench as our laughing in Durham Cathedral when Bishop Headlam lost his false teeth in the pulpit. I had never before thought of knives and forks having a conversation! We were also told to 'empty ourselves' – to get rid of oneself – and to let Christ take over. I can't find any reference to Jesus telling people to do that, but he did tell them to take time out and to pray, as he often did himself, and to take up their cross daily and follow him.

If God has gone to all the trouble to make you 'you' and no one else, it seems to me quite wrong to try and discard the gift of that unique personality. You may be just another model off the human production line, but you are not 'manufactured' in the way that cars are assembled. You may have two arms, two legs, a nose, a face and a pair of eyes just like every other human being, but the miracle is that each one of us is so uniquely different. To try and rub out that precious identity given to you by God seemed to me to be an affront to the Creator. In the equivalent of Chairman Mao's Little Red Book I kept a 'Little 'Black Book' recording memorable remarks from lectures. I also include several of my own personal student jottings, among which I wrote these words: "God may use 'you' as a priest, but he always remembers it is you he is using. He will not make a priest of you but he will make you a priest."

Of course our human nature is often flawed, and we do need a lot of help to get rid of our own personal defects. Our wills on their own without the help of the Holy Spirit are never strong enough to achieve all the changes that need to be made - witness all the horrors that human beings are capable of perpetrating. The required changes take place throughout the parade ground of the whole of one's life. The goal is to become the best possible 'me' that God has created with the help of what we Christians call his grace. Our business in life as human beings is to add to the glory of God's creation and to be a blessing to others.

Our aim in these pages is to trek down the pathways that lead to faith, while wandering along some of the more unlikely routes that God puts in our way, the purpose of which we don't always recognise at the time. It seems obvious to me now that real faith is acquired not just by studying doctrine, nor from prayer manuals, nor listening to sermons, but is an interaction of all these things with our daily experience of life, within the little cosmos that is continually spinning round in every human soul. A computer can open many windows at the same time, but there is only one window through which each one of us can look out on life and find faith, and that is the window of our own soul.

Ordination
Turning one's collar round

Ordination is a little bit like getting married. You don't quite know what lies in store! Our ordination retreat took place in the Bishop's Palace outside Ripon, where we met for meditation in the Bishop's conservatory among the tomatoes and the vine that shaded its roof. Outside, sheep were safely grazing. This all reflected the moorland peace that I so much treasure.

One had already been measured for one's first cassock but more alarming still was the acquisition of one's first clerical shirt, tailored to receive either a linen or plastic clerical collar worn back to front! You had a feeling that you were being changed into something else. I have to confess I had a dread of becoming a hirsute creature dressed in a permanent black suit. Today clerical shirts reflect every colour of the rainbow and adorn both men and women. My suit mostly keeps Wilfrid company in the wardrobe. I did however don black morning clerical dress for our wedding.

I was ordained Deacon in 1955 in St. Matthew's Hunslet, one of the city of Leeds' poorest parishes, before taking up the post of assistant curate at St. Matthew's, Chapel Allerton in north Leeds. Turning one's collar round marks a very definite transition, and makes you much more conspicuous as you begin your new role in life, though the lay person still remains hidden within you. Like a policeman or a traffic warden, you stand out in a crowd or on a train – maybe someone to be avoided! I mostly found it to be exactly the opposite; a sort of icebreaker and an opportunity to engage people in conversation.

The following year I was ordained priest in the historic cathedral of the city of Ripon, a city I knew well, and where the town hall carries the inscription "The watchman waketh but in vain except the Lord keepeth the city." It was a moving ceremony and a very significant step on one's pilgrimage but it was not quite so life changing as one's ordination as Deacon. I celebrated my first communion service with some trepidation.

Jill and I were duly wed two months after I was priested, and spent our honeymoon in Austria, Verona and Venice, surviving when we returned to our new home by removing the traditional half-crown from the champagne cork and by raiding the silver coins extracted from those packets minted to celebrate the Queen's Coronation, now, if complete, worth a lot more. We also made a gift from a parishioner of two scotch eggs last for two meals! Together we have since embarked on many ventures of faith; bringing up our two sons, being available to no end of people in many parishes across the country and later across the world, travelling to many remote places, but first just trying to learn what we were supposed to be doing while still wrapped up in young romantic love.

In 2010 the BBC ran a documentary on marriage; "What is the secret of a long and happy marriage?" they asked an elderly couple. The husband, in his early nineties replied: "Being able to have really good arguments." We have at times had some furious arguments, mostly over pruning shrubs, but always ended with a big hug. To argument I would add preserving a spirit of romance and fun that reaches far beyond holding each other's hand and enables one to survive all the traumas of old age.

Cracking the curate's egg
Chapel Allerton

After four years of study and theological training, almost the very first job I was given was to help the verger move two hundred chairs from the church hall to the vicarage garden for the Summer Fête. With a head still bursting with theology, that was very good for the humility stakes! The verger, Louis Morley, was a lovely man who saw himself as the real educator of new curates.

The collar eventually adjusted itself to its new neck and I learned to greet everything in the parish on two feet, apart from bus queues! It was not long before my vicar asked me to conduct my first baptisms and to run through the service with three families beforehand. Being trained at Warminster was one thing, holding real live babies quite another; virtual babies electronically programmed to cry and wet their nappies all through the night had not then been invented! Holding newborn babies was not a skill I possessed. I had never ever held a babe in my life. One of those three mothers, who had given birth to twins, kindly allowed me to practise on her new offspring. A less helpful mother might have decided to defer the baptism, fearing I would drop them in the font!

Knocking on the doors of those families I thought about the people living either side. I would often knock on their doors too. One of the other great challenges you had to meet was preaching, and talking about the Gospel in public. This was still mostly done by means of a parsonical monologue known as the sermon. How refreshing it would have been at times to be interrupted! Some of the best sermons I found myself preaching in those early years were in people's homes and more often than not the homes of non-churchgoers who wanted to argue the toss with me over what I believed. As St. Peter says you have to be prepared to give a reason for the faith that is in you. You have to speak from your heart.

A little later, at one of those group baptisms that took place at St. Matthew's, my new wife was a guest among the large crowd of parents and godparents. By now I was a little more skilled at baby holding; one father nudged Jill in the arm, not knowing who she was, and whispered "He'll make a good father one day!" In mid-January 1956 our elder son Simon was born in Leeds Maternity Hospital; fathers just paced up and down the corridors in those days till it was all over. Parenthood was then a much more hit and miss affair, you learnt by your mistakes!

To welcome our new son and my wife home to our rather damp Victorian cottage, I got the bedroom so warm with a roaring coal fire that Simon developed 'prickly heat' in the middle of the severest cold snap of the winter! I later met the secretary of the church council on my way to the church. He congratulated me on the birth of our son and offered some words of wise advice: "Feed him whenever, I've had five and I ought to know!"

Then there came the day when I took my first wedding. The priest of an adjoining parish, Father Mowl, had asked for someone to take a wedding during his absence. I was volunteered by my vicar, who suggested I might as well make any mistakes in someone else's parish rather than his. I would have married any couple who had presented themselves with the correct names. The bridegroom was a soldier and he arrived in the full dress uniform of an army corporal, a proper red coat with epaulettes sword, the real McCoy. To give us both confidence, having been a soldier so recently myself, I told him that this was also my first wedding!

After a ceremony with no mishap I congratulated the happy pair on being the first couple I had ever had the privilege to marry. The bride then turned to me and said "If I'd known you'd never taken a wedding before I would have fainted on the spot!" She had put all her trust in me. Fr.

Mowl later came to thank me and over coffee he offered me a cigarette which I declined, never having smoked in my life. I made the comment that at least I had something left for my money, like rose bushes or a new garden rake. He was of the bells and smells persuasion, rather high church, and made the riposte "Ah well Francis, you see you are setting your heart and mind on things where moth and rust can corrupt, but our smoke goes straight up to heaven!"

One of the verger's jobs was to ensure I conducted a funeral service properly, which he always did with great aplomb and dignity, except on the occasion when I failed to turn up! I had to attend 'Potty' classes (Post Ordination Training) conducted by Canon Wood, one of our retired clergy. His reading of the Old Testament was impressive. I recall his rendering of the story of Elisha healing a sick child which concludes with these words 'And the child (pause) sneezed (pause) seven times' rendered in a loud dramatic voice, with undue emphasis on the words sneezed and seven.

I had warned the Canon that I would have to leave early, but we got so bound up in our discussion that we all forgot. I only remembered as I cycled cycling home, when I passed the funeral procession driving up the hill to the church! The vicar kindly stepped in, but I had to ready myself for the interment. I was slowly becoming a fully qualified practitioner of hatches, matches and dispatches.

Long before the days of health and safety at work, an extremely agitated and irate lady knocked on the vicarage door. "It's cruelty to h'animals like, vicar, putting that barbed wire right h'along't top of t'owd churchyard wall. My cat's always walked along that wall and if yer don't take h'it down h'immediately, h'I 'll report yer t't RSPCA."

The Vicar gave her a cup of coffee, saw her out, and thought no more about it. Some months later there came another knock on the vicarage door. "Excuse me for troubling you Vicar, I'm from the RSPCA." Another cup of coffee ensued and again the matter vanished from the Vicar's mind. Many months later there was yet another knock on the vicarage door. "This 'ere cat o mine Vicar, Seein h'as t'wer so fond of t'owd churchyard like, I wonder h'if you'd be kind enough to 'ave im buried there?" The Vicar responded saying: "Well, if you like to go and see my verger and tell him that I know nothing about it, that'll be all right". He had a vision of the old churchyard becoming the sanctuary and final resting place for a whole host of pets, even budgerigars!

The crowning climax was Louis' solemn report to the clergy and churchwardens one Sunday morning in the church vestry. "This 'ere cat like vicar. I give it a right good send off like. I dug a 'ole three feet deep like under t'old oak tree like, then I laid't cat out all proper like in one of them strawberry chip baskets like. I gets me a bit of rope like and I lowers it down like. Then I gives it the one, two, three like..." By this time we were all convulsed with laughter. Louis, preserving a suitably solemn countenance throughout, was conscientiously reporting that he'd done his duty by the cat. Of such is the stuff of life, and so I continued to be 'educated' by dear Louis as well as by my vicar. Man does not live by religion alone but by every experience sent to him from God above.

Leeds city trams trundled past our home in those days. Visitors came and went. I attempted to teach R.E. in the

Church School, and took the Sunday School. It was always assumed that because you were young you would automatically be good with children and young people. Sunday afternoon is a notoriously soporific time of day. Thanks to a reverend gentleman rejoicing in the poetic name of Elfinstone-Fyfe, I once succeeded in covering all the children, myself, and the church hall floor and tables in Plaster of Paris, making Palestine models out of match boxes and sticky brown gummed strip then plastering them white; their parents were not amused! That was long before Sellotape had been invented. Our very first washing machine was my wife, assisted by my mother's old copper posser! All our buckets were zinc, washing up bowls were enamel and draining boards were made of wood. Plastic, nylon and tights were distant clouds on the horizon.

From the very beginning our home was always open to all comers. In 1956 Imre Nagy made his desperate appeal for the rest of the world to help the Hungarian people as the Russian tanks rolled into Budapest to put down his people's desperate bid for freedom. He met no response and lost his life. Hundreds of Hungarians fled to the West. Many churches were asked to respond. So it was that Cornelia, a young Hungarian girl, came to live with us in our home. After all these years I have eventually deciphered her own surname as Nagy.

She was only with us for three weeks. Upon leaving she wrote a lovely poem in our visitors' book; when translated it reads like this:

Like the bird in its nest
Like the traveller finding fresh water,

Like the babe on his mother's breast
I desire this peaceful home.

This was followed by "I thank you for your kindness, for your love, and for your hospitality. I have found a home here to replace my own." We were not to know then that Hungary would play an important role in our lives in later years, turning away thousands of refugees fleeing from terrorism and the Syrian civil war in 2015.

The Bahai Faith

Also in our visitors' book is an entry by a lovely young Bahai. The Bahai faith emphasises that all people are part of God's creation. Bahá'u'lláh, founder of the Bahá'í Faith said, "The tabernacle of unity hath been raised; regard ye not one another as strangers. Ye are the fruits of one tree, and the leaves of one branch." People of nearly every background, in every nation, have become Bahá'ís. I am afraid there is no translation of his Arabic script in our visitor's book, but we still possess the decorative little brass cheese knife he gave us.

The Baha'i faith was founded in the mid-19th century in Iran. In 1844 Siyyid 'Ali Mohammad, a Shiite Muslim, proclaimed that he was "the Bab," "the Gate," an interpreter of the Quran with special religious insight and prophetic abilities; he was the "Hidden Imam." The Bab's prophetic message spread in Iran, which angered both the government and the Shiite leadership. He was arrested and then executed. One of the Bab's disciples, Baha'u'llah, continued to spread the Bab's teachings, which eventually evolved into the Baha'i faith, and it is Baha'u'llah who is most typically known as the founder of the tradition.

The Bahai faith teaches that God is utterly transcendent and ultimately unknowable to humanity. Of course that is where the Christian faith differs, as we believe that God has made himself known through the person of Jesus Christ. We shall consider this in detail in our closing chapters. God's manifestation is understood in Bahai to come not just through the Bab and Baha'u'llah, but also through the world's religious prophets. The Bahai faith also teaches that religion is the most powerful force for the transformation of human conduct, human relationships, and the structure of society. Since the 1979 Islamic Revolution in Iran, Bahais have been systematically persecuted as a matter of government policy.

I was also invited to represent St. Matthew's on the local United Nations Committee by their secretary, a Mr Dressler, I forget his Christian name. He was of Polish extraction. We often met in the home of a retired Professor Carter, and we used to hold several functions to try and involve the local community.

We had a lady in the Parish whom we christened 'purple Mrs Hall' to distinguish her from the other Mrs Halls. She was very elderly and fell seriously ill, and the vicar asked me to be with her one night as she was in no fit state to be left alone. The church's task is all about caring. But how do you enter the experience of the elderly when you in your mid-twenties are thinking of life stretching out in front of you – and they are wondering about death? Discussing this with my uncle, I remember saying to him 'At first a babe is hardly conscious of the world into which it has been born.

Ask a four-year-old where China is and it cannot really understand, even if shown a map of the world. A young child is not aware of the feelings of the adolescent, the adolescent of the newly married, the newly married of parenthood or the feelings of middle-age, nor the middle aged of being elderly. You only really understand each successive stage of life as the years lead you there. So when we think of the life of the world to come we shall only really understand when we enter it – just like everything else.' I have now *nearly* experienced the lot!

We so often make the mistake of imagining any future existence as a continuation of what we already know; for many the main expectation is meeting up with loved ones. I believe it is far more likely that life will be lived in an entirely new dimension. Mathematicians will tell you that there are far more dimensions than the three to which we are accustomed. I am married to one – a mathematician, not a dimension! Just think of every successive generation wanting to meet their forbears, some of whom may even have been Neanderthal! It has got to be something different, an entirely new experience of life, lived beyond the restrictions of time and space, lived in another dimension and on a different plane; a mystery, a wonder beyond our imagining, just as our earthly life is a mystery, a gift which we encounter amid the present dimension of our existence. Let us always leave space in life for Mystery.

The time came for us to move to my second curacy. In 1957 we had entertained the Bishop of Melanesia, who tried to persuade us to go to the Fiji islands. We were somewhat tempted, but it would have been very difficult with Simon only being a few months old. In 1958 we moved to Hayes, a nearby parish of St. John's, Shirley, where we had been married. In August 1959 William, our second son was born; his arrival kept being postponed. I was out picking blackberries when he finally entered the world. No prickly heat this time round! When older he and his brother developed the habit of sharpening their teeth on lumps of the coke stored outside the back door.

Hayes

New skills were learned from a new rector. Both my first vicar, Bill Purcell, and the Rector of Hayes, Eric Smith, provided me with very good training, though in quite different ways. Bill was forceful, almost dictatorial in his conduct of meetings, which always ran to schedule. Eric Smith was diffident, shy and often allowed church council meetings to run past midnight discussing who would make the sandwiches at the Summer Fair!

A new accomplishment came my way in the form of conducting a ceremony for the blessing of the May Queen. Clergy are expected to be completely versatile! I also had to 'look in' on my first Brownie meeting. I thought I had stumbled upon a pagan ritual. All the young girls seemed to be worshipping a toadstool. Most young men never encounter Brownies at worship!

The church ran two youth groups, the Junior and Senior Challengers. I became closely involved with the senior group and remember talking to them about ordination and its meaning and sharing in many of their functions just as I had in the AYPA in Winchester. I treasure the red all-steel garden spade they gave me when we left, wonderfully light, and still in use! It had to be welded once and is nearly two inches shorter on one side than the other. Rather well-worn, like my ordination bible. Faith becomes well-worn too when used properly! In the 1950s around fifty young people or more filled a whole side aisle on most Sundays at Evensong.

I also assisted a retired army officer, Major Binyon, who ran a youth group for non-church youngsters in his own home, a large manor house type of property. I remember one of them coming up to me and asking why I wore such a funny collar round my neck. Looking directly into his face, I asked, "And why are you wearing bootlaces round yours?" That was the latest male teenage fashion at that time. Those bootlaces became a bridge that led to an ongoing friendship.

Our new home was in a small cul-de-sac of just over twenty houses; it is surprising what a difference that makes, as everyone passes the same way to reach their own house. In Hayes Lane there were 280 houses, with very little neighbourly contact. One of our close neighbours was Mr Gilliver, whose wife was dying of cancer. We spent many hours together, which helped enormously when she eventually died. He used to work at Bromley South Station, which was being demolished at that time. One day, knowing that I was a bit of a carpenter, he arrived clutching a heap of planks from the dismantled station building; a gift of love if ever there was.

Out on a baptism visit, I met a father who had built the most wonderful wooden model of a steam engine for his son. I asked him how he had found such a perfectly round boiler. "It's the half of a large old wooden mangle roller," he said. "You can have the other half if you like." So the boiler of my train, still welded to its metal spindle by generations of water, is mounted on pieces of the old Bromley South Station with a wooden tender to match. It now lives in my study and has helped entertain all sorts of children. That train is a sacramental reminder of Mr Gilliver, who lives on as one of those thousands of friends who have helped me on my way.

While in Hayes we were asked by the CMS (Church Missionary Society) if we would entertain two young Chinese nurses from Hong Kong. They made a wonderful etching of a Chinese river scene in our visitor's book and much enjoyed looking after our two young sons. They also told us of the grim times they had experienced as young children during the Second World War and how one could never be quite sure what sort of meat might turn up in a stew.

I was not to know during my time at Hayes that one of the young choir boys would one day retire to Potterne, only a very short distance from our home in Devizes. He had heard my name mentioned at a talk given locally by George Carey, a former Archbishop of Canterbury. Keith introduced himself and his wife. Much later over supper he showed us a picture of himself as a choir boy with me as a curate. He is now a churchwarden!

After completing your second curacy, you undertake the charge of your first parish. I was invited to consider two country parishes in the Weald of Kent. With my love of a garden I thought I might end up exhibiting Delphiniums, so I declined. The Bishop of Rochester, Christopher Chevasse, was one of the old school of bishops, and not used to his suggestions being set aside, so I was forced to look elsewhere, and with the help of my former theological college, ended up in charge of two other country parishes on the Isle of Wight.

CHAPTER THREE

FAITH ON THE HOOF

An Island Parish

Arreton Vicarage on the Isle of Wight was a large rather and gracious eighteenth century house with an even larger overgrown garden and a derelict apple orchard. A stream formed the boundary on the east side of the garden. It came complete with a stable block dated 1782. Inside were the original stalls and mangers. A year or two after we arrived an eighty-two-year-old man knocked on our door begging me to let him look in the stable. Like many an old man, he was revisiting his past. The stable loft had once been his home when serving one of my predecessors as his coachman.

For a moment I thought I had returned to the Garden of Eden. Rooks greeted each dawning day, as they had in my childhood, and the garden, if not bounded by rivers, was at least bounded by a stream, From my study I could see the steam train puffing its way from Ryde to Ventnor.

My mother and my brother came down from Yorkshire for the Institution Service in May 1961. All the local Incumbents were invited, and who should be among them but one Fr. Harold Mason, the vicar of the neighbouring parish of Godshill, my mother's first boyfriend! He was curate of Elland in the mid-1920s. Of course on the Sunday she had to go to Harold's mass at Godshill. She was then invited to his home. He was married to a young wife who was exceedingly kind to my mother. They had four children. Thereby hangs a tail.

We only discovered years later how that marriage had come about when Jill was in Odstock Hospital in Salisbury having a skin cancer removed from her nose. In the next bed, believe it or not, was a lady from Godshill who knew Harold well. The village had watched with keen interest as their vicar spent more and more time at the village Post Office. Too much time, some thought! He then announced that he was going to be married. They had all expected it to be the Postmistress, who was about his own age, but to their surprise he married her daughter!

Soon after our arrival I discovered the remains of a vintage car in a lean-to shed adjoining the stable. It was all rather a mystery, a mystery that was only solved when I made my first call upon 'Whitey', the retired village Headmaster, who still lived with his bachelor son in the old School House. I was warmly welcomed. Comfortably ensconced in an old armchair I was offered a glass of whisky, a drink that had never before passed my lips. That was followed by another; I forget if there was a third! As you will hear later we have eaten our way through mountains of hospitality; now I was learning to drink my way through hospitality as well! "By the way, Vicar," said Mr White, "we owe you some rent for that garage where my son keeps his vintage car." Mystery solved. The parish had been vacant for about six months. I had already been in post for a further three months. Whitey went to a drawer and withdrew a fistful of those old purple paper cash bags all filled with the bulky old half-crown coins then in use. He had been storing them assiduously week after a week – over forty of them. Eventually I struggled home with my pockets drooping with half-crowns, and just a little whisky worn! Thereafter, whenever I experienced one of those grey days that we all have, I would call on Mr White, collect some half crowns, knock back a noggin or two of whisky and the world would suddenly seem a better place.

Another interesting character was Len Orchard. He had been verger of St. George's Arreton for many years but was now retired. I thought to myself, oh, oh, another verger, perhaps he will think it is his duty to bring up the new vicar in his first incumbency. Shades of Louis Morley! I needn't have worried, but it was on my third or fourth Sunday that he came up to me and announced "Vicar, if you preaches more than ten minutes I'll get up and go t't' pub!" He did on one occasion too.

A year or two later he broke his leg and I visited him regularly for several weeks. He began talking, and telling me all about his life. He was a good talker. After a time he began to tell me about his own faith, which meant a lot to him; for Len this was full of hope based on a very simple trust in the Lord. On one visit he said to me, "You know Vicar, I think I should have become a vicar!" I replied, "I know one thing for certain Len, you'd have preached for much longer than ten minutes!" He nodded. It was interesting for me to recall how a layman thought about his faith, without ever having had any training in theology; that is something a priest often needs to remember and understand.

Another village character was Norah Calloway, who ran the village shop and went out of her way to help all her customers. She was a spinster. I made a point of calling quite often as this was the place where you could get to know a lot of your parishioners. She was also a pillar of the Methodist Church. One day when I popped in there was a very long queue. A member of our church choir was buying a birthday card for her husband. She was looking for a card with the word 'husband' printed on the front. The delay was because Norah was busily searching all her boxes of cards stored beneath the old mahogany counter. Eventually a muffled voice announced somewhat impatiently "I know I have got plenty of spare husbands tucked away somewhere!" It took her a long time to live that one down.

Who should turn up one day on our doorstep but 'Prince Paleologus'. No kidding. He claimed to be the last living descendant of the last Emperor of Constantinople. He offered to copy some of our ancient parish records for us. I could see no harm. This was long before the days of microfiche, and the mice in the church chest had already nibbled away at some of the first pages of our earliest records which began shortly after 1534, the year when the keeping of Parish Registers became obligatory. (Latest research on the Internet exposes him as an English eccentric who was often to be seen striding the streets of Newport. His second wife still piously continues to defend her title as Princess.)

He was very self-effacing and became a regular visitor. Seated at our large dining table he set about his task with meticulous detail, working for several hours at a time while occasionally sipping a glass of milk and delicately eating a digestive biscuit or two. He claimed to be married to a princess descended from the Pacahonta Indians. He and his wife had four daughters whom we met when invited to his home in Newport; they lived off Social Security and child benefits. He considered paid work beneath the dignity of his office.

He also conferred titles and knighthoods! Some time after we left the Isle of Wight the owner of Arreton Manor, one of the Arreton churchwardens, whom I knew well, became 'Count Slade de Pomeroy'. The Prince considered conferring titles an honourable way of turning the odd penny or two. Mr Slade, as he was in my time, was in fact a Midlands businessman, who had come to the Isle of Wight on holiday and snapped up the derelict Arreton Manor at a rock bottom price, much to the annoyance of many local landowners.

What lessons did one learn from this strange encounter besides boasting that one has moved in more royal circles? I think never to make a quick judgement, because you never know what lies hidden behind the face of anyone who comes your way. The original parish records are now held safely in the Diocesan Archives, and on microfiche – but maybe somewhere hidden away in the parish are the beautifully hand-written copies made by the Prince Paleologus at our dining table.

The winter of 1963 was a winter that those who experienced it will never forget. On Boxing Day my brother and I were playing snooker on our large dining room table; with its oak leaves removed and raised to full height it becomes a very passable billiard table with a slate bed. A strong east wind suddenly swept up the Channel. We kept opening the shutters to see how the storm was progressing, as we had as young boys in the Dales.

My brother wrote in our visitor's book "It snowed and it blew and it blew and it snowed." In the morning we awoke to drifts of up to five or six feet deep in places, with no sign of a thaw. The Isle of Wight was hit for six. Normally enjoying a very mild climate, the Island was at one stroke plunged into an Arctic winter. All transport drew to a halt. I couldn't even walk to my parish of Newchurch because of the depth of the snow. There were only two snow ploughs on the whole of the Island, and the farmers did not then possess the modern machinery they have today.

My wife and I set off to deliver milk on our sledge to some of the elderly living down the farm tracks. Like rabbits hiding in their burrows, most of my parishioners remained in their homes for several days. They had never had to deal with such a situation before. Coming from the Yorkshire Dales, it was child's play. The Arctic conditions continued well into March with little let up. Eventually roads were opened, though not all, and I was able to drive to Newchurch.

A strange thing happened in that village. Two neighbours who had fallen out with each other and never spoken for years resolved their differences and became friends. In Leeds in 1958, passengers on the trams were all chatty and full of kindness to each other. I have noticed that snow always seems to have this sort of calming effect as it drowns us all in a wonderful silence.

One day there was a loud knocking on the front door and a somewhat aggressive retired military gentleman announced that he was going to report me to the Archbishop of Canterbury. Major Smart lived in the Newchurch parish. He had attended the annual Remembrance Day service that I had conducted the day before. I always found preaching on Remembrance Sunday a bit of a challenge. War is a total contradiction of all that Jesus came to teach mankind and is regarded as totally abhorrent by most people. But such are the vagaries of the human spirit that brutal evil sometimes has to be destroyed when all else fails.

This problem perpetually haunted Leo Tolstoy. In his great novel *War and Peace*, having fought in a Crimean War and written about the battle of Borodino, he comes to the conclusion that war is totally futile and adds these words of wisdom: "Everyone thinks of changing the world, but no one thinks of changing himself". He battled with this thought throughout the whole of his life. The Syrian conflict is further proof of the futility of war. It is high time that in all political debate the UN and all the world's leaders placed the human victims of conflict as the very first item on their political agenda instead of national self-interest.

That said, there is a great need to commemorate those who have died in battle and all the human grief involved, but I have always felt constrained to deliver a forceful message of Christian faith at the same time. After all,

Remembrance Sunday is one of those days when you always have a considerable congregation. I readily admit that I may have expressed myself badly; it was after all my first Remembrance Sunday sermon, or maybe the faith I was talking about was too strong meat for the retired major. But there he was on my doorstep.

I invited him in, gave him some coffee, and we talked for quite a long time and became very firm friends. That is often how the Gospel is best communicated, in a one-to-one conversation. My wife and I were invited to supper, and he gave me some seed from a wonderful broom hedge he had grown in his garden. Two years later a similar hedge graced the northern boundary of our vegetable patch, where I once grew a species of cabbage where one plant weighed in at fourteen and a half pounds!

But that was not the end of the story. Some years later when the struggle in Rhodesia (now Zimbabwe) was reaching its climax, there was another knock on the vicarage door; it was my close friend Major Smart again, this time reporting the Archbishop to me! "What's this Archbishop of yours doing Vicar, saying it might be right to use force in Rhodesia?" The wheel had come full circle. I remembered the knockings on the vicarage door of my first vicar in Chapel Allerton, and the cat lady and the churchyard; I was obviously becoming a fully-fledged vicar!

Every year the 'Harvest Supper' was held in the village hall. There was still a 'high' table at which sat the Vicar and the Churchwardens and the Treasurer and their wives. A certain Mrs Morey always provided the most superb sherry trifle, which had a habit of arriving on this particular table. One year while we were struggling through a rather solid jelly trifle covered with a thick layer of Indiarubber custard, a little voice from the 'Kids" table pipes up, "Cor Miss they been and put some poison in it!"

As a curate I had never attended Ruri-decanal or Diocesan Conferences. As an incumbent it was considered a matter of etiquette. Frequently I came home wondering what all our debating had to do with parish life, and the presentation of the Gospel. More often than not the debates concerned rather abstract theological issues, the question of raising money, and at that time ecumenism and church unity were also coming to the fore. Crossing the Solent added a certain amount of romance to the occasion, but more often than not when I returned home I would wander around my garden to recover. I am comforted that Archbishop Robert Runcie in his autobiography describes how he also resorted to wandering round the gardens of Lambeth Palace after such occasions!

Church finance is always a problem and in the early sixties both my churches needed to be re-roofed. One of my parishioners, Frank Fisk, a very wealthy farmer, lived with his sister in Apse Manor, where King Charles was reputed to have spent a night before being caught and imprisoned in Carisbrooke Castle. One night, while drinking a lethal mixture of cider and whisky and eating the farm's sweet chestnuts roasted on the bars of an old 'Esse' stove, Frank said to me "What are you doing about the church roof, Vicar?" I replied, "Well, Frank we have raised a thousand pounds (quite a considerable sum in 1963) and the Diocese are going to lend us another fifteen hundred pounds." No more was said. More whisky and cider was drunk, more chestnuts roasted; then in his own inimitable manner Frank

muttered quiet...
pounds vicar? We ...it help if I lent you fifteen hundred
but we'll use that ...arge any interest... yes we will,
everything's all done." ...decorate the church when

Some months later, wh... ...more driving to Apse
Manor I met Frank in the mid... ...a narrow lane high up
on his farm tractor.

"You'll be wanting that money I pr... ...ed you sometime
soon Vicar, won't you?"

"That's just what I've come to see you about, Frank."

"Tell me Vicar" he responded, "How do you get money
out of a deposit account? I've only ever put it in before!" I
quickly enlightened him and the roof was duly repaired.

On another occasion Frank once said to me: "I can't
understand anyone not believing in God; when I look across
this island with all its beauty and watch my lambs and
calves being born it's all so miraculous". Later his sister
committed suicide by throwing herself off the cliffs at
Shanklin. In his sorrow he asked me if I would inter her
ashes under a very special oak tree on his farm. Rules and
regulations about burial after suicide were not so relaxed in
those days. I just knew that it was right to do what he
asked, and that was a very special moment for both of us.

It was during our time at Arreton and Newchurch that
we first began camping, an enterprise that was soon to take
our young family to the Yorkshire Dales, and to Wales,
where we climbed Snowdon via the Pyg Track when William
was only four years old. Approaching the summit the mist
came down and almost reduced vision to zero. I was pushing
one boy up by his belt and my wife the other. Those coming
down mostly made encouraging remarks: "Not far now little

feller, well done", but one b.. muttered to his wife
"They need reporting to th.a Fancy bringing such a
small child up the Pyg T.er a day like this."

Soon Scotland and t.er Hebrides were added to the
list of our adventure.w years later we set out for the
Isle of Mull, visit.na, then travelled by ferry from
Tobermory to th.indswept island of Tiree. Later on
arrival at Sout.Jist we set out to walk from Lochboisdale
to Lochmad.v before crossing to Ardnamurchan for a boat
back to Tobermory. As early as 1965 we made our first
family excursion to the Continent, across France to
Switzerland and returning via the Black Forest. This was
to be the first of many such escapades, culminating in 1973,
with our first adventures behind the Iron Curtain that took
us to Yugoslavia, Bulgaria, Romania and Hungary. That
was the last journey we made together as a family.

In 1962 we offered an African family the chance to
holiday in our home. They were very surprised that we still
put 'grass' on many of our roofs. We then had no idea how
much a part Africa was to play in the future development of
our faith. Fertz and his wife and their young daughter
Tumie paid us a second visit in 1967 just before we left the
Island. I often wonder where their life's journey has taken
them.

The garden was restored to its former glory, though not
the orchard. Frank Fisk showed me how to trap the
pheasants that made their home there, though not how to
kill them. That task fell to Norah, my eighty-year-old
churchwarden in the Newchurch parish. "The thing to do
vicar, if you can't bring yourself to ring its neck, is hold the
bird upside down by its feet, lay its head on the ground and

place a stout strong gre LIFE
side, and pull for all your w

Every Sunday I used to co it, put a foot
Saints Newchurch together wit fails, I know
lady from the Arreton parish. Fre d take her to
speed that surpassed even Patri ather garrulou
somewhat frenetic update of all her p on-stop with a
once vouchsafed the shattering informatic e. Giving a
good clean living woman and always change affairs, she
twice a week! Before leaving home she alwa she was a
husband Percy full instructions on how to occu knickers
time. Percy was going to do this, Percy was going ve her
and a host of other things besides. I would say to his free
semi-invalid, "Don't you worry Percy, she's with me for the
next hour or two, you just do what you damned well like!"
His eyes would sparkle and he would return a knowing
wink. He dared not speak.

Freda was one of those persons to whom you could be
outrageously rude, tell her to shut up or pack it in, and still
be on speaking terms the very next second, largely because
she herself just never stopped talking! That was the reason
why she attended church in the other parish. One Sunday
morning, while returning home, Freda, smoking and
wringing her hands, began declaiming at length about how
she was always living on her nerves. Norah, the lovely quiet,
peaceable soul that she always was, seized her moment to
interrupt and said "Freda, when I get like that I always bite
an apple!"

Plants play an important role in my life. 'Eike' Eldridge
used to tend the Arreton churchyard, and would picnic with
his lady friend on top of one of the table top tombs! They

married. I still possess a species were both elderly, gave me, telling me that whenever I of Crassula always think of him. That was in 1965. looked at it ever since, though only by a miracle! In I have kept it into the greenhouse and it was killed 2012 I forgot a leaf must have fallen into a tray of by the frost. I had stood in the greenhouse the previous compost we had during a spring clean I discovered spring. The following year during a spring clean I discovered the leaf had rooted and grown into a small plant! Eike, Norah Mary, Mrs Blow and many more have places in my living garden of remembrance.

I took communion to two elderly spinsters who lived all on their own in the old family home. The sitting room was adorned with a large number of corn dollies, and every bit of wall space was decorated with the Christmas cards of years past. "I must give you something for the church" the elder sister would say to me, and immediately burrow in her capacious bosom from which she retrieved large numbers of £1 notes with no embarrassment whatsoever. No theology of the doctrine of the real presence, or the principles of schematic theology, was going to help you in such situations! At this level your faith is wrapped up in people, in being alongside them, sharing with them in their experiences, and learning from them too, sharing your faith and your love. People came to Jesus grasping at the hem of his garment looking for help. Blind men called after him asking for their sight, lepers came looking for cleansing, struggling just to be beside Him. Sometimes the only help you can give to others is your presence; being beside them and leading them to God's presence and his love.

If you have never read a tiny book entitled *The Practice of the Presence of God* by Brother Lawrence, then you should. Part of his monastic duties, besides his devotions, involved doing the washing up, and on one occasion he had to travel to Burgundy to order wine and rolled over three casks in the process! He began to discover that he was 'often more united to God in his outward employments, than when he left them for his devotions, and by doing little things for the love of God.'

The book continues: 'Many fail to make progress in their spiritual lives because they get stuck in penances, and particular religious exercises, while they neglect the love of God which is the end of all our endeavours, and that we have no need to change what we have to do in life, but rather to do for God's sake what we commonly do for our own.' So perhaps when others come to us in distress above all else we need to reflect God's presence and to become a channel for his love.

From hamlets to tower blocks
Birmingham

The time came to leave another Garden of Eden. Our elder son was to become a chorister at Lichfield Cathedral. The Bishop of Birmingham at that time was Leonard Wilson, the former Bishop of Singapore, who had been imprisoned and severely tortured by the Japanese in the notorious Changi prison. He invited me to take charge of the parish of Kingshurst. Changing our life among the rural rides of the Isle of Wight for a large re-housing area on the outskirts of Birmingham was a rather daunting prospect. Would we cope with all the tower blocks after the thatched cottages of England's rural Isle?

On a second visit the Bishop heard me out for about eight minutes; there then followed a long pregnant pause. When you have said all you have to say, made all your excuses short of saying that the cats wouldn't settle, you yourself become speechless. After that long, deliberate silence Bishop Leonard leaned forward, looked me straight in the eye, and said "And what the hell do you think I felt like when they asked me to be Bishop of the whole damned lot? When are you coming?" We went!

Bishop Leonard had experienced life at the raw edge in Changi prison. The moments we shared together made a lasting contribution to my faith, and in retirement we had the privilege of visiting Changi. At one Diocesan Conference he told us of some of his experiences; how he was tortured and beaten by his guards, and also how he had given communion to fellow inmates by passing consecrated grains of rice through the bars. After the war he sought out his Japanese torturer and forgave him and he was eventually baptised. Leonard was a man whose great faith had been refined like gold in the assayer's fire – St. Peter's words, not mine. True faith goes on being perfected and changed every day in all our lives.

Years later in the parish priest's home on the island of Kalangala in Lake Victoria, surrounded by a small circle of friends, I celebrated the Eucharist in much the same way. "Would you mind using ordinary bread?" said Henry. No problem. Henry then asked if Coca Cola would do instead of wine! We had no books other than a Bible; I chose a reading, and then kept silence before I consecrated the bread and

Coca Cola using the prayers I know by heart. I think that in both instances the simplicity drove home the full meaning of Christ's body broken for us, and the need for all our lives to be continually rebuilt by his love.

What Bishop Leonard had not told me in that interview was that eleven thousand new souls would be moving into my new parish within the first eighteen months of my ministry there. We found out by discovering the footings on the far side of a busy double carriageway! The parish of St. Barnabas, itself very new, was to absorb one tenth of the new housing development of Chelmsley Wood, then one of the largest housing developments in Western Europe.

The local Council of Churches accepted this challenge and formed a team of visitors to call on new residents on Sunday afternoons. I was apologising to a Caribbean lady for the fact that our church was some distance away across a busy dual carriageway. "Well vicar," she said, "If I wants my shopping I goes over there, and if I wants the library I goes over there, so if I needs God I'll come and get him!" That has a message for all of us. Africans often walk miles to get to church.

One young girl stays with me throughout my ministry. Christine was nine when she developed a severe form of leukaemia. I visited her several times in the local children's hospital, the last occasion being on Christmas Eve. I had previously told her that I was awaiting a major operation on my spine, believing it would help her to think I would soon be sharing some of what she was experiencing. On arrival, before I could say a word, she gave me a beautiful smile and told me that I looked very tired, and asked how my back was. I had come to visit her and she was visiting me. Christine was to die within a matter of hours. That a nine-year-old child should be thinking of me amid all her own suffering just before she died was a very humbling experience and has a lesson for us all.

My parishioners all lived 'on the Kingshurst' and were largely people re-housed from the slums of the centre of Birmingham. Christenings were still conducted in groups of three or more families. One of the benefits of a modern church was that you could turn the chairs around to face the font. I always asked the parents and godparents to gather near the font and made sure all the young children stood in front; nothing worse than being five or six and looking at a load of adult bottoms!

On one occasion many of the uninterested men folk were holding their own private conversations at the back. Coming to the blessing of the water, I always asked the question "What should we use water for first thing in the morning when we get up?" I usually got the reply for which I was angling, but on this particular occasion a five-year-old girl piped up, "Please to make a cup of tea." There was much laughter, but from that moment onwards there was reverent silence; even the men paid attention. That little girl did more to focus their attention on the words of the Gospel than any words of mine.

St. Barnabas Kingshurst was a poor church. On our very first Sunday the hymns were sung to a badly-played piano, so bad that our chorister son had to walk out when *Lift up your Hearts* was played to a tune nobody knew. An organ fund was launched, and after a great battle with the Diocesan committee responsible for church music a new electronic organ was purchased – unheard of in those days.

The great day came for its dedication. The Lichfield Cathedral Choir was invited to lead our worship. Our son's eighty-year-old cello teacher offered to transport our two boys, an offer I declined as he was very frail. While driving Mr Broadhurst and the boys from Lichfield to Kingshurst, somewhere near Castle Bromwich, a shaking Parkinson's hand began to wave in agitation: "It's somewhere there that I ditched a light aircraft in 1917," he said. Never underestimate the elderly!

Shortly before the visit of the Cathedral choir the ladies set to work to make their own bright red choir robes. After the dedication I provided the local weekend news reporter with the usual information they demand; I also let slip that some of the choir ladies had made their magnificent new robes using a 'maternity pattern.' Instead of a short paragraph hidden away on page twenty-five the local paper boldly sported a front-page banner headline announcing, LOCAL LADIES USE MATERNITY PATTERN FOR CASSOCKS. I had no regrets, as the publicity was a great boost to our growing church community.

Our young people did their best to raise money for the church. One Saturday they held a jumble sale. Afterwards they burned the residue at the back of the church hall, including pile upon pile of plastic shoes. High into the air there arose a dense black mushroom cloud resembling the explosions at Hiroshima and Nagasaki. Ladies on their balconies, their washing covered in plastic smuts, waved their arms angrily, pounding the air with a battery of four-letter words and threatening to call the police. The police, in the form of a man on a bicycle, duly arrived. "It's a very naughty bonfire vicar, and I'm afraid I'm going to have to ask you to put it out." This we duly did. The leader of the local Labour Party was holding his Saturday morning surgery in the back room of the church hall. He had observed the drama and offered the youngsters the use of a council skip just across the road, into which they unloaded the remaining items from the bonfire. In it all went, including two dead televisions and a great deal of left-over clothing and knick knacks. Some time later the skip caught fire! The televisions exploded with loud reports, the fire brigade was called, and once more along came the same friendly policeman on his bike. To add to the drama, a bride and her father arrived in their horse driven cab for her wedding. The following Sunday I congratulated the young folk on raising £50, the police and the fire brigade!

A Family Service was introduced; invitation slips were sent out for several months to get it established, then one month we gave them a miss. Not a soul turned up, even the organist was sick. I could have buried my head in my hands; instead I made some outstanding visits to a nearby high-rise block of flats. One lady mistook me for the local football pools man come to collect her coupons; recovering from the shock, she greeted me with "Nice to see you vicar, especially on a Sunday." The church often has to go to the people.

There were many poor families in the parish. I was often in contact with the Birmingham Housing Authority and sometimes the Prison Service also. Winson Green once asked me to visit one of the prisoner's wives; her husband was very anxious to discover if his family was all right financially. When I called she was entertaining another young mother, so talking about money was a little difficult. The lady showed no signs of leaving, so in the end I was forced to broach the topic. Her visitor immediately announced that her husband, a long-distance lorry driver, had sent her £60 the previous Thursday (a lot of money in 1970) and that she had found it quite difficult to spend it all by the next Thursday, adding 'But I managed.' It was probably meant to last two weeks, but many families didn't plan that far ahead; that's how they lived, from pay day to pay day.

One year Mothering Sunday fell on April the 1st. The Scouts, Cubs and Brownies and their leaders were all present with their banners. Before my address I asked the Scoutmaster to move the reading desk into the centre of the nave, and others to re-arrange chairs around it, and to do one or two more unlikely things that I now forget. Everyone did exactly as requested without question, until I called out "April Fool"! There was much consternation and laughter as they put it all back. Afterwards the Scoutmaster came up to me and said, "I thought we would at least have been free from that sort of thing in church, vicar!" The young people thought it was tremendous fun.

My wife worked fulltime at the Erdington School for Girls, where she became the head of the Maths Department. Surprisingly that endeared her to all the other working mums in the parish as it identified her as 'one of them'. Consequently we had to have some help with the housework. One morning we forgot to put canker powder in the cat's ears, a two-person exercise. When Mrs Watts arrived I grabbed the cat whilst she dusted Wilfrid's ears. Leaving the vicarage she then popped into the local Co-op to do her shopping. A lady from the flats overlooking the vicarage promptly blurted out for all the world to hear "I saw you on the floor with the vicar, Mrs Watts!"

Life in Kingshurst was never dull and opened one's eyes to how some of the rest of the world lives. One afternoon a young girl of about twelve or so began talking to me while I was cutting the front grass. "Why are you wearing that funny collar?" she said, and then asked what I did and if I was married. To my complete surprise she followed that by saying: "If you want a bit, you can have some." Pastoral theology lectures left you totally unprepared for a remark like that.

One morning while working at my desk the phone rang. It was Bill Purcell, my first vicar, now the Archdeacon of Dorking in Surrey, asking if I would I consider becoming the vicar of Camberley. Our days in Kingshurst drew to a close. At the same time I had been invited to travel to Malawi to represent the Birmingham Diocese, which was linked to that small land-locked African country. I had to choose between visiting Africa or the parish of Camberley. It was to be Camberley. Our two teenage sons had been excited at the prospect of spending time in Africa and at that age disappointment is not so easily managed. To compensate, between parishes, we took them camping behind the Iron Curtain, visiting what were then Yugoslavia, Bulgaria and Romania and ate luxurious ice cream in all three capital cities as well as Vienna! This was to be the first of at least twelve extensive journeys by car that my wife and I made across much of Eastern Europe, including the former Soviet Union, during the next twenty years They were to have a long-lasting effect upon the roadmap of our life, especially when the Iron Curtain began to crumble.

The people of Kingshurst and Chelmsley Wood made a huge contribution to the growth of my own faith. As

Christians we all nurture each other's faith, and as individuals that faith is never static. It goes on growing under the guidance of the Holy Spirit and within the fellowship of the world wide Christian family as we build upon the foundation of Jesus teaching and his revelation of God's love.

Marching in step
Camberley

St. Michael's Church Camberley, built in 1851 stands beside the busy A30 London Road. On the north side a large churchyard borders the extensive grounds of the Royal Military Academy and the Staff College. St. Michael's, officially designated as Yorktown, is where the grand old Duke of York marched his men to the top of the hill and marched them down again. Sadly the historic Duke of York pub is now no more. While walking from the vicarage to the church I would sometimes hear the strains of the RMA band. By the time I was half way along the two hundred foot crazy paving path my wife had laid, I often found myself marching in step!

Camberley has changed beyond all recognition since the early 1970s. The former church of St. George's that had stood in the town centre had only recently been demolished, with the intention of building a new church on the Old Dean housing estate. The site was going to be sold for approaching two million pounds, as the price of property had boomed. This was quickly put on hold with the sudden onset of the winter of discontent in 1973 within weeks of our arrival.

The vicarage was approached by a long drive bordered

by rhododendron bushes and sweet chestnut trees. Just beside the main entrance there stood a semi-derelict church hall. One cold dark November night, my predecessor took pity on a tramp and allowed him to use it as a 'stop over' - how else can you respond to those verses in St. Matthew's Gospel "I was a stranger and you took me in, naked and you clothed me?" The bush telegraph soon got to work among the vagrant community and by the time we arrived there were upwards of a dozen men in regular occupation of the 'Hut' as they called it. The Hut had only two electric light bulbs and one cold water tap, but it was a haven for men of the road. No questions were asked, no registration made. No decontamination. They came and they went under the guidance of their king and leader, known to all and sundry as 'Danny'. The loo kept on being damaged beyond repair, so there was no sanitation other than the rhododendron thickets in the vicarage garden!

Six months after our arrival the local Health Authority condemned the "Hut"; either it was to be closed or we would have to furnish it with proper beds, bedside lockers and washing and cooking facilities at an estimated cost of £60,000, all to be spent on what was effectively a ramshackle tin hut. In addition it would have to be registered and run under the direction of a suitably qualified warden.

The proposal was much debated by the church council. In theory it was just the sort of thing a church should undertake; in practice it was probably unattainable, and a somewhat dubious plan for a totally unsuitable building. There were articles written to the local paper, some very negative and others saying 'What a wonderful idea,' but never any offers of real practical help. The new proposals would have been anathema to those professional vagrants; demolition was the only practical solution. Most of my new friends were found alternative accommodation, either in a Salvation Army Hostel, or one of the dreaded reception centres. After the closure some of them would still turn up on the vicarage doorstep.

That year provided an insight into the life lived by so called men of the road. They too, like us, have to tread their roadmap of life. They loved the "Hut" because no questions were asked. It provided some sort of roadside freedom. I soon discovered that there were problems behind all of their lives. An Irishman called Kevin had been conscripted to fight in Korea and developed what we would now call post-traumatic stress disorder. To dispel his constant nightmares, he took to drink. He would be dried out; then the nightmares would recur, so he returned to the bottle, and so the process went on with no real solution. We contacted his sister in Ireland, but the family did not want to know. He had always been a 'weak' character, they said. More of his story emerged when later we took him by car to the reception centre at Newbury. Who was to blame - Kevin, or the society that took over his life and sent him to fight? There is no easy answer. A battalion of my regiment, the Greenjackets, was in fact posted to Korea, and I could as easily have been among them as was Kevin.

Bill was an entirely different sort of man, another swarthy Irishman. He turned up asking for work; he was in luck as the churchyard maintenance was causing a major problem. He set to with a will and when sober cleared far more than the average man and in much less time, but at other times you would find him spread-eagled beside the shade of a table-top tomb with an empty cider bottle or two beside him, dead to the world and all its problems.

To maintain the near quarter acre of grass around the vicarage, we kept geese. One evening I went to ask the local publican just across the road from the "Hut" if I could help myself to some old iron Vono mesh bed-frames perched on the top of a skip. "Of course vicar, help yourself," he said. There were four. Surprise surprise, who should be in the pub but my friend Bill with one of his mates. "Don't you worry vicar I'll give you a hand with 'em." That meant crossing the busy A30 London Road, no mean task, choosing a suitable moment to transport four iron bed frames with a half-drunken Irishman. Their cost had also increased by three pints of beer! Safely stowed Bill says to me "Now would yer be in the whay like of givin me a wee h'lift to Bagshot Park? H'i wants yer to see my old 'ut where I lives like." One could not refuse. Bagshot Park was then home to the Army Chaplain's department where he lived courtesy of the senior chaplain who rejoiced in the surname Pew!

"Na these days," he continued, "Yer canna use t' main entrance hany more like, cos of't Princess and h'all er security like, but ha' knows a whay round t' back like, where we shouldn't be goin, but as yer wi me like hit'll be h'alright!" So I took my well-oiled Irishman through the illicit gates. On reaching the farm in the middle of the park Bill says, "Now yer could be doin wi some straw like for your wee chickens like. Ha knows t'farmer very well like. You be stopping ere like while ha goes and h'asks him."

After about five minutes he returned with two enormous bales of straw one on each shoulder, saying "Now t'farmer

was na there like, but ha knows ee won't be minding like."
As he stuffed them into the back of my Hillman Minx estate
he continued, "Now just h'over there like there's two der-hi-
lict greenhouses full of old bamboo canes and ha knows you
could be usin' them as well." Off he went and there I was
sitting in my car, in my clerical collar, with two nicked bales
of straw in a place where I had no business to be. The
bamboo canes duly appeared and were safely stowed. We
still have a few to this day. We progressed further into the
park to view his little 'home', a very wee corrugated iron
workman's road hut.

Later we erected a garden shed for him in the
churchyard to which I ran an electric light. I could have
easily found a flat in the town, but he refused, he'd have
been on someone's books. A new claw hammer, a smart pair
of secateurs and several other gifts wandered my way,
including a set of clapped-out jemmy tools and some
eighteen-inch pneumatic drill bits, all of somewhat doubtful
provenance! Come a Tuesday he would be asking for a 'wee
loan' against his next week's wages. This was always
deducted the next pay day and he was meticulous in seeing
that it was all done correctly. If he asked for more I would
send my wife to speak to him. She was much more able to
say NO than I ever was. "Now how yer lives with that wee
dragon of a woman ha just cannay himagine!" he would
sometimes say to me.

I treasure the ability I developed of talking to the rough
and ready of this world in their own language, many of
whom have hearts just like ours, only a bit more bashed
about. They provided good company, taught you a lot about
life and how it is love that saves and heals, not book

theology, though that has its place. The stories involving Bill are legion. Once I was nearly assaulted by one of his friends, who used to hover around him on pay day. "You're a wicked vicar," he began, "letting my friend Bill live in that wretched hut without any heat". He became rather aggressive and I thought he was about to strike me. Then he used the word 'bollocks.' "And bollocks to you mate," I replied. That was the last thing he had expected a vicar to say and he burst out laughing and was totally disarmed. Had I quoted the Bible at him? Some days later I saw him in the town with a large black eye. Bill must have thumped him one after I left. "You don't talk to MY vicar like that you don't" – Bang!

Before Bill, there was Tom. He also lived in a hut in our garden. One day he had an accident and broke his leg in the London road, the victim of a hit and run driver. He had just been paid and everyone thought he was drunk. He gave our address as his next of kin. When Jill went to visit him in hospital they all assumed she was his wife! He begged her to find his clothes, which had been steam-sterilised and placed in a black bin liner, insisting he was not drunk and could prove it. From his trouser pocket my wife slowly extracted some sodden old one-pound notes and a few accompanying coins, his week's wages, exactly the amount he had just been paid. She laid the notes on the ward radiator to dry. He had not been drinking. but was never able to work in the churchyard again. Those experiences help one understand the challenges that face so many men and women and the huge task that Jesus himself faced as he proclaimed his vision of the Kingdom of God.

While wrestling with the Hut there were extensive plans

in the pipeline for building a new church on the Old Dean, a large housing estate attached to the parish. The design I inherited was for a massive church centre with consultation rooms and offices for social services, besides the provision of an equally large church building. The old St George's site was still unsold. The two million pounds had evaporated into thin air overnight with the outbreak of war in the Middle East. The world was plunged into crisis as the price of oil suddenly crashed, bringing the advent of the three-day week and the winter of discontent, with many of the supermarket shelves noticeably emptying overnight. The value of the St. George's site dropped like a stone. The sale was delayed. The land in the town centre was eventually sold but for a much-reduced amount; a more suitable church was built in 1979 together with a new church hall for St. Michael's.

Another aspect of church life at St. Michael's was our association with the military. Sir Hugh Beech, the Commandant of the Staff College, introduced a civilian sponsor scheme by which local people befriended some of their overseas officers. Among several, we hosted an Egyptian family. The overseas officers' children were mostly educated at one of the local primary schools of which I was one of the governors. Just before Easter one year the school put on a children's passion play. The daughter of the Israeli officer was given the task of reading the story of how all the horrid Egyptians perished in the crossing of the Red Sea. Sitting next to me was the son of our Egyptian friends. This was a rather sad and embarrassing moment and could almost have amounted to racial discrimination these days. He needed a lot of comforting.

On another occasion we invited the family of the Kuwaiti officer to Christmas lunch. They arrived late with a great tray of stuffed vine leaves. Our family members were at least a dozen, and included a rather unusual Irishman suffering from diabetes who had collapsed outside my study window one morning after which he came to church nearly every Sunday. He always sat on the left side of the church next to my wife. He was a socialist and once muttered to my wife, "Good socialist hymn this!" He rode an uninsured moped with perpetual L plates, but was very kind to my father-in-law, who was suffering from Parkinson's disease. We also became his next of kin! When we came to clear his flat we found it filled from floor to ceiling with mail order goods, most of which were unopened.

Later in the year we received a return invitation to feast with the Kuwaitis. We accepted. We were only three, my wife and I and my mother-in-law. They had prepared a meal for twelve, thinking those they had met at Christmas were all part of our extended family. We applied the 'wedding feast technique' and began to scour the highways and byways. We hastily phoned Jill's brother and his wife asking if they 'fancied dinner on a sheik.' They upped sticks and travelled from High Wycombe. A more worthy gathering eventually sat down to a whole lamb which had been quartered, cooked, and then put back together again!

My Camberley congregation seemed to be rather serious and sombre after our light-hearted Birmingham folk. I thought back to my April Fools' Day service at Kingshurst. Trying to brighten things up a little I would include a joke or two in the sermon. The trouble was they thought my every word was gospel truth! Much later our deputy organist took up lodgings with us and as a consequence gained an unusually deep insight into our family life, as well as having at times to care for the geese and the chickens. Together he and our lady churchwarden produced a parish pantomime. In one sketch the church treasurer came on stage dressed in clerical collar, green welly boots and gardening clothes and addressing the churchwarden, said "I think I have got greenfly all over my Cinerarias, darling!" Then the churchwarden turns to reveal a large yellow '20p off' sticker on her back saying in a loud voice, "I've just had a *marvellous* idea" – one of my wife's well-known pet phrases – and so it went on, taking the mickey in a riotous way. What a change! Once you have got that far, you have made it. You have developed a bond, which is what our Christian life is all about, and you can really begin to share the Gospel message in a lively way. Jesus often adopted that technique and told story after story when he attended dinner parties, some of which we hear about in the Gospels. He rather made fun of the dour scribes and Pharisees at times, often with deep sarcasm.

Diocesan Synod in the Guildford Diocese was a very different animal to that in Birmingham. Before the onset of the year of discontent, you arrived to a glass of sherry. At one session the Synod was again debating a proposed 'Decade of Evangelism.' This had been on the agenda for a long time, may be for nearly all of its ten years! The debate became bogged down once more in a lot of rather complicated theology. After about an hour and a half of tortuous discussion the Dean of Guildford, Tony Bridge, a rather flamboyant personality and an accomplished artist, rose to his full stature and pronounced from the floor of the house in his loud stentorian voice this masterpiece of literary shock and awe: "It would help a little if we all got our f...ing fingers out and preached the f...ing Gospel!" With those words he at once sat down. He didn't just say f...ing either, but used the full version, in frequent use in some circles. There was a stunned, electric silence which no one knew how to break, not even the Bishop, whose face became as purple as his shirt. All the other members on the platform were fidgeting with a selection of contorted facial expressions, hardly daring to look each other in the eye. The silence continued for some time until the Bishop somehow or other pulled himself together and muttered, "Don't record the F word in the minutes. Mr Secretary". The trouble was that Tony had put his finger on what was really needed, and they all knew it.

As a vicar one is brought into close contact with death more often than most people, and one has to pluck words of appropriate comfort for the bereaved from whatever source springs to mind amid the particular circumstances. One particular brush with death stands out more in my memory than any other. It concerns the brother of a lady called Ethel. She was one of those friendly and faithful souls who had taught in Sunday School all her life long, probably from her early teens, repeating word for word what she herself had been taught in her time. I was called to Ethel's home late one afternoon when a neighbour telephoned to say that her brother had just died. Nothing, but nothing, that I had ever learned at theological college could have prepared me for the particular encounter with death that now awaited me.

On being ushered into the living room, where the fire was burning cheerfully in the grate, there was her brother, still seated in his high-backed Windsor chair beside the hearth, pipe in hand, and looking straight in my direction. Without more ado Ethel began to discuss arrangements for the funeral. From time to time she addressed her brother - "Now this was always one of your favourite hymns, wasn't it dear?" He somehow seemed to be having a hand, if not exactly a word, in making his own funeral arrangements. It was almost as if she expected him to say 'Yes dear' while another lingering puff came out of his still smoldering pipe!

Now our human existence is basically a matter of what happens between our birth and the moment we die. The dividing line between the two can often be very slender. But so often we want to sweep death under the carpet, even try to pretend that it does not exist, unless it becomes totally unavoidable. We do ourselves no end of harm by taking this attitude. We tend to hide our real feelings and emotions, covering our souls and our inward wrestling with the vestments of a dulled or fearful imagination. This is a very negative approach to those whom we have loved.

Our Christian faith, on the other hand, enables us to come to terms with death, and reminds us of the way our Lord dealt with his own death, where he showed compassion for others, especially his mother, and even those who had crucified him. He conquered death and the fear of it by putting it into a proper perspective with his closing dying words – "It is accomplished" – and by entrusting his soul into the hands of his Heavenly Father. The message of the Cross is the real answer to the question that young barrow boy asked me in the army all those long years ago: "What's going to happen to me when I die?" Ethel's brother was duly laid to rest in St. Michael's churchyard, but his presence has remained with me more than most.

Another totally different experience also stands etched in my memory. Undertakers will occasionally confront a vicar with a fait accompli. The phone rings. "We've arranged a funeral for 2.30 on Tuesday, Vicar, that'll be all right won't it?" On this particular occasion it wasn't. I had a long-standing commitment made more than six months earlier to be the guest speaker at the Annual Meeting and Luncheon of the local branch of the Industrial Life Assurance Offices Association. I explained to the undertaker that I could take the funeral, but would arrive only at the very last minute, and would arrange for people to welcome the mourners. As luck would have it I was able to return to my vicarage a little earlier than expected and for some reason providence directed my steps to the churchyard to check the location of the grave, something I usually took for granted. I looked and looked but it became obvious that no grave had been dug.

Returning to the vicarage, I was greeted by the undertaker walking across the extensive vicarage lawns. He was of a ruddy complexion and announced cheerfully, "Everything's all right vicar, we're all ready for you."

"Everything's not all right, no grave has been dug," I replied.

"My man dug it this morning, Vicar. I know he did. Everything's all right, come along, there's nothing to worry about, they're all waiting for you."

Very reluctantly, he finally agreed to accompany me to the churchyard. His face dropped a mile and his normally rosy cheeks became ashen grey. I was right. We had no grave! We did the only thing possible. The situation was explained to the family, I conducted the first part of the service and we left the coffin safely locked in the church while we attended the funeral feast, not a comfortable experience. I phoned another local grave digger whom I knew quite well. "Well Vicar," he said in his broad Cockney accent, "By ve time I've mide mi littul motor go and gavered mi tools togever, it'll be arf past five before we gets a grave dug, Vicar. It's hard work in that dere part of de churchyard, vicar!"

Only by the grace of God were we prevented from enacting in real life a scene I once saw performed by the inimitable Dave Allen on the show that bears his name; the verger led the vicar (Dave!), the undertaker, and all the funeral guests to circle the churchyard searching for a non-existent grave! Had I had no faith in the Holy Spirit before, it was now firmly established! Someone other than myself had picked up my feet and taken them to look for that grave.

Then there was Camberley Kate. Kate was a rough-spoken Yorkshire lady who lived in a tumbledown house beside the Lamb Inn, a local pub along the London Road. Her house was home to upwards of fourteen stray dogs at a time, with some of whom she slept in her double bed! It was a familiar sight to see her walking them to the old Camberley town centre, each dog tethered to her 'cart', a little box mounted on a pair of old pram wheels. There she begged funds for their upkeep. She was even featured once or twice on the television, and still is from time to time. Her financial affairs were administered by the local Baptist Minister, but she fell out with the Baptist congregation, or rather they had fallen out with her because she was heard by some devout soul swearing her head off at her dogs in the town precinct! After that episode she attached herself to the Anglican Church. We are always regarded as being an inclusive church, and there are many reasons why people join us, but surely this must rank among the most bizarre!

Taking tea with Kate was a very risky affair and required more than the usual amount of courage. The milk was often accompanied by a generous dose of left-over washing-up water that was already standing in your mug, with the odd dog hair sometimes in evidence floating on the surface. On one occasion she bared her bosom to my wife and said, "Look dear, I've got the mange." She once very generously donated some large boxes of dried milk powder for use in the church coffee; it was only later while disposing of the packaging that we discovered the label 'Unfit for Human Consumption'!

Reports of our travels in Eastern Europe were sometimes featured in the church magazine. In 1978 we set out to travel the length of the former Soviet Union in a little yellow Fiat, the model on which the Russians designed their basic Lada. Should we break down we thought they might be better able to assist us. All our Eastern European friends hated the Russians and said we were courting arrest and imprisonment! We wanted to see for ourselves what their ordinary folk were like, and they proved to be as welcoming as all the people we have met on our travels abroad.

After crossing Europe we headed for Kiev campsite in the Ukraine. It was there we met our Russian friends , Boris and Stella, before continuing to Rostov-on-Don and Sochi on our way to Tbilisi in Georgia. The journey home took us across the Caucasus mountains to Moscow and Leningrad before stopping at Helsinki and Stockholm and finally reaching the ferry terminal for Harwich at Gothenburg, a journey of over 7,000 miles. That was in 1978 in Uncle Brezhnev's time. This was all made possible by a Canadian priest, Bob Birtch from London, Ontario, who took charge of the parish during our absence. He is still affectionately remembered by the people of St. Martin's, and until recently we used to exchange greetings with his widow.

In the autumn of the same year, while working at my desk one morning, the telephone rang. "Cyriac Arpad here from Cluj-Napoca in Romania. I am in London!" I arranged to meet him at Ascot station and brought him back to the vicarage. He told us how he had been travelling across Austria and some rather doubtful story about their car having caught fire. He joined me for Morning Prayer each day and preached on the Sunday. We took him to London, to Canterbury to meet the Archdeacon (my mother's former rector in Elland), and to visit my brother in Yorkshire.

Before we went north, Cyriac received a series of mysterious phone calls from Bucharest which led to our meeting another priest at Heathrow on our return. He was dressed in a long, belted fawn raincoat and a trilby hat, the brim of which was turned down, partially hiding his face. He didn't behave like a priest and never entered the church, except under duress on their last morning when both he and Cyriac spouted prayers in Hungarian in the sanctuary, leaving me on the sidelines in the choir stalls. Back in Camberley Cyriac behaved quite differently, and the two of them went up to London every morning, returning home quite late in the evening. When asked what they were doing they informed us they were visiting theological bookshops and museums. We begged them to have supper with us on their last evening. Not long after their departure, there were reports in the press and on the news about the mysterious disappearance of two former Romanian citizens from their home in London!

Visiting Romania once more the following year, we met Arpad, now his old normal self again. However, while walking to lunch we were in conversation with David Laslo, another close Romanian friend, and asked how the priest was who had accompanied Cyriac on his visit to the UK. "What priest?" David asked. "He was travelling on his own." As we were on the way to lunch with their Bishop we thought it best to drop the subject, remembering how that 'other' priest had born so close a resemblance to a James Bond spy. Lunch comprised chicken claws in a bowl of broth, a Romanian delicacy!

During my time at St. Michael's, Paul, who had played the organ since he was fourteen, completed ten years as organist. He had an inimitable way of skilfully incorporating the music of *Happy Birthday* into the verses of a well-known hymn, and always gave a superb rendition of *Rudolph the Red Nosed Reindeer* after the Christmas midnight service. Tributes were paid at the main morning service and he was presented with ten cans of Courage beer by the Churchwarden and his wife, who also gave him a kiss, or two! For those who may not know, it says in the Acts of the Apostles that when Saint Paul was journeying to Rome along the Appian Way he broke his journey at a place called the Three Taverns, where he stopped and took Courage! It's all too easy to go on turning the handle when you have been in a parish for ten years. It was time to consider leaving Camberley. Both my wife and I owe a great debt to all our friends there. At our farewell party we were presented not with a gold watch but a substantial garden ladder, presumably to help us climb the next steps along the roadmap of our journey which took us to the parish of Long Sutton in Somerset.

Bathing in Bath and Wells

Long Sutton

We left Camberley with some misgivings. The old Victorian vicarage at Long Sutton was undergoing extensive renovation, which continued long after we arrived. We inherited yet another severely-neglected Garden of Eden and even another old stable building that predated the vicarage by a century or two. While we had been at Camberley Jill's father had died, and her mother had moved from Burwash into a flat nearby. She was now to live with us for the remainder of her life.

It was quite a challenge restoring the old vicarage to its former glory. Upstairs the floors were very uneven and furniture had to be propped. The garden was an equal challenge, but after a year or more it became yet another pristine Garden of Eden – with a magnificent flower border running the eighty-foot length of a four-foot-high south-facing stone wall. Delphiniums and other perennials grew in clumps of five, all raised from seed.

Long Sutton was linked to two other parishes; Long Load, where barges of coal once came to the landing stage there, and the historic Parish of Muchelney, which included the site of Muchelney Abbey. This former Benedictine

Monastery was founded by King Athelstan in 939. What makes Muchelney church famous is the fabulous 17th century ceiling stretching the length of the nave. Each panel features an angel, some of which are rather décolleté, and some bare breasted altogether. They are thought to be a symbol of purity. I wonder how many parishioners have gazed upwards during some of the lengthy sermons of days gone by!

From at least 1228 the vicar was appointed by the Abbot of Muchelney, who was also responsible for providing the vicar with bread and ale every day, plus meat twice a week, and eggs and fish the other five days. This was even kept up after the dissolution of the Abbey, but a pint never came my way.

The church at Long Sutton is equally historic, with a magnificent 15th century mediaeval carved pulpit, containing beautifully gilded figures of the saints. The pulpit is in fact older than the church itself. A distinctive feature of the parish in those days was Peter Lamb, a rather dishevelled elderly retired priest, a familiar figure who wore a distinctive peaked cap as his two dogs walked him round the village. He would accompany the hymns rather erratically on his somewhat screechy violin. On his 70th birthday we presented him with a large bottle of Lambs' Navy Rum. This sort of presentation was becoming a habit, though this time round I could find no biblical justification!

The parish was governed by a retired senior churchwarden known as the Brigadier; he had sort of been in charge from time immemorial. There were ways of getting around him. When caught short he would announce that he was going to 'privatise' himself. I often wonder what he did when he nationalised himself? Once I had got to know him, I chose an appropriate moment to ask. He gave a sort of military chuckle, more perhaps a snort, and walked away!

As at Arreton all those years before we formed a village youth club which met at the vicarage. They volunteered to run a stall at the annual summer fete held in the newly-restored garden; the contents of their table somewhat bemused the ladies who ran the more traditional stalls.

My wife and I volunteered to deliver meals on wheels, an excellent means for a new vicar to get to know some of his housebound parishioners. Later in retirement in Devizes we delivered meals there also. Two men stand out in my mind: Mr Weeding, to whom I would chat while Jill cut his grass, and another gentleman whose name I can no longer recall. He suffered from severe itching all over his body and had constantly to rub himself with E45 cream. One day he took me aside and said, "I would like to give you something for the Ugandan school you support. Tony Blair gives me my heating allowance and I don't really need it". He then handed me a small well-stuffed brown envelope. When I got home I found it contained five hundred pounds, all in £20 notes. We were dumbfounded. In 2003 he had his reward when we brought Bishop Jackson and his wife Dorothy to stay in our home. We took the Bishop to visit him. I shall never forget the expression on his face; it was one of sheer joy. He just has to be added to my large cloud of witnesses to faith.

I often visited an elderly man in Muchelney who always told me the same story of his experiences in the First World War. I conducted his funeral, and twenty years later, when visiting the family to buy vegetables, his son greeted me by name and told me he remembered all I had said at his father's funeral. I had long forgotten, nor can I recall his father's name. Sometimes we scatter seeds of faith that may take ages to grow; it is a rare blessing to see them germinate years later.

One morning as I was taking my wife and her mother to Long Load for the morning service, we passed a freshly-killed rabbit lying beside the road. I have often had to wait for my wife, and now I had two ladies to wait for! We were running rather more than late. I refused to stop. On arrival I accompanied Clarissa to the church; Jill immediately got back into the car to collect the road kill. I took my time in the vestry and put on my surplice, which would steam when held in front of the electric fire. I slowly gave out as many notices as I reasonably could – still no wife. As I was about to announce the first hymn she arrived breathless to take her seat beside her mother. A loud stage whisper echoed round the little church – "Did you get it, Jill?"

"Don't be so conspiratorial," my wife replied with as quiet a whisper as she could.

Another loud stage whisper followed: "What does conspiratorial mean, Jill?"

By this time the congregation was convulsed and I had to announce the first hymn to halt the laughter. I was hardly able to do so – the organist had selected "Dear Lord and Father of mankind forgive our foolish ways"!

During my time floods occasionally prevented my reaching the parish, but never anywhere near so severe as those of 2014, when it was isolated for weeks. The angels must have looked down with wonder as a local supermarket delivered supplies by boat to the church for distribution. The monks of old were no fools when they built their abbey on high ground.

During our time at Long Sutton we continued our travels in Eastern Europe. Canadian priests and their wives took up residence in the vicarage for a month while we visited and revisited our friends in Yugoslavia, Bulgaria, Romania, Hungary, Poland and Czechoslovakia, as it then was. Our Bishop was also very interested in this part of the world and gave us every encouragement. We once made a rendezvous on Karcag station with a young Hungarian girl we had got to know; we boldly displayed a large Tesco bag for recognition. Her family gave us a wonderful welcome and a typically Hungarian meal, including lashings of the famous goulash.

We revisited Miroslav and his family in a remote part of Yugoslavia, near the city of Nish. It had all been pre-arranged and we arrived only one hour late to find them preparing a sucking pig for our evening meal. The intestines had been cleaned and were hung up in a lilac tree. As guests of honour we were given his parents' bed, and the evening meal was unbelievably gourmet – freshly-roasted sucking pig and all the accoutrements, followed by home-made desserts smothered in freshly-made rich creamy yoghurt, accompanied by glass after glass of Slivovitz. The next day we were taken to meet some nuns, who entertained us with milk and honey!

Some of our parishioners were rather suspicious of our travels in the former communist lands and thought that besides being tourists, we must also be 'fellow travellers'. We learned a great deal about the challenges of everyday life in what were then known as the Comecon countries;

many goods were in short supply – things like sewing needles, batteries, aspirins, vegetable seeds and much more. Our boot was always laden with the most unlikely goods. This is a time in history that can never be repeated and we were privileged to travel there by car so freely. Our visits were a lifeline.

Our stay in Long Sutton was short. After only three and a half years I was invited to consider the parish of Stockbridge in the Winchester Diocese. At the time we wondered about making this particular move. It was somewhat pressured, but in hindsight it was to have more far-reaching implications for working out the roadmap of our life in the future than we could have ever possibly imagined.

Trout Fishing on the River Test

Stockbridge

In the summer of 1987 we left behind yet another 'Garden of Eden', one that had only barely reached its prime; not to take up salmon fishing in the Yemen, but fishing for men (and women!) in the Test Valley. Stockbridge is a small but historic market town that straddles the famous river Test, home to one of the most renowned trout streams in Europe and also to an equally prestigious fishing club. I possessed just the right sort of story for the annual Angler's Club dinner. During my time at Hayes I had encountered a story-telling bus conductor who entertained his customers from a seemingly limitless supply of amusing tales and anecdotes. Seeing a clergyman board his bus was grist to his mill and prompted him to tell the story of a seaside vicar taking an evening stroll along the pier, accompanied by his three attractive teenage daughters. At the end of the pier stood a lonely fisherman.

"Have you caught anything?" asks the vicar.

"Not a solitary fish, vicar, my bag's empty and I've been here nearly all day."

"Then you should become a fisher of men like me," said the vicar.

Eyeing the three young girls, the fisherman replied, "Well excuse me for saying so, your reverence, but you do seem to be using the right sort of bait!"

We can turn this story into a parable – all anglers have to be extremely patient, casting their lines time upon time before finally making a catch. The same is true when trying to help people find faith; you require persistence, patience and the ability to listen, but above all respect for those you are trying to encourage. As we have seen, the seeds of faith you sow may only come to fruition much later, when you have taken many more steps on your own life's journey.

Stockbridge Parish Church was then a rather damp and mouldering building and for a while one wondered where life was leading us. The parish included two other church communities, those of Longstock and Leckford. Stockbridge in the daytime has all the appearance of being a thriving market town, but at night its population is only in the hundreds. On arrival I inherited a lady known as Nan, the fount of all local knowledge. Her sitting room was also home to a magnificent mynah bird. I would often consult her, saying "I've come to pick your brains, Nan." After having called several more times I once again repeated my customary greeting "I've come to pick your brains again, Nan" at which the wretched bird broke into fits of uncontrollable laughter! It must have looked up the word 'brain' on the Mynahnet! I had to greet her more circumspectly after that.

Stockbridge has many claims to fame. It was founded by the Romans, who laid a causeway of compressed chalk to create a crossing of the River Test. The Prince of Wales, the future Edward the Seventh, had several assignations with Lily Langtry in Stockbridge and is reported to have fallen into the river on one occasion while returning to his lodgings! During the First World War the old railway station was used by many of the soldiers as they settled into some of the staging camps nearby. In the Second World War, Spitfires were secretly assembled and flight tested, often by female test pilots, on the grass runway beside the old racecourse.

The Parish of Stockbridge is in the patronage of St. John's College, Oxford. As patrons they make the appointment of a new vicar. Our six-year stay entitled my wife and me to a visit to the college every third year, where we spent several days hearing lectures and sharing in university life. One memorable lecture was on Beatrix Potter. We also dined in the Great Hall and met the Chaplain, who was researching a book on the Christian Socialist Movement of the 1920s. Once more Harold Mason's name popped up, the same Harold who had been curate of All Saints Elland, my mother's home town, and her first true love! There are books all over our home inscribed 'with love from Harold'. Any thought of her marrying him was immediately quashed by her father, who besides making me toffee pipes and walking sticks was an ardent Conservative and engineered Harold's removal from the parish. My mother promptly married the next curate!

Of course we already knew a lot about Harold, and we had learned a great deal more when I was appointed Vicar of Arreton on the Isle of Wight. The Chaplain had no idea that Harold had ever married and we supplied him with a great deal of material, especially about the Battle of the Flags at Thaxted, where Conrad Noel was Vicar and where Harold was his assistant priest. Known as the Red Vicar of Thaxted, Conrad was a prominent British Christian Socialist. At Thaxted he flew the red flag and the flag of Sinn Fein alongside the flag of St. George. This led to a continuous battle with students from Cambridge, who made attacks on the church to remove the flags; eventually a consistory court ruled against his flying inappropriate flags.

The population of Stockbridge almost doubles during the daytime as staff and pupils pour into the schools, and the local shopkeepers arrive with the staff who run its many famous restaurants. Stockbridge is in the Winchester Diocese and my duties often took me to the Cathedral. It was of course full of memories for me. One day as I was passing the back entrance to the old Green Jackets barracks I fell into conversation with an old soldier. He asked me who had been my platoon corporal and sergeant. Yes, he knew Corporal Scott and told me roughly where he was now living, not far from King Alfred's College. I looked him up on the elector's lists in the public library, and later knocked on his door. He was old and rather weak. Over a cup of tea he told me that I was the only one of all the National Service men who had passed through his hands who had ever taken the trouble to go and see him. There were tears in his eyes.

We shared many memories. I reminded him how one morning he had overslept and how one of our squad had assembled us outside his bunk to march us to breakfast mimicking his words of command "Squaaad…squad….shun. Ma-ooove to vee layft in fwees…. Raaight tarn!" and how he stormed out of his bunk and marched us round the parade ground three times in his slippers and pyjamas. We both laughed till we could laugh no more, and then he asked me to pray with him.

Over the years, as with most of us, my faith has had its ups and downs, its doubts and challenges under moments of stress, all of which can weaken our resolve and cloud our vision, but moments like that add a new depth and meaning to life and help you to soldier on amidst all the cruelty in the world. Shining through the darkness are moments of blinding certainty when one feels God's presence amid the ordinary moments of our daily lives, a presence that takes you far beyond all knowledge and understanding. "God is not apprehended by reason but by life" – (Tolstoy, *War and Peace*.)

Longstock set particular store by the observation of Plough Sunday. An old hand-plough was always placed in the chancel. I prepared what I thought was a suitable sermon based on Jesus' words "Whoever puts his hand to the plough and looks back is not fit for the Kingdom of God." When the service was over a master ploughman came up to me and said, "That was all right Vicar, but you got one thing wrong, we always look back these days when we are ploughing to make sure we are laying a straight furrow." Just a trifle deflating, but I think we all know what Jesus meant, that when we set out to accept his way of life as the pattern for our earthly pilgrimage we need above all else never to turn back.

One Sunday at Longstock, just as the idea of women priests was beginning to be floated, I had a lady come to preach on behalf of the Church Missionary Society. I was a little late arriving and she was already dressed in cassock and surplice. I greeted her and went to the vestry to find her skirt neatly folded on the back of my chair! My mind boggled. What would have happened had I arrived early? When putting my cassock on I never take my trousers off! I had to stay at the back of the church chatting to parishioners to allow the reverse operation to be achieved with appropriate decorum and modesty. Was this what women priests were going to be about? After a long struggle we now also have women bishops; hopefully we can now get down to carrying out the late Dean of Guildford's demand that we get on with preaching the Gospel! St. Paul said that in Christ there is neither male nor female, slave nor free, but we are all one, and that when we follow Christ and his way of life we all become a new creation. As a priest stands at the altar, gender is not really an issue; what is of most importance is the celebration of what Jesus did when he sacrificed his life on the cross so that we might be forgiven and become part of his Kingdom on this poor troubled earth, an earth that is so hurt and divided by what many human beings often do to one another. He died above all else to show us that true humanity to which God calls everyone

Back to the nitty gritty of life and the need to maintain church buildings, but with no apology for mixing up a little philosophy with the hurly burly of everyday life. That's where philosophy and theology need to be firmly rooted. In the course of time I inherited another military gentleman as churchwarden – a retired army general, quite a contrast to the Brigadier. He was to mastermind plans for the restoration of Stockbridge Church, which involved the re-tiling of yet another church roof and the replacement of almost the entire floor to create proper ventilation. It is now a beautifully-preserved example of rather better than average Victorian neo-gothic architecture.

Upon completion, we then undertook the restoration of the old fourteenth-century chancel which had been left behind when the old St. Peter's was demolished and replaced with the new church in the High Street. This was all done by voluntary labour under the direction of local antiquarian experts, and involved removing all the soil that had encroached upon the walls to a height of nearly three feet in places. Its rededication was a moving moment.

The parish of Leckford also possessed a very historic building but only had a population of just over sixty souls, so an attendance of eight or so represented just over 7% of the population, far above the national average. This was boosted at harvest time by large quantities of apples from the nearby Waitrose Estate, as well as some of their employees. The organist used to play a rendering of the theme music for *The Prime of Miss Jean Brodie* as a church voluntary at Evensong!

Perestroika and Glasnost

The fall of the Berlin Wall

During our stay in Stockbridge profound changes took place

in the Soviet Union and Eastern Europe when President Gorbachev introduced 'perestroika' and 'glasnost', restructuring and openness, and slowly but surely the Iron Curtain began to crumble. Nan Clay, besides being a mine of parish information, would also very kindly sit with my wife's mother when needed. One evening in the early summer of 1987 she received a mysterious phone call from a French lady in Strasbourg. Nan knew next to no French but very carefully made a note of the telephone number. In a rash moment Jill had promised nearly all our Eastern European friends that we would meet them 'anywhere in the West' if they managed to obtain a visa. Jill, a reasonably fluent French speaker, returned the call and the lady informed us that she had Simeon and Olga Felecan with her and would we go and collect them! Simeon was the Dean of the Orthodox cathedral in Cluj-Napoca whom we knew well and with whom we had travelled to Moisei, a monastery in northern Romania.

We dropped everything, took Jill's mother to a friend and left immediately for the continent on a night ferry. With the help of the Orthodox Church in Paris some car parking was arranged and we awaited their arrival at Notre Dame. Simeon and Olga were rather late, the reason being that they been advised to park their old Dacia car somewhere near the Eiffel Tower. Later we transferred many items into our car, but a short way out of Paris over a light supper I became distinctly uneasy. No way would I have left our car there. We turned back and drove both cars in convoy to Boulogne. The Dacia was safely parked in the ferry carport. Among the many items transferred was a quite ordinary 'cushion', with which we were told to take especial care.

Simeon had a powerful voice and sang beautifully in the church. We took them to Westminster Abbey to meet Canon Trevor Beeson, who had a special interest in Eastern Europe and in orthodoxy, and with whom arrangements were made to receive one of Simeon's theological students from Cluj. The time soon came for us to return them to Dover on their way to recover their ancient Dacia from the friendly port staff of Townsend Thoresen. We heard nothing more of them for about six months, and then one day a postcard bearing only the postmark 'Munich' came through our letterbox informing us in French that they had decided 'définitivement' to remain in the West. The cushion, which some London friends collected, should in itself have been sufficient proof to warn us of their ultimate intention. It had probably been stuffed with jewellery and other valuable items.

We tried repeatedly to contact Simeon via the Orthodox Church. The saddest thing was a letter we received from their daughter, Cornelia, asking why they hadn't heard from us and wondering if they had done anything wrong. Our only option was write to their old address, to no avail.

But that is not the end of the story. In 1989 our Czech and Polish friends came to visit us. Guy, a Czech architect, had repeatedly said that never in his lifetime would he set foot in our home. I had studied history and assured him that one day changes would come. I was proved right, and they were our guests. We were all overjoyed. We are still in touch with both families.

The closing months of 1989 saw even more dramatic events taking place all over Eastern Europe. Large numbers of East Germans were finding their way into Hungary, where parties were being held beside the Iron Curtain to celebrate its dismemberment. Arguments were taking place in high places about how to contain the widespread challenges to the Communist system in all the satellite countries, but on November 9th the people of East Berlin began to tear down the Berlin Wall itself in full view of the media. Emotions and expectations were running high.

All on my own one December evening I was watching the TV News when suddenly Nicolae Ceausescu appeared on his balcony to address the militant crowds in Bucharest. This scene was perhaps the most poignant of all. The man who had been used to orchestrated adulation at every turn was facing an angry mob. The expression on his face suddenly clouded as he began to realise that no more adulation would ever again be forthcoming. The last bastion of the Communist Empire was crumbling before the eyes of the whole world. For a moment I was part of that crowd. I seized a bottle of Cyriac's slivovitz and raised a toast to all our Romanian and East European friends. I instinctively knew we had to visit as many of them as we possibly could during the following summer to share their new-found freedom.

Our travel plans ran rather wild. First we set sail for Helsinki aboard the Finnjet (then the fastest and largest car ferry in the world) to spend over two weeks in Leningrad with our friends Boris and Stella. Unexpectedly an illicit tour of Estonia was added to our itinerary, to visit Boris and Stella's friends in Tallinn and Tartu before camping wild just north of Pskov in the Soviet Union on our return journey to Leningrad. We then crossed Scandinavia, heading for the port of Gedser in Denmark. Travelling from

Gedser by ferry to Warnemunde, we were ceremonially welcomed on board by the Captain as their first ever Western visitors. On arrival in East Berlin we drove down Unter den Linden to the Brandenburg Gate, acquiring a little bit of the Berlin Wall as we left! Lutherstadt, the birthplace of the Reformation, lay on our route to Dresden as we travelled to our friends in Czechoslovakia, Hungary and Romania; a rather bizarre route across Europe.

A further climax was welcoming our Russian friends Boris and Stella the following year, 1991. At Heathrow they were mobbed as VIP guests. We showed them as much of England as we could, visiting the families of both our sons and my brother in Yorkshire. While there we learned that Gorbachev had been deposed and was being held prisoner in the Crimea. Our friends panicked and were beginning to make plans for remaining in the West. In the event Gorbachev was released and they returned to what was to become St. Petersburg.

Three months before Christmas a young Bulgarian girl called Sonia wrote asking us to sponsor her visa application. We had first met at the roadside when buying tomatoes from her grandmother in the monastery town of Bachkovo in 1973. Instead of staying for two weeks she found employment in a local pub. She went home for Christmas, but promptly returned to marry one of my Stockbridge parishioners, and all because we had stopped to buy her grandmother's tomatoes in 1973! How chance meetings affect all our lives' journeys. She now lives in Canada.

Our busy life in Stockbridge continued. The town's ancient Courts Leet met once a year under the chairmanship of the Lord of the Manor, in our time Rosalind

Hill. We were summoned by the chairman of the town council, Laurie Stares, who acted as the Town Crier, and who opened the proceedings by ringing his bell accompanied by a very fine rendering of Oyez! Oyez! My attendance as Rector was obligatory. One of the perennial items on the agenda was ragwort picking on the meadows by the river Test. Ragwort is poisonous to cattle.

Once a month I used to take communion to some of the elderly residents of Rosalind Hill House. The warden was a rather boisterous North Country lady. One Wednesday she had forgotten to make preparations. I tapped on her door and was greeted by a loosely hanging shoulder strap. She was not at all fazed! Later her son was involved in a horrendous motor-cycle accident. I became a regular guest in her flat for a while, and my wife and I both visited her son in Salisbury hospital.

Here hangs another parable. What sustained her during that difficult time was not the church's teaching or dogma, but the love with which we all tried to surround her, and especially our little church congregation there. I think that must be something of what St. Paul means when he talks about the fellowship of the Holy Spirit. She came to believe that she and her son too were also surrounded by God's love.

I also used to visit the Little Dean nursing home to take communion to some of the residents there. Among them was a titled lady. One morning on arrival the staff told me she had forcefully requested that I go to her first. I soon discovered why. She was still the owner of some racing stables and one of her horses was running that morning. I don't think she asked me to pray that it would win! Also resident in one of the privately-owned flats was Fanny

Cradock, the famous television cook, who invited my wife and me to tea. The flat was in a terrible state, with a rather dirty and messy kitchen. She still got into town from time to time, though the shopkeepers dreaded her arrival because of her rather fierce and acerbic temper, but she was fun and added a rather different air of dignity to the town.

Jill's mother fell on the stairs and began to deteriorate; someone had to be in attendance nearly all the time. We became eligible for the attendance allowance. In due course an inspecting officer came to assess the situation. While we were talking in the lounge, Jill's mother kept on calling repeatedly from her room upstairs; the climax came when she exclaimed "Jill, I can't pull my knickers up!" The gentleman blinked and as he left said "If anyone needs the attendance allowance, you two do." It was granted. After having received only one week's payment, Clarissa died in Winchester Hospital.

Roland de Corneille, a Canadian priest who had acted as locum while we were in Long Sutton, asked if he could do another exchange. We thought that perhaps with the Iron Curtain now safely undrawn the time had come to visit all those Canadian priests who had helped make our East European adventures possible. During their domination by the former Soviet Union, those visits had become something of a commitment. In June 1954 the Soviet Union gave Romania and Bulgaria the gift of the Friendship Bridge that crosses the Danube, a bridge we had crossed many times. In a different way we also provided a bridge of friendship to all our East European friends; a lifeline between their lives and ours and the freedoms to which they themselves aspired.

In 1992 we travelled to Toronto, our first international flight, to take charge of two of the city centre churches. On Sundays driving Roland's ancient automatic Oldsmobile was a somewhat daunting experience as we navigated the eight-lane carriageways. We made many good friends with whom we kept in contact for several years, particularly one family, whose son I baptised.

While there we drove around Lake Ontario, visiting Quebec and Vermont before heading for Stockbridge, Massachusetts and returning by Niagara Falls. After a month in Toronto we visited two other families, Bob and Nettie Sinclaire, who lived on the shores of Lake Huron, and Bob Birtch and his wife Yvonne near London (Ontario), whose home, an old railway station, had been towed to a site in the woods by a ginormous transporter. Heading for Calgary, we travelled to Vancouver on the 'Rocky Mountaineer' to visit my niece, whose wedding I was to conduct soon after we got home. Motoring across the Rockies by camper van, we made our way back to Calgary before flying home.

Stockbridge is part of the Romsey Deanery, a large group of individual parishes led by a rural dean on behalf of the Bishop. The Romsey Deanery was to play a larger part in our lives than we ever could have imagined at the time, because of its link with the Diocese of South Rwenzori in Uganda. In 1991, as part of the Diocesan exchange programme, I was invited to host an African archdeacon and his wife, Andrew and Naomi Nghima, from Kasese in Uganda. As there was no email in those days we lost contact for eleven years, but their visit to Stockbridge was eventually to lead to a very close relationship with Uganda that was to make a tremendous impact on the remaining roadmap of our life's journey.

After thirty-eight years of parish ministry I fell to thinking about retirement, hoping that some different opportunity might present itself. In 1989 we had purchased Homelea, our retirement home in the village of Barton St. David in Somerset, another garden with a house in it. We took up permanent residence in June 1993. Perfecting one more Garden of Eden had its attractions.

CHAPTER FOUR

PUT OUT TO GRASS

Retirement

Shortly after arrival in Somerset we embarked on our final
East European tour. Our aim was to circumnavigate the
Baltic and travel to Poland after crossing the Baltic
Republics; a plan we had to abandon. All our friends begged
us to avoid the Lithuanian/Polish border because of the
vandalism affecting nearly all foreign vehicles at that time.

Our outward journey was by Scandinavian Seaways to
Hamburg, from where we travelled to Travemunde before
once more boarding the Finnjet for Helsinki. Accompanying
us were some sixty pairs of children's shoes donated by the
owner of a Camberley shoe shop and destined for Romania.
We stayed for a few days with our old friends Pauli and

Sirka Laukkanen in Hameenlinna. Crossing the Russian frontier in 1993 was now a doddle; the young customs lad only made a cursory inspection of one or two items, but among them he unearthed a large box of garden seeds; for several years a former Camberley parishioner always gave us two black bin liners full of out of date seeds. He couldn't bear to see them burned. Our hearts fell. "мой сад! мой сад!" he shouted excitedly – "My garden! My garden!" A couple of dozen packets sped us on our way! Soon we were once more guests in the home of our Leningrad friends, Boris and Stella.

Sadly they were no longer allowed to cross the Estonia frontier. From 1973 a new Iron Curtain had effectively closed the frontiers of the Baltic republics to Soviet citizens. We first visited our friends in Narva and Tallinn before being welcomed by Tarmu and Saima in Tartu. During our stay their son arrived home with a severely-damaged car he had bought in Holland. That finally put paid to any attempt at crossing the Lithuanian/Polish frontier. Friends in Riga helped us board a small Black Sea Russian warship which had been converted to a tourist vessel; once more we were sailing the length of the Baltic Sea, this time to Kiel in West Germany.

With no booking we were forced to accept the only unoccupied cabin, a luxury suite boasting three portholes and all mod cons. We survived the two-day journey by living off the few dollars left us by the ship's purser, gifts from a procession of visitors to our luxury cabin and a large cake given us by some new found friends in Latvia. Another gift of seeds had already earned us some coffee and ice-cream in a small roadside coffee shop. On leaving we noticed a beautiful front garden, and not wishing to waste our remaining seeds we knocked on the door of total strangers.

From Kiel we once more drove to Chomutov in the Czech Republic. For the first time the Catholic priest greeted us with open arms. He had longed to do so on many previous occasions, but in communist times, fearful of the spies attached to every church congregation, he had always looked past us as we shook hands. In those days he over-filled the sanctuary with as many young altar boys as he dared, not being allowed to run any form of youth group.

Guy, our host, was outraged that before being allowed entry we had still been forced to purchase Czech crowns, and promptly changed them into Hungarian Forint travellers' cheques. Cluj in Romania was our final destination, where we were to unload our cargo of children's shoes. As we crossed the frontier we encountered pretty young girls with trays hung around their necks like those used by cinema usherettes, not laden with ice-cream but with large bundles of Forint notes purchased by passing English pounds through the car window! Jill also waged a charm offensive and persuaded the official cashier to accept the traveller's cheques, boldly forging Guy's signature.

Before leaving Stockbridge we had been invited to consider an exchange by the Vicar of Stockbridge, Massachusetts. Though no longer able to stay in my former parish, he and his wife were more than happy to borrow our home in Somerset. So in October, just in time for the fall, we once more crossed the Atlantic to gain more experience of our Anglican church overseas. It was an opportunity we could not pass by. Living in their parish was a Romanian Professor, Pauli Petrescu, and his wife, who had first fled to

Munich before arriving in the States. Did he recall a Simeon Felecan, we asked? "Yes, yes," came the eager reply "We both escaped to Munich. He had a very fine voice." Pauli informed us that Simeon was still living in Munich and promised to contact a London friend from whom we later received Simeon's address in the local suburbs. Unexpectedly, travelling to the States provided a renewed means of contacting Simeon and his family. So another rather momentous year came to an end.

For a few months we enjoyed munching the grass of retirement, then early the following spring an advert appeared in the *Church Times*: 'Chaplain required to serve part-time in the Helsinki and Riga in the Diocese of Europe. Would suit retired priest.' That was just the sort of opportunity I had hoped would arrive. I applied immediately, but received no acknowledgement. Later we were to attend the wedding of Jill's French pen friend's nephew, Jean Francois, in Montpellier. After seven weeks I rang the Diocesan Office: "Yes there is someone considering the post, he has a Finnish wife and it seems likely he will accept." That seemed to be that.

We immersed ourselves in creating our new Garden of Eden but in the autumn of 1994 the advert reappeared, now for the full-time post of Helsinki, no longer linked with Riga but with Tallinn in Estonia! I immediately rang the Diocesan Office in London and within two weeks was called for interview. We already possessed an intimate knowledge of Eastern Europe, especially Estonia, thanks to our travels there with Boris and Stella, as well as close friends in Finland; we were offered the job on the spot.

The eighteen months respite in Homelea provided a

time when I could relax and engage in some serious study, which later included the history of both Finland and Estonia, as well as the Provoo Agreement, with which the new Chaplain would be heavily involved. It was suggested we travel the following January but our departure was delayed until the following April.

Finland and Estonia
The Helsinki Chaplaincy

Travelling the Baltic by steamer was no novelty. This time we were aboard an excellent boat run by Finn Carriers, a container vessel delivering its cargo to the Helsinki docks at Sompasaari. This is quite a luxurious way to travel the Baltic. There are only a dozen or so en-suite births for private travellers. The cabins are spacious, and you dine in style with the captain and crew.

We arrived in Helsinki during a snowstorm just before midday on April 1st. Frozen snow still lay in the streets of the capital. A welcome party piloted our car to our new home in Mannerheimintie, one of the main thoroughfares leading out of the city. We had already visited the flat in mid-January, encountering a severe snowstorm which brought the Finnish rail system to a halt. 1995 proved to be even more severe with the coldest winter for many years, the temperature frequently falling to minus 25 degrees centigrade. Helsinki harbour and the Gulf of Finland became solid ice.

We had only a few days to settle in Mannerheimintie before conducting the Holy Week and Easter Day Services, the busiest and most important celebrations of the Christian year. Our worship then took place in one of the large chapels situated either side of the imposing Lutheran Cathedral that stands high above Helsinki harbour. Our congregation consisted of a core of regular worshippers, but every Sunday was different. Each week visitors came from all over the world; some were with us just the once, but others would be working on all sorts of different contracts. We were in effect an open door to all English-speaking people. Hardly a Sunday passed without our entertaining new members of the congregation to Sunday lunch.

Soon after our arrival Charles Vane-Tempest, who had given his life to keeping the Chaplaincy in good shape, sat me down in front of the parish computer. Every week a news-sheet was produced and printed and then copied on the copying machine. As he showed me what to do, he assumed I knew almost everything. In fact I knew nothing! I had hardly ever used a computer, except for a short preparation course; I could type and highlight, but that was about all. Just in case of problems, we had brought my wide-carriage typewriter.

After the first two weeks I gained a little proficiency but had not learned how to print pages five to eight without printing the first four pages. I saw a delete button. Was that what I needed? I pressed it. "Are you sure you want to delete?" Yes, I replied, and as I closed the programme down it asked me a second time "Are you still sure you want to delete?" Yes. Finally as I set about closing the computer it asked me with additional emphasis "Are you really sure you want to delete?" YES! I shut the computer down. The next time I tried to open it I was unable to access anything; the church accounts, the membership list, the Electoral roll, the magazine records – they had all gone. Nor was it possible to call up any word processor programme. Nothing! The screen was just one big black blank displaying a night sky of flickering white dots. I spent a very uncomfortable weekend!

The following Monday a Swedish-speaking Finn, a computer wizard with an English wife came to fix it. It took him several hours to recover all the lost material! There is a sort of parable here. Our brains are in some ways very similar to a computer, so you need to be very careful, the whole of your life is stored there!

A chaplaincy 'parish' is not like any parish back in the UK and has a camaraderie all of its own including expats, some with their Finnish spouses, overseas residents and students and visiting businessmen; you are also involved in a special relationship with members of the Diplomatic Corps. In those days that carried the privilege of diplomatic status, a diplomatic passport, a diplomatic car and duty-free drinks and petrol. This was repeated in Tallinn, the capital city of Estonia. One was also personal chaplain to both ambassadors.

Arrangements had been made for the visit of the Rochester Cathedral Choir long before our arrival. They arrived in mid-April. The choir was hosted in the Athletics Stadium just behind our flat. The choir men complained that they had only been given paper sheets. The choirboys tore theirs to shreds! No real publicity had been put in place and the attendance in the Cathedral was embarrassingly low, consisting mostly of a few parents of some of the young Finnish choristers. After the performance I suddenly realised that the conductor was about to give his own choir a vote of thanks, so I hastily rushed forward to take his place.

It was a different story in Tallinn the following Sunday. The Estonian Revolution against the Soviets was known as the 'singing revolution'. On the tenth and eleventh of June 1988 spontaneous mass night-singing demonstrations took place at the Tallinn Song Festival Grounds. At the same time approximately two million people joined hands to form a human chain of three hundred and sixty miles across the Baltic Republics; Estonians, Latvians and Lithuanians all holding hands. The Estonians are into singing in a big way and the opera house was full. Their performance was followed by encore after encore. Our Tartu friends Tarmu and Saima joined us.

Not long afterwards I received a frantic call from our Ambassador in Tallinn: "Francis, I have just received orders from the Foreign Office that we are to hold a service on Sunday May 7th to mark the fiftieth anniversary of the end of European hostilities in 1945. We can't possibly use the service provided here in Tallinn, the Estonians think the war ended five years ago when the Russians left! I 'll arrange a flight for you and we must discuss this together." I soon found myself sitting in his office, drafting a revised service on the theme of reconciliation on sheets of A4 paper while he continued his diplomatic business over the phone. Arrangements were made for the German Ambassador to read one of the lessons. I had to preach.

All of our experiences in Eastern Europe seemed to have prepared me for this particular moment. In 1990 my wife and I and our Russian friends Boris and Stella were standing in the Raekoja Platz, Tallinn's mediaeval Square, when it was suddenly invaded by an enormous crowd of workers carrying banners in Russian, Estonian and English that read "LIQUIDATE THE CRAZY KGB GANG!" An elderly Estonian Lutheran couple standing next to us had tears in their eyes and told us that they had never expected to see their country free from Russian rule in their lifetimes. At that moment we ourselves became part of Estonian history.

In 1991, as Soviet tanks attempted to stop the progress towards independence, the Estonian Supreme Soviet, together with the Congress of Estonia, proclaimed the restoration of the independent state of Estonia and repudiated Soviet legislation. People acted as human shields to protect radio and TV stations from the Soviet tanks. Through these actions Estonia regained its independence without any bloodshed.

Our experiences among the many friends we had already made in Estonia, and the fact that we had visited every country in Europe at one time or another with the exception of Lithuania and Albania, enabled me to pursue our theme of reconciliation in an unique way. We had friends in Warsaw, and while in Wroclaw with Jan and Anna we had visited the concentration camp of Auschwitz. Later our Czech friends took us to Terezin, and in 1978 we had journeyed by car across the length of the former Soviet Union from Tbilisi to Leningrad. It was a privilege to address so large a crowd; pursuing the theme of reconciliation, I was able to draw on my intimate understanding of so many East European countries and all the suffering they had endured, among them both the citizens of Estonia and of the former Soviet Union. After the service I was invited to dine with the Ambassador and his wife. What should I wear? I needn't have worried, he was wearing a polo-neck light blue pullover. Before we ate we played a game or two of table tennis and watched ourselves on the Estonian Television news bulletin.

About a year after the visit of the Rochester Cathedral Choir, their Archdeacon paid a second visit to Estonia. We were both invited by the Dean, Gustav Pier, to take part in the Lutheran Confirmation service taking place at Puhavaimu, the church where our English congregation is privileged to worship. Neither of us had realised that this actually meant 'confirming' some of the candidates. We are probably the only Anglican priests to have ever done this. In our church this is the prerogative of the Bishop. In the Lutheran church it is the Pastor who confirms; that is logical in a way, as he is the person who has got to know them and has done all the teaching and preparation.

In Helsinki we were to become very close friends with some of the Embassy staff, the Defence attaché and his wife, and the head of the Consular Department, Bill Whitton, in particular. Among our new parishioners was the new South African Ambassador, with whom we developed a very close relationship, and were invited to small evening parties at the South African Embassy. He agreed to open our annual Christmas bazaar, one of the highlights of the chaplaincy year. To our surprise he began by leading us all in prayer for about eight minutes or so before finally declaring the bazaar open. He then let on, politely, that we had hung the South African flag upside down! There was also an annual Christmas party at our own embassy, and from time to time we were invited to other embassy functions; on one occasion for some reason to a Taiwan Embassy party.

One of the first baptisms I took was held in Kokkola,

way beyond Tampere, Finland's second city. Many expats were married to Finnish wives. We would invite ourselves to stay with the family on the Friday evening and by arrangement would conduct the service the next day in the local Lutheran church. When invited to tea in a Finnish home you always remove your shoes before entering. At the christening party we were all sitting in our stockinged feet; one or two of some of the men's toes peeped through a sock. You noticed which men had the best wives!

There were several 'mixed' marriages. The Lutheran Pastor and I would share the occasion using part of their service and part of ours. When we first arrived we found the Lutheran church rather more formal than ours; I remember how several of their pastors enjoyed our more relaxed Anglican way of doing things. The Finns love our English Christmas carols and each year the Chaplaincy Choir provides the traditional service of nine lessons and carols in the great Lutheran Cathedral. On this particular occasion I more or less dragged a somewhat reluctant Dean to the back of his cathedral to shake hands with more than a thousand of his flock who always attended. He had never thought of doing so before and much enjoyed it.

Our family soon christened me the 'Flying Chaplain.' As a consequence of the Porvoo Agreement the work of the Chaplaincy expanded considerably. Besides Tampere, English language services were already held in Turku, the former capital of Finland in Swedish times, and in Kotka to the east of Helsinki on the way to St. Petersburg. Many more were to be added. Carol services were legion and included Oulu just south of the Arctic Circle, where there are only five hours of daylight in the depths of the winter months. In addition to the normal duties of a parish priest I was also responsible for implementing the provisions of the Porvoo Agreement, by which the Anglican and Lutheran churches were to be joined in full communion after a break of well over 300 years.

A Moment of History
Anglicans and Lutherans United

In 1992 The Porvoo Agreement united the Lutheran churches of Scandinavia and the Baltic Republics with the Anglican Communion. This was an historic occasion; the first time that two mainstream Christian Churches had come back together since the Reformation. The Agreement was signed in Järvenpää in Finland and concluded with a joint act of worship in the ancient Finnish cathedral of the city of Porvoo, hence its name. Anglicans and Lutherans United became a good team!

In 1938, the then Archbishop of Canterbury invited representatives of the Estonian and Latvian Lutheran Churches to Lambeth Palace to discuss the possibility of closer contacts and fellowship between the Anglican and Baltic Lutheran churches. This process was interrupted by the war years and only came to a formal conclusion with the signing of the Porvoo Agreement and the formation of the much wider Porvoo Communion in 1992. It was very early days when we arrived in 1995, and the public signing ceremonies were yet to take place.

Besides the normal duties of the chaplaincy my remit was now much wider, as we were all in the very early stages of making the Porvoo Agreement a reality. I was called upon to represent the Anglican Church to many church groups in both countries and also in Latvia, and to make presentations at the meetings of the Anglo-Scandinavian Pastoral Conferences.

The Porvoo Agreement was first officially signed on Sunday September 1st 1996 in Trondheim, Norway. Preaching at the service in Trondheim's Nidaros Cathedral, Bishop Richard Holloway, Primus of the Scottish Episcopal Church, sharply criticised his own Anglican tradition. He began by making some fairly controversial remarks about episcopacy. What the press did not publish was his flamboyant suggestion that all the Bishops should toss their mitres into the river Thames! I wondered if the message also applied to the Lutheran Bishops present.

Our Archbishop's brother, Robert Carey (Bob) was a member of my new church family in Finland; he had asked us to convey his greetings, which we duly did during the civic reception that followed. In addition the local Anglican Norwegian Chaplaincy laid on a magnificent reception for all the British representatives. That set me thinking. They were all going to arrive in Tallinn the following weekend!

Shortly after George Carey arrived in Tallinn I had his rather distressed Chaplain on the 'phone. "Can you provide a spare alb for the Archbishop?" British Airways had lost all his luggage, including his mitre! Was this the fulfilment of Richard Holloway's surmisings? The alb was eventually used by the Chaplain, the Archbishop being duly robed by his Estonian Hosts. Many of the same 25 bishops and five archbishops met for the second signing ceremony in the ancient Tallinn Cathedral on Mount Toompea. This was followed by another civic reception to which we were accompanied by our Ambassador, Charles de Chassiron, a close supporter of our fledgling Anglican congregation that met in the ancient Lutheran church of Puhavaimu by the kindness of Gustav Pier, the Dean.

One of the bishops' wives and Mary Tanner, a representative of the World Council of Churches, helped us to organise the evening festivities in Puhavaimu, where we entertained no fewer than eleven Bishops and other English representatives. A few doors away was the local pizzeria and restaurant. Pizzas were duly ordered and two kindly bishops, still clad in purple and sporting pectoral crosses, offered to help pay and came with me to collect them. The normal clientele consisted of young folk aged between seventeen and twenty-five enjoying themselves in a way totally unknown in Communist times. Many tables were occupied and the restaurant was filled with the strains of loud pop music. Our entry produced a dramatic silence as all eyes turned in our direction. They had never seen the like in their lives. The pizzeria ran out of cardboard boxes.

Mary Tanner went with Jill to a local hostelry to acquire a goodly quantity of dark Estonian Saku, a beer of exceptional quality, and comparable to the best English stout. A memorable evening was had by all. Some of the pizza was left over; the elderly retired Estonian Archbishop humbly asked if he could take it home for his wife. The infrastructure of the Estonian Lutheran church had all but been destroyed by the Soviet occupation and he had absolutely no pension. We all parted, mutually looking forward to meeting for a third party at the final signing ceremony in Westminster Abbey on November 28th.

We took advantage of that occasion to take a few days' break and return our Citroen to the UK. The ceremony in Westminster Abbey was attended by the Queen, who also added her signature to the official document. Communion was administered in several parts of the abbey and the Archbishop of Wales squeezed Jill's hand as he gave her the chalice. But we were not to meet for a third party. Perhaps he knew that. The bishops met somewhere, but all my Finnish friends and my wife and I, without more ado, were somewhat brusquely ushered out of the abbey by the head verger into the cold of a late November evening. We took counsel and nearby we found an Olde Worlde Baked Potato Bar where we passed the rest of the evening celebrating.

Besides helping to build a very close relationship with the Lutheran church we were also in close contact with the Orthodox churches. There are magnificent Orthodox cathedrals in both Helsinki and Tallinn. During the week of prayer for Christian Unity we used to process around Helsinki, visiting various churches on the way. Once we concluded by entering the great Orthodox Cathedral, where prayers were read for the whole world. One Easter one of our parishioners invited us to attend the ceremony of the 'New Fire' on Easter Eve. A long procession of worshippers meanders to the cathedral, mounting the steps to the main entrance where their candles are lit; the whole building eventually becomes flooded with Light.

The Finnish Jewish regiment in the Nazi Army

The position of Finland during the war years was very

ambivalent. In the 'Winter War' Finland was attacked by the Soviet Union; the Finns gave the Russians a very bloody nose, their troops on skis adopting guerilla tactics overwhelmed the Russian infantry. Though the Finns will never say they were invaded by the Germans, they later allowed them free access across the country. A second struggle ensued and Finnish troops fought alongside the Germans. At the time the Nazis were bent on eliminating the small Jewish population of Finland and already held eight Jews who had escaped from the Baltics. Seven of these were executed, but one escaped after the intervention of General Mannerheim, the Finnish 'Churchill'. Somehow he managed to persuade the Germans that they needed every single man capable of fighting the Russians to help drive them back to Leningrad. So unbelievably a Jewish company was formed, the only Jews whoever fought alongside the Germans throughout the whole of World War II. Karelia once more became a battleground but was eventually ceded to the Soviets after the end of the war.

Among our friends at the Embassy club nights was Peter Martin, whose father's identity was given to the "Man Who Never Was." Documents relating to Major Martin were planted on the body of a tramp which was dumped in the Bay of Biscay and later washed up on the shores of Portugal. This has been the subject of several TV dramas codenamed 'Operation Mincemeat'.

Peter's personal account makes fascinating reading and includes a full history of his father's career. During the war this was interrupted by a mysterious posting to the USA where he somehow disappeared off the radar screen into oblivion. Major Martin never quite understood what was going on, but so far as 'Operation Mincemeat' was concerned he was listed as dead and buried in Huelva cemetery, though in reality living life as a civilian. The body laid to rest there was in fact that of Glyndwr Michael, a Welsh vagrant who might otherwise have languished in an unknown grave.

Another of our duties was to visit Peggy Pertunen, who had married a Finnish biologist and came to live in Helsinki during or just before the end of the Second World War. She developed quite a role for herself in Finnish society. During our time she was an elderly widow, but she loved entertaining. On one occasion she recounted the story of how as a young bride she had helped her husband's study of bed bugs by allowing him to place some of his specimens in the nuptial bed. You can't get more romantic than that!

During our monthly five-day visits to Estonia we travelled the length and breadth of the country. At first we were hosted by several of our new parishioners, the church accommodation having been severely damaged during the war. We had to build up the chaplaincy almost from scratch. The core congregation was much like that of St. Nicholas Helsinki, and very international. The churchwardens were the Earl of Carlisle and another titled gentleman, who like many of the other Estonian expats had come seeking to make a better living abroad. Quite a few Estonians also attended to improve their English.

Among our number was a retired Estonian teacher, Aino, who had been compelled to teach her children the Russian version of their national history. We possess some of her textbooks. She had been forced to teach atheism, but was now a seriously practising Christian, with others like her who had experienced both German and Russian brutalities in their country. Bible study took on a rather different slant and brought our study of early church history very much alive. Their contributions were never 'armchair' observations, but were drawn from their own first-hand experiences of persecution, giving a new relevance both to the persecution of the early Christians and to so much of what is still happening in our world today.

Charles de Chassiron drew our attention to the Headley Trust foundation, which was offering £25,000 for the restoration of art projects in Eastern Europe. It was decided that Jill would draw up a suitable application. At his suggestion she began with Arthur Ransome of Swallows and Amazons fame. It is not generally appreciated how closely Arthur Ransome was involved in the Estonian struggle for independence in the early 1920s. After the start of the First World War in 1914, he became a foreign correspondent and covered the war on the Eastern Front for a radical newspaper, the *Daily News*. He also covered the Russian Revolution of 1917, coming to sympathise with the Bolshevik cause and becoming personally close to a number of its leaders, including Vladimir Lenin and Leon Trotsky. In Russia he met the woman who would become his second wife, Evgenia Petrovna Shelepina, who at that time worked as Trotsky's personal secretary.

In October 1919, as Ransome was returning to Moscow on behalf of *the Manchester Guardian*, the Estonian Foreign Minister, Ants Piip, entrusted him to deliver a secret armistice proposal to the Bolsheviks. At that time the Estonians were fighting their War of Independence alongside the White Russian movement of counter-revolutionary forces. At great risk, Ransome had to cross the battle lines on foot. To preserve secrecy the message had not been written down and depended for its authority only on the high personal regard in which he was held in both countries. He delivered the message to the diplomat Maxim Litvinov in Moscow. To deliver the reply, which accepted Piip's conditions for peace, Ransome had to return by the same risky means, but this time he had Evgenia with him. Estonia withdrew from the conflict and Ransome and Evgenia set up home together in the capital, Reval, today's Tallinn.

Besides her research into Arthur Ransome, Jill assembled all sorts of other local information, including the part the British Navy played in the War of Independence, and a history of the British war graves in the Tallinn cemetery. Also included was a history of Puhavaimu Church. Her efforts resulted in the church being awarded the full grant of £25,000 for the restoration of the 57 wooden oil-painted panels crafted in the seventeenth century by the German Artist Elert Thiele. These are mounted on the front of the galleries surrounding the nave.

There is a sequel to this story. At a party held at our Estonian Embassy we heard how during the Second World War the caretaker of the local cemetery buried all the British war graves under dead flowers, leaves and other rubble to protect them from vandalism. After Estonia recovered her independence in 1991 she got her son to uncover the graves and brought them to the attention of the British War Graves Commission. I cannot recall her name, but she was invited to a party at the Embassy and awarded the MBE for her bravery.

The Ambassador asked me to contact a certain Danny Krepka, who was much in need of counselling. Thereby began a long-lasting friendship that continued well after we left. Danny had served in the Falklands War and had been traumatised by his experiences. While there he had rescued a British helicopter pilot from his sinking helicopter. By an extraordinary coincidence that pilot in later years was posted to the staff at the Yeovilton Air Base and was looking for maths coaching. Yeovil Sixth Form College, where Jill was then teaching, gave his name to my wife, who provided him with personal tuition. How the circles of the world turn around.

Danny had been a Corporal in the King's Royal Rifle Corps in which I had also served. Every time we met he stood to attention and we 'presented arms' to each other. His father was of Estonian origin and on returning to his home country he met Helga, who slowly nursed him back to health and weaned him from the worst of his alcoholic addiction. They lived in a wonderful country house in the west of Estonia. He caught and smoked his own salmon and had built a wood sauna. He also had become close friends with the Earl of Carlisle and we had some wonderful parties in his home.

On one occasion Danny took us to visit some Russian ladies whom the Soviet Army had left behind after their hurried departure. He used to befriend them, providing food and clothing and raising money. They lived in the shoddy collapsing former army barrack room blocks. He also led us to the site where many Jews were murdered by the Nazis, where there is a small memorial pillar. After my time he became one of the most bizarre churchwardens ever appointed! Danny eventually died, but during his life he had done all he could to follow Jesus' last wish that we should all love and care for each other.

We are still in touch with his widow, Helga. On one of our later visits to Estonia she described how life was good to her in communist times when many workers received paid holidays. She once had a week in Sochi, and also described how on another occasion she had helped accompany two wagonloads of pigs from Moscow to Vladivostok on the Trans-Siberian Railway and got into trouble for 'shovelling shit' in the wrong place on some of the platforms! Her description, delivered in her broken English, was hilarious.

I was also invited to visit the Anglican Congregation of St. Saviour's Riga. We left by bus and were to be met at the Riga bus station by the Lutheran Pastor who was then in charge. He had returned from exile in the States, just as Gustav Piir had done from Canada. We arrived in a blizzard and were lucky to complete the journey, but the bus station was totally deserted. It was dark, cold and still snowing heavily. There was one solitary telephone; fortunately we had the Embassy number. As luck would have it the caretaker picked up the phone and provided us with the number of our hosts, Arthur and Issy Sanderson. Arthur was in charge of the British Council. Issy hired a taxi and came to meet us. It was a dangerous ride to their home. It was there that Arthur introduced me to single malts, Lagavulin, Talisker and Laphroaig among others. I have hardly ever touched a blend since!

On the Sunday we were welcomed by Dr Juris Calitis. I had been invited to conduct an Anglican service. The

Anglican prayer books had obviously not been used for some time and were rather dusty and hidden away in the church vestry. During the communist period the church had been used as a disco for university students. At a loss for a name, it had been christened "the Anglican disco!" The keyboard must have been left over from the disco period and the organist trotted out the hymns as if they were pop songs. Perhaps she had been their disc jockey.

After the service Issy took us to the crypt, where a team of helpers was preparing a hot meal for some of the many Russians who had been left all but homeless after the departure of the Soviet authorities in 1991. During Soviet times many Russians had been imported as part of a Russification process. There were also Russians living there from much earlier times. During the communist period they occupied a very privileged status, provided with superior flats and the best jobs. Now the tables were turned.

A member of our Puhavaimu congregation who worked in the prison service also played a considerable role in the Salvation Army, which at that time had taken over an old Soviet cinema which they had turned into a simple but unusual 'citadel.' We always exchange calendars with Raivo at Christmas. They had also built a shower unit and changing rooms and provided clothes and all sorts of other assistance. Breakfast was served in an adjoining room to about thirty very poor people. We sat down with them as Raivo's guests. In that part of the world knobs of fresh butter were placed all over the bowl of porridge instead of milk. Occasions like these gave us a considerable insight into Estonian life, as did visits to many other churches and homes all over Estonia. In a small country parish with an impossible mediaeval church they had what they called a summer church and a winter church. The latter was part of the Pastor's house turned into an 'Upper Room.'

In 1990 Boris and Stella's friend Tarmu had been high up in the communist system and boasted that his herd of cattle was among the finest in the world. He proudly showed us his charts of their milk production, claiming it was much superior to that of Western farmers. He drove us everywhere. We went for ride on a speedboat and dined at the best restaurant in town, where he pointed out their national poet, who was seated in the upstairs balcony. Life was riding high. On our second visit in 1993 we enquired after the cattle. He drew his hand dramatically across his throat. He had given one or two to his friends and kept a few at his country home, but the rest had been slaughtered as it was now no longer possible to export his milk to Leningrad. The new Iron Curtain was closely monitored by guards on both sides, even along the shores of Lake Peipsi around which we had driven to Pskov in the Soviet Union with Boris and Stella three years earlier.

Our elder son and his wife visited us while we were in Helsinki. We all travelled in our car on a family ticket to stay at Puhavaimu. The theory was that we could all have got in had we not had any luggage, and a baby and its cot. We hired another car for the family on arrival. Our friends at Tartu hosted us all at their country farmstead. We had a wonderful reunion in the August of 1996, our son Simon helping the party flow along with his accordion, and what a magnificent feast was prepared by Saima and Tarmu.

Simon and his family were not the only family visitors. My brother came to Helsinki and also a disabled cousin accompanied by her wheelchair. As a diabetic, she had lost both her legs above the knee and just fitted into the lift to our flat, which was on the fifth floor. She expressed a wish to see reindeer. Finnair were magnificent and made her wishes come true, a shining example of how ordinary folk rally round those in need. She saw the sun set and rise almost at the same moment. Former parishioners turned up too. Briar, from Stockbridge, came with us to Estonia and Danny's wife Helga accompanied us to her sister's home in the south of the country. Her sister's husband had been deported to Siberia and forced to make stout wicker baskets. He had returned after many years and was still making beautiful baskets out of sheets of aspen wood. He was not the only Estonian we met who had suffered the rigours of deportation when Estonians were shipped to Siberia in their thousands.

In 1990 Boris and Stella took us to meet Ivan and his wife Olga in Narva. They had met in one of the gulags. She had been taken as a small child and miraculously had survived the fierce Siberian winters, though not her mother. They told a harrowing and almost unbelievable tale of the conditions they had to endure. Ivan was running a factory for the disabled that made filters for diesel motors for the factory in which Boris worked.

A teacher called Tonya, of Ukrainian origin, was called on to act as our interpreter. She also became a close friend, and she and her daughter Tanya visited us in later years. We took her to Wellesbourne, where she had grown up as a child, and the shop where she had bought sweets was still there. The Methodist church were very kind and found Tanya's name in the baptism book. Her father had responded to an appeal from a close friend saying how life was now good in the Ukraine. He made the biggest mistake of their lives and eventually they left the Ukraine for Narva. Tonya's husband worked in Ivan's factory.

On a subsequent visit Tonya took us to the home of another very elderly couple who had the most excellent wood-burning sauna. They made it especially hot, so hot that we developed a sort of deep tomato sauce hue. The husband, a man of upright military bearing, was yet another Siberian escapee. His wife had given him up for lost, but never remarried. One morning he turned up at her door having travelled much of the way from Siberia to his long-lost home on foot. He had survived, he said, by standing straight and by his military discipline; another deep insight into Estonian life.

A neighbour of ours from our home in Barton St. David who was an avid participant in competitions won lots of prizes, among them a toy Formula One pedal car. Would we like it for the children's hospital in Tallinn? Every Christmas Puhavaimu had a carol service helped by a choir from one of the local schools and organised by Sister Mary Venard, an elderly Catholic nun. Of course we replied, but how about bringing it yourself? She did. It was as well she was with us as we crossed the Gulf of Finland. The customs showed keen interest in the car, but my diplomatic passport helped solve the issue. Denise came with us to present it to the hospital and the chaplaincy is still supporting the children's hospital to this day.

Hazel, a former teacher friend of Jill's from Farnborough College, also came. She was in touch with a less traditional church and had already visited a group who were trying to help young children. Travelling to the south of the country, we met a pastor who felt that the Lutheran church he was serving was far too traditional and ought to be experimenting more. He had erected a new building some distance from the main community. We only met in passing, but were invited to return on another occasion.

On our next visit we spent a night in his home; they were hosting a very poor family all of whom were to be baptised the following day. His church was not far from a beautiful lake which had been a communist resort and holiday centre. It was now largely deserted. He and the family waded into the lake to waist depth. Jill wanted me to follow, but I was wearing the only pair of trousers I possessed! I went as far as my knees. The whole family was totally immersed one by one. We celebrated with a party afterwards, another rich memory. No tourist ever set foot in these parts.

*****

Our time in this part of the world was sadly to draw to a rather abrupt end. We had to return home for family reasons. My wife left for England alone just before Christmas while I stayed behind to conduct some very important services over the whole of the Christmas period. David and Marna Gowan were holding a party at their home to welcome the newly-appointed Ambassador. Both were regular worshippers and very supportive; David was temporarily in charge of the Embassy and Marrna had recently been elected churchwarden. Beforehand I visited a partially-sighted lady to take her communion. I suddenly realised I had forgotten to place my clerical tab in my shirt. I couldn't have turned up at the Ambassador's party improperly dressed. I thought of the Vicar of Dibley and the scene where Dawn French found herself in just the same predicament. Taking a Fairy Liquid bottle, she sliced off a section to act as a substitute collar. I asked my friend if she had some strong white card and a pair of scissors and did the same, the only difference being that in Dawn's case her tab still sported the word 'Fairy'!

The party at David and Marna's home was a sumptuous occasion. David in particular felt very sorry for me having to return to an empty flat and kept plying me with an unlimited supply of red wine. I am normally quite a talkative soul and this provided an excuse to recount even more of my large fund of stories. Fortunately I was returning home by tram. Instead of the normal double tram, a single section came along headed for 'The Depot.' The Central Tram Depot was right opposite where we lived, so I had no worries about dismounting. I must have descended into a deep comfortable stupor, because the next thing I recall was a loud growl from the burly tram driver informing me in his best guttural Finnish that he wasn't going any further. I stumbled off his tram and somewhat hazily dragged myself across Mannerheimintie to my front door.

A final trip had to be made to Tallinn for the ordination of Ain Leetma. Ain had received his training for the priesthood in a San Francisco Catholic theological college and was to be ordained into the Anglican Church to succeed me at as Chaplain. Bob Carey came to lend his support. I was invited by Gustav to prepare an order of service based on our Anglican ordinal, but including other provisions required by the Lutheran Church drawn from the Augsburg Confession of Faith. He was ordained by the Lutheran Bishop. Church unity at its best and put together on the hoof! Jill returned to Helsinki for our final farewells and with much sadness we returned to our home in Barton St. David.

The morning after I completed the final revision of this chapter, I awoke thinking of all the hundreds of other people whose lives had touched ours in those three eventful years, including Ian Harland, the Bishop of Carlisle, who was among those feasting with us in Tallinn at the signing of the Porvoo agreement and who later insisted on doing Sunday duty in Helsinki enabling us to travel to the North Cape; we conducted a wedding together followed by the marriage feast on a popular Helsinki island. It all came flooding back how later that had led to our stay in Roseland Castle, their home in Carlisle.

There was Anna-Liis, Gustav's secretary, who took us on a tour of Saaremaa, a large Estonian offshore island, and all the people we met there; the cups of cocoa and digestive biscuits and cheddar cheese that we shared with Gustav late at night when we made all our plans for the Estonian chaplaincy, and the kitchen sink that Jill transported as 'hand luggage' for the newly-restored guest house. The flow was unstoppable – hundreds and hundreds more of all the people who have become part of our lives.

There were the archdeaconry meetings and synods held across northern Europe in Stockholm, Oslo, Hamburg and Berlin as well as the Anglican Lutheran conferences in Stavanger and London. This all represents an outpouring of love and fellowship, a living parable of how Jesus' vision of the Kingdom of God can begin to shape our daily lives here on earth. Meeting all those people amid their ordinary daily lives with all their problems, especially those whose faith has been tested to the limit, is truly inspirational and makes a lasting impression on your own faith. What impressed the ordinary people of Jesus' own age most as they gathered in their thousands to hear him was his presence among them, and the way he spoke as he shared with them his vision of the Kingdom of God in parable after parable. Faith is so much more than belief and is built from among those with whom we have begun to share our own understanding of God's great love for all mankind as we all tramp the road of our earthly pilgrimage.

In the January of 1998 we returned to our home in Somerset to resume real retirement and re-immersed ourselves in our half-completed Garden of Eden. During this period we celebrated the millennium. A computer became a must; I began to hone the skills I had developed in Helsinki to become a quite accomplished silver surfer. Gradually the story of our East European adventures began to take shape and we took our full part in village life; Jill began helping out in the nearby charity shop and I was in demand among the local parishes.

One of our near neighbours, Adrian, had suffered a stroke which left him with a severe speech impediment. 'Yes' was one of his favourite words among his very limited vocabulary. He had played chess, and I helped him to relearn all the basic moves one by one. Gradually he began to think ahead and slowly recovered the power to suggest his own moves. His vocabulary also began to increase. The names of Bishop and Knight arrived, and the word 'jump' as knights can hop over other pieces on the board, and the word 'square'. This was all very exciting.

After a year or two we began to realise that in later years we would not be able to cope with a garden whose soil consisted of solid marine clay, and our elder son suggested that we ought to think of moving a little closer to our family while we were still energetic enough to do so. In the July of 2001 we moved to Devizes, to yet one more garden with a house in it, and set about constructing our final Garden of Eden. Over sixteen years it has raised considerable sums of money for our projects in Africa which began with our first visit in 2002.

CHAPTER FIVE

AFRICAN ADVENTURES

There is something particularly precious about the first time you set foot anywhere, but perhaps nowhere more so than in Africa. It has a particular magnetic pull that draws you back again and again. No account of the roadmap of my faith would be complete without mention of the hundreds and hundreds of Africans who are woven into the very fabric of our life's experience. The churches are lively and the people you meet full of faith and hope, even among the poorest communities. Ask an African how he is and he will always answer 'fine', accompanied by a large grin. I once commented on this to an African priest and he said "Yes, we do always smile, but sometimes that smile hides a lot of suffering."

Archdeacon Andrew Nghima and his wife had been our

guests in Stockbridge in 1991 sponsored by the Winchester diocesan Romsey link. Shortly after our arrival in Devizes in 2001 I wrote to Andrew exploring the possibility of paying a visit to Uganda, and in response to my snail-mail letter to their eleven-year-old postal address I received a reply by email! It was from the Diocesan secretary, Jackson Nzerebende, saying that sadly Andrew had died in a motorcycle accident, but his wife Naome would love to welcome us and that he was sure there would be lots of things we could do; he even offered to arrange a local safari trip. A tour of the Masai Mara and Serengeti game reserves was already in place, organised by a local ecological travel company in Zanzibar who kindly adjusted our itinerary to include Uganda as our first destination. I replied to Jackson enthusiastically, but declined the offer of visiting the local safari park, saying we wanted to meet people rather than elephants!

Watching the wildebeest crossing the Mara River is an unforgettable sight. Our safari also included visits to local villagers, a school and a hospital, but wonderful as that sort of experience can be, the close friendships we were later to form all over Africa were of much more lasting consequence. Besides our very close involvement with the church in Uganda we were to develop equally close contacts in Rwanda, Ethiopia, Kenya, Tanzania, Zanzibar, Botswana, Zambia and Namibia and visit two of our most vibrant chaplaincies in Cairo and Dubai. In this chapter it is only possible to include the highlights of the many 'human safaris' made to so many wonderful African communities which began with our welcome to Kasese in October 2002.

Uganda

Kasese is a small market town in South-West Uganda that grew up because of the cobalt mines close by. It was once served by a rail link that was abandoned during the time of Idi Amin. Our very first flight was via Cairo with Egypt Air; as you approach the runway of Entebbe Airport the waters of Lake Victoria rush to meet you just before you make dry land. Our first night in Africa was spent in the Namirembe Guest House overlooking the hills that surround the capital, Kampala. While registering we were asked to complete a large census form; one of the compulsory questions was headed 'Tribe'. We wrote British! We relaxed for the next day or two. Namirembe Guest House is a truly wonderful place where you meet people from all over the world.

Then followed a seven-hour journey by road to Kasese, where we were warmly welcomed by Jackson Nzerebende. I well recall that first meeting. Looking me straight in the eye, as had Bishop Leonard Wilson, Jackson said "I have a good feeling about this meeting." We were welcomed by his wife Dorothy and spent our first night in their home. We were scheduled to move to the guest house next door for the rest of our stay, but never went. In eight of the next eleven years we became guests in their home.

On our first Sunday morning we attended three church services in the old cathedral: the local language service at 7 am; the English service two hours later, at which I gave the address; and shortly after that the main act of morning worship, including the confirmation of a large number of young people and some older candidates. This preceded the ceremony of Jackson's installation as the new Dean. We finally left the cathedral at about 2 pm! Next there followed a big party, speeches, feasting and much dancing. What an introduction to Africa.

Our very first duty was to visit Naome and her family in the foothills of the Rwenzori Mountains. What a wonderful welcome we received. From that first visit there has grown a long-lasting relationship with the whole family. It has been a joy to watch her young family grow and make their own particular contributions to their local community.

During the following week our itinerary included visits to several remote and almost inaccessible mountain villages. High in the foothills of the Rwenzoris, the fabled 'Mountains of the Moon', lies the tiny village of Kitabu. Its all-purpose church building had only been completed earlier that year; the altar rails then consisted of two lengths of undressed 4x2 timber and the windows were still unglazed. The welcome given by the children was unbelievable. In Uganda grandfathers are treated as toys and as many little hands as could tried to grasp mine as they propelled me down the slope from their school to the church. Several choirs each sang their welcomes. Gifts of large handmade clay pots were presented, speeches made, and a spirit of wonder, praise and thanksgiving and an overwhelming atmosphere of love and fellowship almost awed one to silence. Their worship was enthusiastic, even boisterous, and totally welcoming. Besides being presented with gifts we were also presented with their Parish Plan – their aims and ambitions for the future. I wonder, have we lost our way in our supposedly advanced societies hell-bent on making money, or has the Third World something to teach the so called First World?

So began a long lasting friendship, now continued by

email. At another village, Rwnsande, a 'marquee' made of poles and old sugar sacks provided shelter for a large crowd. Before being confirmed, some of the young children were first exorcised. There is still much spirit worship in some of these remote communities. Some forty to fifty people were confirmed. During the celebration of communion that followed, Jackson had to call for extra plates and glasses to serve the bread and wine. Then a young girl came to him with a towel over her arm, a washing-up bowl, some dark blue soap and a plastic bottle of warm water for him to wash his hands, just as they do in most African homes before you eat. No fancy silver-topped vessels in this part of the world. It was all so natural and brought home the simplicity of how the first Christians washed their hands before celebrating the sacrament.

In 2008 that so-called First World began to experience the devastating effects of the 'credit crunch'. A financial balloon went pop. Many people's livelihoods came under threat and homes began to be repossessed. When the world banking crisis began to bite, I remember talking to an older man who serviced our gas boiler; like us he had frequently travelled to Africa. In conversation he remarked "We may have lost 5% of our GDP (Gross Domestic Product) but we've still got the other 95%. In some of the parts of Africa I visit they would be glad to live off the 5% we've lost!" Of course getting the economy right is important, but not just as a source of money-making; we do need a thriving economy and employment to help people make a useful contribution to society and to share fellowship with one another so they can grow into true humanity as we all tramp the roadmaps of our individual lives. But as our African experience was already beginning to prove, there is so much more to life than year-on-year growth and GDP.

Just before the end of that first visit, Jackson took us to one side and whispered that he had been shortlisted to become the next Bishop. As a boy he had grown up in the South Rwenzori Mountains herding goats before one of his older brothers, a successful tailor, decided to pay for his education. Early the following year we received news that he had been selected. We decided that a bishop-elect and his wife needed to step outside Uganda before embarking on their new role in life. They came to Devizes the following July. On their first night Dorothy kept saying: "What's happening? It's already seven o'clock and it's still light!" During their visit we arranged our very first garden party to raise funds for his new diocese, an annual event that is now in its sixteenth year and which over the last eight years, with the support of many other friends, has helped fund the building of the Bishop Jackson School.

The Bishop Jackson School

The Bishop Jackson School is managed by FIPHAI (Fighting Poverty with Hands on Initiative), which was founded with the purpose of building a school for orphans and poor children living in a very poor neighborhood on the outskirts of Kasese that housed refugees who had fled the war in the Rwenzori Mountains. Over a period of eight years we saw the buildings grow from a bare site to the school it has become today. A boundary fence was first erected and large numbers of bricks were made by local unemployed young lads from the on-site clay. As the years progressed the classrooms slowly took shape before finally being roofed with sheets of corrugated plastic. In 2013, on our final visit to Africa, we saw the school up and running with over 26 staff and 250 pupils, fourteen of whom are supported by Devizes bursaries. Now it has approaching 700 pupils.

At first it was a very daunting prospect, but the Africans' cheerfulness, perseverance and determination to succeed add a totally different dimension to Jesus' vision of the Kingdom of God that he set out to achieve here on this earth. That vision was never meant to be only a passport from this world to the next; it was also a direct challenge to us all to help bring the values of Heaven down to earth, a message our broken world needs more than ever before.

While visiting Base Camp, a rather poor parish on the outskirts of Kasese, just as dusk was falling I was invited to bless a Mother's Union gardening project. Two years later we found the church thriving. The windows had been glazed and a small youth centre was under construction. We were presented with a woven tray of high quality garden produce. Thanking them, I jokingly said God must have been working overtime when I blessed their garden! It was their leader's reply that was much more significant: "What we have learned to do is to organise our poverty." That stands alongside Mother Theresa of Calcutta's statement "As we have done so much for so long with so little, we are now qualified to do anything with nothing." Another clarion call to our over-organised consumerism if ever there was.

Rwanda

In 2004 we made two visits to Uganda; on our second visit

before returning to Kasese we left Kampala for the island of Kalangala, the largest of the Ssesse Islands just off the northern shores of Lake Victoria. It was there that we first met Henry Maguzi. Henry had charge of the town of Kalangala and sixty other small islands, a Herculean task if ever there was. The link with Kalangala came through a local branch of a charity called SUBI, supported by our former village of Barton St. David.

We were due to be met at the island's only ferry port by a lady called Liz. The old ferry by which we travelled was very dilapidated and only set sail when there were enough passengers to pay for the diesel which came aboard in cans. On arrival Liz was conspicuously absent, so we were bundled aboard the one and only bus by the rest of the passengers. Dusk falls quickly in Africa and the dense forest became pitch black as we penetrated deeper and deeper into the jungle. Liz met the bus as we arrived in Kalangala and dumped us in a little café lit by a single candle. We waited in the semi-darkness before some moments later she arrived with Henry, the parish priest, an entirely unscheduled meeting. We ate a simple meal and amid the gloom Henry quietly informed me that I was to celebrate, preach and baptise five children the following morning! One of the ways by which my faith was deepened by our African experiences was having to entrust everything I spoke into the hands of the Holy Spirit. There was no electricity on the island, so that was my only available resource that night. This was to happen time upon time as we met more and more church communities.

Henry's church stood on the site of one of the earliest missionary churches ever built in that part of the world. On that first visit it had no windows and was occupied by flocks of swallow-like birds that flew all around us. One all but dive-bombed me while I was preaching; I seized the opportunity of making this a visual aid. "You all saw that bird, didn't you? It flew in through one window, heard the Gospel and then flew out through another to take the good news to the rest of the world, which is just what we are called to do!" Henry has been a close friend ever since. We travelled in a small boat to some of his sixty islands, distributing bin bags of clothing and were guests in the home of some wonderful people on one of the more remote islands.

Henry has served in two Kampala parishes since leaving Kalangala. On one visit we were invited to two family graduation parties; in each case the church choir was present and played a prominent role singing hymns, but also accompanied vivacious dance tunes, another real insight into local life. Through Henry a close relationship was forged with the Namirembe Diocese, where later we were guests at the opening ceremony of the new Diocesan Synod Centre. The project was started during the Idi Amin period and then held in abeyance for many years. Outside there is a plaque commemorating one of the architects and many others involved who all lost their lives at the hands of Idi Amin's henchmen. The Kabaka, the constitutional monarch of Uganda, was a guest at the party that followed. The local Mother's Union fed several hundred people that day with all the food cooked in the open on wood fires!

Earlier that year we had transported a vanload of bicycles, sewing machines, cutlery and many other items to Operation Sunshine in Folkestone to help fill a forty-foot container for shipment to Kasese. The clerk registering our small part of the cargo suggested that we visit Cyangugu in

Rwanda, a diocese supported by the retired Bishop Ken Barham. So after leaving Kalangala we were met by Bishop Jackson for our third visit to Kasese, and later were driven across the bush to Kabale, from where we travelled by bus to Kigali, the capital of Rwanda.

The onward journey to Cyangugu near the Congolese frontier was made in a local minibus crowded with Africans, and we were deposited on the roadside by the entrance to the Cyangugu Guest House. As we wondered quite where to go, who should pull up beside us but the Bishop, who tossed our luggage into his car and drove us down the long drive. On the Sunday we worshipped in the Cathedral and later visited their farm project and a local tea plantation.

On a second visit two years later, I celebrated and preached in the wonderful new cathedral and had the privilege of giving communion to Bishop Geoffrey on his first visit to his cathedral since returning from major surgery in the US for the removal of his thyroid. Amos, the vicar of the Cathedral, hosted us and invited me to conduct a course for a large group of trainee lay leaders. He also took us to visit the sites where three new churches were to be planted to replace those destroyed during the genocide; we pledged our support. The memory of a very old woman dancing for joy because her church was going to be rebuilt in her lifetime will remain with us forever. We were accompanied by Vincent, another priest with whom we now keep up a regular email correspondence. In 2015 he was given charge of those three churches, one of which is now a magnificent new brick building. Rwanda had already made huge strides since the 1994 genocide.

While worshipping with one of those three small congregations a town official accompanied by an armed guard burst in and challenged us, saying we had no business to be there. He ordered us to attend a people's court that was taking place to judge some of those involved in the 1994 massacres, and promptly escorted us across the road to join the proceedings.

Visiting a tea plantation, we met a group of young people meeting in part of a destroyed school who entertained us with some drama. The most impressive moment was when the part of the cripple in the story was taken by a young girl who had herself been badly crippled amid all the violence that had taken place. How brave of her, and what a message that conveys. Despite the genocide there is now a wonderful atmosphere of reconciliation, and somehow people are managing to overcome the memories of the scenes of utter desolation they all experienced. In one church an elderly lady showed us the still bloodstained floor and the bones of a large number of people who had perished there despite seeking refuge. She herself had narrowly escaped after being wounded with a machete and thrown down a well.

On the final day of our last visit to Africa in 2013, who should arrive for breakfast at Jackson and Dorothy's home but Bishop Geoffrey; we struggled to recognise each other as we met on the veranda and then embraced as our memories cleared. We had not met since I gave him communion in Rwanda.

Ethiopia

In our early years in Devizes David Stables had given a talk about ACET, his education project in Ethiopia which provides primary education for poor children continuing to university where appropriate. Ethiopian Airlines allows you to break your journey in Addis Ababa, besides offering double the normal baggage allowance. We met David, who introduced us to Bisrat, one of his former pupils, who now runs the Addis branch of his charity. On a second visit they invited us to have supper with Birhan Woldu, the child we all saw rescued by a television crew in the 1984 Ethiopian famine. Birhan was then a shy retiring girl but has since become world famous for her own charity work. Meeting Birhan made a lasting impression upon us, as did the Coptic churches in Lalibella hewn out of solid rock bearing their long silent witness to faith. The Addis chaplaincy has a wonderful outreach to the Sudanese refugees who even then were fleeing from the ongoing civil war in South Sudan. In 2006 Simon and Ruth accompanied us to Addis as a joint celebration of our respective golden and silver wedding anniversaries before continuing to Kasese. Later still our granddaughter Alice and her friend spent some time in Uganda during their gap year.

At our golden wedding, instead of presents we had requested contributions towards the new cathedral roof. Early in 2009 we were once more in Kasese to attend a large thanksgiving service. On our very first visit all that existed was a framework of roughly-built three-foot-high walls, within which were a pile of roof girders overgrown by vegetation and home to flocks of grazing goats. While taking an evening stroll to view the magnificent newly-completed cathedral, Jill tripped on a small pebble just outside the back door, fracturing her leg. Charles Habagatsi, the vicar of the cathedral, ran to our assistance and she was carefully

L-R my mother, Grandad Chadwick, Grandma Chadwick, Bilton 1936

The 'Garden of Eden'

Francis Anthony Chadwick (left) in
about 1941

Coverdale, winter of 1941

National Service, Bodmin, January 1950

Francis in his workshop
in Leeds, 1958

Arreton, Isle of Wight, 1963 –
the Big Snow

Front of Arreton Vicarage, 1964

Our arrival at Kingshurst parish, Birmingham Diocese, 1967

In Wroclaw, Poland, 1986

Being welcomed into the Nghima family home, 2002

Family with Bishop Jackson and his wife Dorothy

Naomi with some of her family, 2013

Kasese, new cathedral building under construction

The completed cathedral

Celebration service, 2010

Jill demonstrating her recovery after breaking her femur in 2009

Bishop Jackson with workers in the early stages of classroom construction

Classroom nearing completion

Welcome by children on our final visit in 2013

Some of the younger children

Namirembe, Kampala. Dedication of completed diocesan offices

The Kabaka of Uganda (centre)

Entertaining a Rwandan priest, Namirembe Guest House

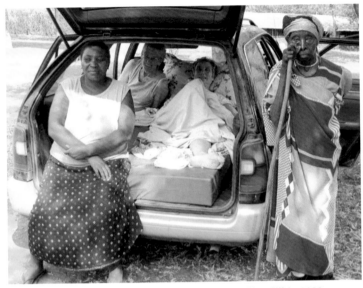

Dorothy and Bishop Jackson's mother tending Jill in 2009

Kitabu Church, built in 2001

Children leading us from their school to the church, 2002

Mother's Union teaching project

Mother's Union literacy class

Kalangala (Ssesse Islands), Lake Victoria, arriving by boat 2006

Kalangala Parish Church - Henry Maguzi and congregation

One of Henry's many remote island churches

The baptism ceremony. Enamel bowl serves as font

Rwanda. Cyangugu Cathedral built after the 1994 genocide

Bishop Geoffrey with other clergy and a visiting American minister

Our farewell to
Bishop Geoffrey
on our final day
in Kasese

Planting a new church in Rwanda, 2006

Elderly lady
dancing for joy

The church under construction, 2016

Tanzania, new church under construction near Dar-es-Salaam

Buzu, site of new Mothers' Union hostel

Jill laying imitation foundation stone, 2010

Dr. Trish outside old children's cancer ward, Dar-es-Salaam 2006

Dr. Trish at the opening of the new children's cancer ward, 2011

Garden party in Devizes to raise funds for Bishop Jackson School, 2017

Ethiopia, 2006

Visiting the Anglican Chaplaincy, 2005, Cairo Cathedral

Sumatra - before lunch in the home of our guide's family, 2005

Fiji - the vicar returning home with our supper

Fijian village church, 2005

laid across the back seat of a car and taken to the local clinic (no ambulances in this part of the world). The following morning she was placed on a mattress in an estate car and taken 40 kilometres to the local Hospital; an X-ray confirmed that she had indeed broken her femur. That night was spent in the Bishop's garden, the car covered by a mosquito net. Throughout the night she was attended by the Bishop's wife, while a security guard also kept watch. The following Sunday evening a flying doctor team from Kenya landed at Kasese airstrip to take us to the Aga Khan Hospital in Nairobi. During our eleven-day stay I made a trip to the local market to buy flowers and fruit. The stall holders had never seen a 'Mzungu' (white European) in their market before and asked why I was there. As I left they said they would pray for Jill, more witnesses to faith, and on my second visit the flowers and fruit were a gift. We are still in touch with the hospital bank clerk who changed our dollars.

The following year we were back. I had to preach at another big thanksgiving service in the cathedral, this time for 'the recovery of my wife's left leg' – Beckham's foot and all that! To close I invited them all to say thank you to God. Shouting 'thank you' simply doesn't work, but you can shout WASINGA. To each of my three 'hip hips' everyone responded vigorously, each shout of Wasinga louder than the last! Wasinga's three syllables just lend themselves to crescendo.

Tanzania

Trips to Kasese were sometimes preceded by visits to Dar-es-Salaam. We had been introduced to Joyce Kibaja, the Diocesan Mothers' Union President, who escorted us to many of their local branches and churches. A large number of those churches were either new buildings or still under construction. Because of increasing congregations a new building was often built around an existing one before that was finally pulled down. The welcome we received from the local clergy and Mothers' Union members was tremendous.

The first item on our 2006 agenda was entitled 'The closure of the Ilala Deanery.' Far from closing down it was their annual general meeting, attended by all the MU branches in the deanery. Each group presented a report and a financial statement and provided an item of entertainment! There were several choral pieces; one group provided a dramatic presentation of the parable of the prodigal son. Two Mothers' Union members, provocatively dressed as the wanton women with whom the young man indulged himself in riotous living, slowly advanced towards me with utter abandon, rolling their eyes invitingly and contorting themselves into every alluring posture possible! All far removed from the often dreary sessions that might take place back home. The whole occasion was sheer drama from start to finish. On another of these occasions, which often took place in one of the poorest parishes, we were impressed by the way MU members organised the distribution of US aid, carefully noting down the name and address of each qualifying recipient for future pastoral visits.

The number of churches to which we were taken over the years was legion, among them a wonderful trip to Mgorogoro where the members train HIV victims as counsellors. On another occasion we paid an overnight visit to Zanzibar. There we met our friend Richard, another of my email correspondents. He has now become a bishop on the mainland. On a second visit I was to preach in the wonderful Zanzibar Cathedral, built over the former slave market. We also visited the old slave port of Bagamoyo, to which Livingstone's body was taken overland by his faithful porters before it was transported to Westminster for burial. His heart was left in Africa. I have been in touch with the parish priest, John Midelo, ever since.

Joyce also took us to visit the children's cancer ward of one of the town Hospitals in Dar. Working there was Dr Trish, an Irish doctor on secondment for two years; she was struggling with very poor accommodation. At that time we had to approach the British High Commission on behalf of the church in Zanzibar. There we met a young man called Mark from the Consular Department; in conversation we discovered that he was a devout Christian. Knowing how the wives of diplomats are often at a loose end, I suggested he might like to ask them to visit Dr Trish's children. The following Christmas Eve I received a most wonderful Christmas present in the form of an email from Dr Trish telling us how a wonderful team of ladies had decorated the ward, and brought all the children gifts. From those early seeds we helped sow, with the advice and contacts of the High Commission Dr Trish has built an entirely new state of the art Children's cancer ward.

The year after Jill broke her leg we left Kasese by bus for Bukoba on the Tanzanian shore of Lake Victoria. We became close friends with the local parish priest and his wife before flying by local airways to visit our dear friend Joyce

Kibaja in Dar-es-Salaam. In the mid-19th Century early Christian missionaries purchased large tracts of land in Tanzania; among them was a site at Buza on the outskirts of Dar. In 2010 we were taken to visit this site for a second time and stood beside a small pegged-out area of land destined to become a Mothers' Union Hostel for girls. Jill was invited to lay a 'pretend' foundation stone. Beside a small pile of loose breeze blocks there was a bowl of sand and cement and a shovel! After Jill had made some 'pretend mortar' the Mother's Union President then pulled back a curtain to reveal a plaque which read:

THIS STONE HAS BEEN
LAID BY
MRS JILL F. CHADWICK
FROM UK DEVICES
30/01/10

That hostel is now up and running, and for the last six or more years Joyce Kibaja has been the Tanzanian Mother's Union Representative at the meetings of the Mother's Union head office in Mary Sumner House London.

The worldwide church family

I am an unashamed website tourist! In 2005 we took a break from Africa and set out to circumnavigate the world. Wherever possible I contacted all the local churches en route beforehand.

Singapore

The cathedral church of Singapore welcomed us with open arms. From the airport, we were escorted to our hotel. The next day a member of the cathedral staff took us to visit Changi prison, where Bishop Leonard Wilson, from my Birmingham days, had been held prisoner and tortured by the Japanese. I presented them with my copy of his autobiography. Besides building a whole new underground church centre, serviced by a branch of the Singapore underground, the cathedral is host to multi-language Asian worship every Sunday, and also supports the church in Nepal.

Bangkok, Laos and Sumatra

The Bangkok chaplaincy supports Burmese Karen refugees. In Luang Prebang in Laos we found a small congregation of mostly young Christians worshipping secretly with whom we kept contact by email for several years. Our boatman on the Mekong took us to his own non-touristy village, where we met an American-trained Laos Baptist minister distilling rice whisky! We also found a wonderfully active Lutheran community in Sumatra who were hosting a meeting of South East Asian Christians, including a lady from Burma, another email contact.

Australia and New Zealand

In Australia we visited some Camberley friends before youth hostelling our way round the North Island. We visited

Wellington Cathedral and later Christchurch Cathedral on the South Island, which in 2011 suffered severe damage in a succession of earthquakes.

Fiji

The dean of Suva Cathedral gave us a warm welcome and arranged for us to spend a night in the home of a village priest. It is their custom for the village headman to welcome visitors by presiding over the Kava ceremony. You provide the Kava (a powder ground from the dried root of a pepper tree) which is placed in a sock and soaked in water in a bowl resembling a portable font; a half-coconut shell is then filled and continually passed from person to person to take a sip until the bowl is emptied. It has a slightly numbing effect on the tongue and induces a peaceful sleep! The warmth and friendship of the Fiji church is a much-treasured memory.

Los Angeles

LA was our last stop, where we were made particularly welcome by All Saints Episcopal Church, Beverly Hills. Our hotel had enquired about their services and informed us there were 'three showings'. We still have the large welcome pack of this wonderful church community with outreach all over the world, and were presented with a live CD recording of the sermon, laughs and all.

Africa from East to West

In 2007 we set out to emulate David Livingstone by

travelling from Zanzibar to the Atlantic Coast, but not on foot! After being hosted by our church family in Zanzibar we visited more church communities in Dar-es-Salaam before flying to Lusaka in Zambia. There we visited the wonderful cathedral built in 1962 without any overseas aid before flying to Livingstone. Our Windhoek travel company had put us in touch with a wonderful retired couple who ran a little lodge on the shores of the Zambezi in aid of a small school. We stood where Livingstone stood beside the Victoria Falls, where an enterprising group of young African lads held on to Jill firmly as she stared over the edge from Livingstone's pool. Worshipping in the local Anglican Church there was a young man wearing a T-shirt emblazoned with the words 'ANGLICAN CHURCH IN ACTION – SERVICE WITHOUT BOUNDARIES'. Leaving Livingstone, our hosts drove us in their 4x4 to board a small ferry to cross the great Zambezi River to Botswana, from where we travelled to the Okavango. After two days organised by our travel company we were driven across the northern Kalahari Desert to Windhoek in Namibia. There we lodged in the Lutheran Hostel and attended the Anglican Cathedral before finally arriving in Swakopmund on the Atlantic coast, having shared in the worship and fellowship of all the Anglican churches along our route.

Our African extravaganza concluded with one final visit in 2013. I have only scratched the surface of our African adventures. None of this could have been accomplished without my wife, my ever-constant travelling companion. It is impossible to include all our African friends, that great cloud of witnesses to faith, who by showering their love and fellowship upon us have helped deepen our Faith beyond all measure. It is perhaps no accident that Jesus sent out his disciples two by two!

*****

The time has now come to turn from all the wonderful witnesses to faith encountered on the roadmap of my life's journey and consider how their faith has led me to an ever-deepening understanding of the Gospel that Jesus committed to his disciples. Faith, like everything else, has to grow and is built brick by brick. The mortar that holds it all together is not cement but the fellowship of all the people you meet on your life's journey. Discovering a meaningful faith in today's fast changing world, so often the victim of violence and greed, can be quite a challenge.

In Part Two we shall examine the growth of the early church after the death of the first disciples and consider the challenges facing religion in the 21st century, including those posed by the advances made in science and astronomy and the enormous changes taking place in our growing understanding of the universe. Then we shall chart the continuing growth and development of the faith with which Jesus inspired his first disciples before finally exploring the personal faith by which Jesus' own life was guided during his time here on earth.

PART TWO

CHAPTER SIX

CHALLENGES TO FAITH IN TODAY'S WORLD

For many millions of people, life is a continuous struggle for survival. Finding meaningful employment in a society increasingly governed by technology can be quite a challenge. All over the world people live in danger of losing their lives, their livelihoods and their homes, while those in highly-skilled jobs live in a highly frenetic world, powered by the ever-increasing pace of change and the financial interests of global companies, driven by the pursuit of many to make more and more money at all costs.

On many television channels a procession of adverts rushes towards you, flashing and flicking speedily from frame to frame urging us to consume, consume, consume.

Your eyes encounter pre-traumatic stress as cars hop from roof top to roof top before descending from the sky along a chute to hit you full in the face, as if designed more for James Bond or Jeremy Clarkson than a family car. In addition we are treated to an almost daily diet of unrest, stabbings and violence, either on screen or as headlines in the daily press. Is this really the path forward for our world, or does it reflect a world spinning out of control as the Gadarene herd of humanity, like those frenzied pigs in the Bible, rushes headlong over the cliffs of consumerism to premature disaster? *(See Note 5, Steve Hilton)*

One of the changes that has been contributory to all this is the advent of television in the early twentieth century. Incidents of violence that used to take days to reach us on the radio are now presented visually from all over the world, tumbling one after another onto a few square feet in our sitting rooms. Of course there are many superb television documentaries, entertaining soaps and dramas, but the proportion of programmes featuring violence and brutality is also significantly high. Do we really have to add to all the violence already taking place all over the world and from which those who are victim would so dearly like to escape? In some instances may this not be just as instrumental in promoting violence and terrorism as the brainwashing of susceptible young people by fundamentalist preachers? Nearly every day faith is also held hostage by the meaningless brutality of terrorism, and people ask how a loving God can allow all this to happen. We will attempt to answer this question later when we look at how Jesus himself dealt with the problem of all the evil and pain in the world.

Today's world is also a daily frenzy of communication, data processing, pressure to meet production deadlines, commuting, high speed travel, Facebooking, mobile ears and the inability for many to escape the noise of it all – a world 'tweeting' away like the contentious woman in the book of Proverbs, whose blathering is likened to the perpetual dropping of water on a rainy day. Amidst the hurly burly of most people's everyday lives there is often little or no time left to ponder where it might all be leading.

William Wordsworth, writing in the eighteenth century, made exactly the same observation. Though written nearly two hundred years ago, these lines sound remarkably like a description of today's world:

The world is too much with us; late and soon,
Getting and spending, we lay waste our powers:
Little we see in Nature that is ours;
We have given our hearts away, a sordid boon!
 - William Wordsworth

The Ever-Increasing Pace of Change

Change lies at the very heart of life, and without it we could not survive from moment to moment. Nothing in life ever stays still. Life is a continuous flow and can be compared to the waves of the sea with their perpetual ups and downs. I have designed and planted many gardens; over the years they have all changed. Tiny shrubs become large bushes and occupy the space where flowers once grew. Saplings become young trees, and what was a sunny bank becomes shaded woodland; each one of us changes as we travel our life's journey. What a good thing! A person diagnosed with cancer longs for things to change. Change is always the pathway to new life.

However, the speed of change in our modern world often appears to be overwhelming. Those of us born towards the beginning of the last century have perhaps seen more swift change than any other single generation in history; most dramatic of all is the rapid increase of the world population from just over two billion in 1930 when I was born to approaching seven and a half billion today.

The 20th century saw remarkable changes in nearly every sphere of human knowledge, not least in astronomy, medical science, natural history and genetics, but above all in the development of the computer and the Internet, allowing speedy access to information and instantaneous communication worldwide. In 1950 the mail service to Cape Town took thirteen days each way. Now emails arrive instantly all over the world at the press of a button, and people are constantly in touch with each other via Facebook and Twitter, both visually and audibly.

I have always enjoyed maps. Maybe when you were young you might have imagined that Brazil was a jigsaw piece just waiting to fit quite snugly into the gulf of Guinea on the African West coast? In 1912 a German professor, Alfred Wegener, proposed that the continents were once compressed into a single proto-continent which he called Pangaea. As late as 1929 Wegener's ideas were still being dismissed; not until the 1960s was his theory finally demonstrated to be true. Up to that time there had been no detailed observation of the drifting and collision of continental plates. My boyish imagination was confirmed.

But perhaps more than all those things has been the change in our understanding of the Universe.

Significant Discoveries of the 20th Century

Electricity

Many of the achievements of the last century could never have come about without our ever-increasing knowledge of the science of electricity. Until the mid-eighteenth century little was known about electricity; lightning was often believed to be the work of angry gods! Between 1745 and 1746 two Dutch scientists invented what is still known as the Leyden jar, a device that stores static electricity. Eventually electricity was proved to be linked to lightning, but Benjamin Franklin's claim to have discovered it by his kite-flying experiment is now generally accepted as a clever bit of personal kite flying to gain him publicity and membership of the Royal Society.

Our knowledge of electricity and its application in modern technology in the twentieth century has led to the computerisation of nearly all industrial production and to enormous strides in the development of medical treatment. We have come a long way from the 15 amp, two pin plugs of my childhood, some of which still inhabit my box of old electrical equipment. We also now know that our bodies act as miniature power systems attached to our own personal national grid that delivers electricity on demand to all parts of our body as needed, which is why we immediately feel pain if we stub our toes, and why distressing news fuels our emotions. You can occasionally experience a slight electric shock when you twist one of your fingers, or when on removing your jumper you hear the crackling of static electricity generated by your own body. While we no longer believe that lightning is a demonstration of the wrath of God it still reflects the wonder of the created world.

Understanding our Brains

Our knowledge of electricity, and the ever-increasing speed of modern computers, has led to a giant leap forward in our understanding of the workings of the human brain. Our brain is made up of a hundred billion cells and there are as many connections between them in a cubic centimetre of brain as there are stars in the Milky Way! Just as my computer processes the words I write, our brains are ceaselessly working as a 'reality processor' turning what is out there into what we can recognise almost instantly.

For the first two years of life our brains are fairly blank canvases, mostly concerned with the development and control of our bodily functions. Though our brains are pre-programmed like our computers to operate our bodies, we then begin to fill them with information developed by our daily experience of life. We create roadmaps of the locality where we live; we grow our own memories and develop our personal aptitudes.

There is strong evidence that the brain patterns we construct in our formative years determine the way we grow up and stay with us for life to become the tramways along which much of our later thinking is conducted. Today over 75% of our young people are constantly addicted to technology from childhood. At Heathrow Airport recently I saw a three-year-old tapping away. Computer games, Facebook, Twitter, tablets and smart phones occupy much of children's time and scientists are now aware that this may pose severe dangers. This is particularly evident in the adult material so readily available and the influence of porn on their attitude to sex; for many today, childhood innocence no longer exists.

Perhaps just as serious is the loss of that childish attitude of trust and wonder. Amid all the technological offerings, little time is left for the development of proper relationships; still less for silence in which one can experience a sense of presence that goes far beyond the constant chatter of our modern world, and which can awaken a childish awareness of spiritual values. *(See Note 5, Steve Hilton)*

What still remains a mystery to the neuroscientist is the development of our consciousness – of what makes ME me and nobody else. During our lifetime all the cells of our body change completely, but the ME of childhood survives, just as a well-maintained lawn remains a lawn however many times it is cut. Our own personal identity is a constant from the moment we wake to memory, the precious gift that gives meaning to all we experience. Yuval Harari in his large volume entitled *Homo Deus*, the sequel to *Sapiens*, his brief history of mankind, dismisses the very existence of the human soul as a baseless reality, but admits that scientists are still baffled by consciousness. No wonder they are. In fact the soul is of the very 'esse' of our existence; the core of our *esse*ntial being. *(See Note 6, Yuval Harari)*

Human beings are a curious mixture of both physical and

spiritual reality. Consciousness and emotions like a 'guilty conscience' cannot be measured by scientific instruments or explained by carefully worked-out equations. The enigma of the soul has to be viewed through an entirely different lens, the lens of spirituality. You don't put reading glasses on to look at the moon, or to drive your car; the latter could be positively disastrous. In the same way it is no use putting on your scientific glasses to discover your soul. Those scientists like Yuval Harari who dispute the existence of the soul are looking in the wrong direction. We have to look into the hidden depths of our own soul.

How can we declare that the soul is an illusion, a reality that does not exist? Anyone who denies the existence of their own soul is hoist with their own petard; their very denial has its source deep within their own being though which they express their disbelief. This is a conundrum. Scientists can locate the existence of other planets millions of light years away but cannot locate the existence of their own soul, so close to hand and hidden within themselves. All science and all religion is only possible because of the Spirit deep inside each one of us that drives all our thinking, and inspires all we write.

Turning Man into God, as the title Homo Deus suggests, only ever leads to disaster, suffering and pain when we consider what man has done to man and to God's creation over the centuries, where so much of our human behaviour falls far below the love and compassion and mercy of God revealed by Jesus to the whole of humanity. Doing so is fraught with as much danger as driving in our reading glasses. The soul is invisible, but there is more to reality than only the seen world. The real evidence of what happens when

Homo abrogates the authority of Deus (Divine authority) and seizes ultimate power for himself is out there for all to see amid all the chaos and destruction that often follows. There is ample evidence of this every time we switch on the news or buy a daily newspaper. *(See Note 6, Yuval Harari)*

What Happens When We Die?

Of course as part of our body, our brain also dies, though many of the body's cells have a life span of their own, and may live on for several hours or even a day. But what happens to the Me that has already survived so many biological changes? Recently at the funeral of a great personal friend, the priest walking up the aisle began the service rather gloomily by pronouncing that we brought nothing into this world and can take nothing out. I question this – what we take with us is the ME that we have become within our lifetime, in the development of which both God and ourselves have played a very significant part. At this point mystery overtakes and surpasses knowledge. *(See Note 7, David Eagleman)*

Natural History

When I first visited the Natural History Museum I was struck by the similarity of the basic structure of all mammals from the dinosaur and the platypus down to each one of us, all seemingly drawn from one basic template. Every skeleton consists of a central bony structure with a head, a tail, two arms and two legs. It seemed to me that the history of all the creatures that have ever inhabited the earth was one gigantic experiment! When Charles Darwin unravelled this mystery in his famous book *The Origin of Species* he was not only severely challenged by the Church but also by Richard Owen, another great biologist; Owen, himself a practising churchman, finally rejected Darwin's theory of evolution by natural selection. Over the years of the 20th century and beyond David Attenborough has revealed more and more of the intricacies of the natural world and in 2008 Darwin's statue was once more given pride of place, returning to its original location in the Central Hall.

DNA - Deoxyribonucleic Acid

All that Darwin discovered has now led to the world changing discovery of DNA, which is made up of molecules called nucleotides. Each nucleotide contains a phosphate group, a sugar group and a nitrogen base. The four types of nitrogen bases are adenine (A), thymine (T), guanine (G) and cytosine (C). The order of these bases is what determines the structure of DNA, or the code that carries most of the instructions used in the development, functioning and reproduction of all known living organisms. It was first identified and isolated by Friedrich Miescher in 1869 at the University of Tübingen, but the double helix structure of DNA was only finally discovered in 1953 by Watson and Crick at the University of Cambridge, using experimental data collected by Rosalind Franklin and Maurice Wilkins. The discovery of DNA has greatly assisted the tracing of our ancestry and has also led to great advances in forensic science.

The Genetic Code

This led to the development of the genetic code, a set of rules defining how the four-letter code of DNA is translated into the 20-letter code of amino acids, which are the building blocks of proteins. Professor Brian Cox, in his own inimitable way, explains how the Orang Utang is our nearest living 'relative' in the created order, possessing approximately 99% of our human genetic code. The most significant contribution of DNA is that it closely links all created life on Earth and shows that all humankind shares the same inheritance with all other forms of life on this planet we call home. How tragic that the genetic harmony of that union is so often carelessly broken by the tragic divisions that mankind inflicts upon itself.

Astronomy – the Radio Telescope

Giant strides in our understanding of the Universe have been made possible by the development of the radio telescope. A great revolution began with the sprouting of numerous strange steel structures on Jodrell Bank in Cheshire in the late forties that led to the eventual development of the world-famous 250-foot radio telescope, which continues to make an enormous contribution to our understanding of the universe. We owe an enormous debt to Sir Bernard Lovell for scattering a great deal of both scientific and religious superstition and bigotry, replacing it with a far clearer understanding of the universe. This enables us by the use of our religious 'antennae' to concentrate on the real message of the Christian Gospel, which is to radiate the beams of spiritual truth revealed by the life and teaching of Jesus. Electromagnetic radiation is effectively used in the treatment of cancer cells, but in the life of our troubled world there are also many other cancers of a more spiritual nature that can only be healed by the radiation of God's love and compassion for all mankind.

The Hubble Telescope

This was followed by the Hubble Space Telescope, launched into low earth orbit in 1990 and still in operation. The telescope's orbit is outside the distortion of Earth's atmosphere, which allows it to take extremely high-resolution images with negligible background light. Hubble has recorded some of the most detailed visible light images ever. Now there are more and more sophisticated telescopes all over the world.

Space Exploration

The mapping of space eventually led to the landing of men on the moon in 1969. The American Neil Armstrong became the first man to walk on the moon's surface as he stepped out into the Sea of Tranquillity. As he put his left foot down he coined those now famous words "That's one small step for man, one giant leap for mankind." While telling the world that he and 'Buzz' Aldrin came in peace, both men talked of being spiritually uplifted by the beauty of the universe, and Neil commented that it made our human stupidities on earth appear even more intolerable. But it was not long before their achievement became politicised, with President Reagan talking about 'Star Wars'. In subsequent years we have landed robots on Mars and put satellites in orbit around most of the planets of our solar system.

Weather Forecasting

Vast changes have boosted the science of weather forecasting. Early attempts were a rather hit and miss affair, but now, with the aid of modern technology and by loading specialised programmes into advanced computers, it has become possible to look at all the factors affecting our global weather from space. Quite a difference from describing a red sky at night as shepherd's delight, words first recorded in the Bible.

Energy

The enormous energy of the sun fuels our very existence. All life on Earth has evolved by the transfer of that energy to the surface of the Earth in the form of chemical energy. This whole process had its beginning in the Big Bang, when that energy was dispersed across the Universe. The most interesting quality of energy is that it never disappears, only changing from one form of energy into another, so that the amount of energy in the whole universe remains constant, exactly the same as when the universe came into being. The fact that energy is always conserved and never destroyed is known as the first law of thermodynamics.

The second law of thermodynamics states that order is perpetually being converted to disorder, a process described as the increase of entropy, from the Greek meaning 'a turning towards' or 'transformation' from one state to another.

The third law of thermodynamics is very complicated and written in language that most of us find difficult to understand.

Spiritual Energy

But beyond physical energy, we should surely take account of spiritual energy. Perhaps we can use the scientific explanations of energy as a parable for what we might coin 'Theodynamics.' The first law of Theodynamics is that God's spiritual energy is eternal and can never be destroyed. The second law of Theodynamics is that the spiritual energy of God's love is constantly being transformed into love and compassion; a process revealed by Jesus and open to be received by all those who make the response of faith.

A close friend of mine once found himself walking along a beach on the south coast where he encountered an elderly couple looking out to sea awaiting the sunset. The clouds on the horizon were tinged a deep rose and bordered by brilliant gold and fading shafts of light; what they were looking at was its residual glow. The sun had already set behind them. They were looking in the wrong direction! That illustrates the third law of Theodynamics; that we have to be turned towards God to allow the energy of his love to flow into our hearts. If God is the ultimate source of all spiritual energy which is mediated by his spirit to all life, when we die that energy is never lost, it returns to God. In the early fourth century St. Augustine, the famous theologian and philosopher, expressed this thought very simply in his well-known words 'Our heart is restless until it finds its rest in Thee'.

Respecting One Another's Knowledge

The last one hundred years have indeed changed our whole understanding of the Universe, and technology has advanced even more swiftly in the early years of the 21st century than any other. I am not alone in claiming that no earlier generation has ever seen more sweeping changes in so short a time space. Modern science has literally moved mountains, changing the landscape of life in many parts of the world, and has completely transformed our understanding of the Universe. In the pursuit of science, mankind has worked miracles for humanity, but we have also reaped the whirlwind. In the field of armaments our discoveries have been turned to evil, causing unbelievable human suffering. It is beyond reason that mankind can at one moment use its knowledge to construct skyscrapers, dams, state of the art schools and hospitals and in the next obliterate whole cities and communities with carpet bombing,

Throughout the centuries, mistaken religious ideology has also caused untold human suffering, leading to almost unimaginable violence and hatred, especially in the Middle East, now the home of so much world terrorism. Science that fails to take account of the values of faith which add dignity and value to our humanity can fall short and endanger all its wonderful achievements. Religion without the benefits of scientific knowledge can lose its way. Only as we learn to respect each other's knowledge can we avoid many of the pitfalls facing today's world. This is the world in which our grandchildren are growing up; they are often much better at coping with it than their parents and grandparents!

Faith and spirituality may take on new forms, but they still need to lie at the heart of our humanity. Amid the rush of 21st century life there are moments when we all need to stand and stare. Many still possess a spiritual hunger that goes far beyond viewing life only in terms of gross domestic product, percentage growth and a successful economy. There is so much more to life than the need to make more and more money. During the 400th anniversary celebrations of William Shakespeare's birth Gregory Doran of the Royal Shakespeare Company, in his 2016 Richard Dimbleby lecture pointed out the relevance of Shakespeare to many of the problems facing today's world. He compared the destruction of the twin towers of the World Trade Centre to the Gunpowder Plot, which if successful would have destroyed the King, the nobility and the government all in one gigantic explosion. In true Shakespearian style he concluded 'There are many who find a God-shaped hole in our secular society.'

Filling that God-shaped hole and struggling to keep the spirit of faith alive amid the violence that has afflicted the whole of recorded history is no new battle. Every generation requires a new presentation of the Christian faith relevant to today's 'modern age', but all too soon time will relegate our modernity to the past. Nothing stays 'state of the art' forever, even less so in an age of ever more speedy technological change. With our ever-increasing knowledge of the universe in an increasingly secular Western culture, where does this leave the proclamation of the Gospel, the Good News? How can our faith help us find a way through the maelstrom of events that seems to hit the news every day? Every generation still asks the question that my nineteen-year-old barrow boy asked while I was in the army: "What's going to happen to me when I die?" We all face the challenge of making sense of our being alive in this world.

In the next chapter I shall explore our need for faith, and some of the dangers that at times have clouded Jesus' vision of the Kingdom of God as we try to find some assurance of where the roadmap of each of our personal lives may lead.

CHAPTER SEVEN

THE GROWTH OF CHRISTIAN FAITH

To help us in our quest to find faith we need to consider how the Christian Faith has grown over the centuries since the death of Jesus and his first disciples. Over time that has led to the development of the church as an Institution. As we look at the progress of Christianity from a way of life to an established organisation we must also explore how the church has responded to Jesus' last command to his disciples to love one another, and to proclaim his vision of the Kingdom of God to the whole world, not just as a preparation for entry to his Kingdom in Heaven, but as a challenge to establish his Kingdom here on earth as well.

The apostle John, the most long-lived of those disciples,

wrote his Gospel much later than the other three, perhaps well into his eighties. With his death, and the death of all those who had known Jesus personally, the church began making the critical transition to the next generation of believers, those who had not encountered Jesus during his life on earth. From about this time we begin to hear the expression 'The Church Fathers' Among them were people like Irenaeus, Clement of Rome, Clement of Alexandria, Cyril and Athanasius, many of whom studied theology at the ancient classical Library in Alexandria. Some wrote in Syriac, a language akin to that spoken by Jesus; and later in the Western Church there were Ambrose, Jerome and Augustine.

In some ways those early Christians and theologians were just like us. They had to think about faith within the parameters of what then passed for 'modern' knowledge, and like us they had to believe without having met Jesus in the same physical way in which he was known to his closest disciples in their lifetime. However throughout the history of the Christian church there are many who have encountered the presence of the risen Jesus in the same way that he made himself known to those early disciples after his resurrection, most notably St. Paul. Many people have heard of his 'Damascus moment' when he had a vision of the risen Jesus while travelling to the city of Damascus. He more than any other apostle laid the foundations of Christianity in Europe and described himself as an Apostle 'born out of due time.'

Travelling in those days was difficult and time consuming. As a consequence there developed a great diversity among local church groups whose beliefs were often at variance with one another – just as there are still divergences to this day. The same was true of the many pagan religions. It is important to remember that the whole of the Roman Empire and the Middle East was steeped in religion and superstition at this time.

Major differences developed among many Christian groups and much argument took place as to whether Jesus was human or divine or both. To resolve this situation the 'Church Fathers', or elders, eventually developed a full-blown theology, struggling to fit Jesus into their inherited monotheistic idea of there being only one God. In the process they developed the doctrine of the Trinity.

Molded by the Jewish monotheistic tradition in which they had been nurtured one can sympathise with their dilemma. They were attempting to marry the Jesus of history to the 'Unseen God', while juggling all the time with the Holy Spirit. They even began to argue over such things as to how the Holy Spirit proceeded, whether it was from God only or from both God and Jesus! In the process of trying to rationalise the Trinity they lost sight of Jesus' vision of the Kingdom and his last command to his disciples to love God and to love one another, and replaced his way of life with a doctrine to be believed. (Professor Keith Ward argues that this led to the Byzantine labyrinth of bad tempered arguments and interminable disputes about the exact nature of the Trinity and the nature of Christ that brought about the radical simplification of Muslim monotheism.) *(See Note 8, Professor Keith Ward)*

Those early theologians were attempting to explain the mystery of God, presenting themselves with the task of solving a giant theological crossword puzzle, searching for clues wherever they could find them, just as science looks for clues to solve the mystery of the universe. In fact they were employing the tools of theology in much the same way as scientists employ their tools, but using reason and imagination rather than testing their ideas by experiment. They had set themselves the impossible task of trying to describe how God is God; a task wholly beyond the capacity of human beings.

The First Two Centuries

Gaius Octavius was born on September 23rd 63 BC in Rome and was the founder of the Roman Empire, ruling as Emperor Augustus from 27 BC until his death in AD 13. It is hard for us to enter into the pagan world of those days with its multiplicity of gods that governed every aspect of day-to-day life in the centuries that surrounded the birth of Jesus. It is interesting to observe that from its earliest days the Christian Church replaced these gods by introducing the veneration of the saints, each of whom was accredited with particular properties. St. Christopher became the saint for the protection of travellers. If you lost your keys, you prayed to St. Anthony. For several centuries Christianity lived side by side with paganism. Pagan temples still flourished as they built their churches, often very similar in style to the Roman temple or basilica.

The pagan world, empowered by Roman authority, must have presented a truly daunting challenge to Jesus, a challenge that also faced his disciples and their first followers. To establish his Empire, Augustus eventually allowed himself to be treated as a god, and emperor worship became compulsory, though he personally never treated the title that seriously. He also conferred the title of 'God' posthumously on Julius Caesar. Christians of the first two centuries saw periods of persecution. At first the Christians were regarded as a peculiar small sect and were only persecuted spasmodically, but by the time of the Emperor Diocletian in the mid third century many Roman citizens were becoming converts and their monotheism was perceived as a serious threat to the Empire, and the possible destruction of the pagan system of belief on which it was based. As the Empire began to falter, persecution increased in ferocity, but as the Christian community began to grow in numbers and to influence the predominantly pagan leadership, the government came under ever increasing pressure; persecution then began to decline and had all but disappeared by the time Constantine became Emperor in the year 306. The historian bishop Eusebius, Bishop of Berytus (modern-day Beirut) and later of Nicomedia, where the imperial court resided, tells us that as Constantine was marching with his army to battle he looked up at the sun and saw a cross of light above it, and with it the Greek words 'In this sign you will conquer.' That eventually led to his adoption of Christianity as the official religion of the Empire.

Though Constantine's Empire was in danger of falling apart completely, despite the many divisions among Christians he saw the Christian Church as a powerful organisation that might just become a very useful tool in holding the Empire together. Determined to resolve the church's divisions, in AD 325 he convened the Council of Nicea, which he himself chaired, to try and restore some sense of church unity. The Nicene Creed which all the squabbling bishops worked out under his chairmanship is still the formative Christian creed of the church today. It has been estimated that by 300 AD, of the sixty million population of the Roman Empire, 10% were Christian.

Constantine was in some ways a rather reluctant Christian and never quite abandoned all his pagan beliefs; he was only baptised on his deathbed. You can imagine him sitting in his chair with all those arguing bishops, getting bored to the teeth! The Jewish historian Josephus tells us that he got so impatient with them all that he tore up some of their written presentations in front of them. Some modern synod meetings can be just as boring! There were benefits, however. Hagia Sophia was built in Constantinople, persecution ceased and the church received his approval and protection. *(See Note 9, Josephus)*

From that moment onwards the Christian Faith changed significantly. It had first been known simply as 'The Way' – a way of life based upon Jesus' teaching and the call to follow his example. Confucius, in the China of the fifth century before Christ, also described his philosophy of life as a way of life.

Confucius

Kong Qui, better known as Confucius, was born in 551 BC. His teaching focused on creating ethical models of family life and public interaction. In the sixth century BC traditional Chinese principles began to deteriorate, resulting in a period of moral decline. Confucius recognized an opportunity. His social philosophy was based primarily on the idea of *ren*, or loving others while exercising self-discipline. He believed that ren could be put into action using the Golden Rule, 'What you do not wish for yourself do not do to others' – the second of the two great Commandments that Jesus gave to his disciples.

Confucius gained employment in what we might call the civil service, but felt that his teachings had made little impact on Chinese culture. He died in 479 BC. During the fourth century Confucius became a recognised sage and philosopher who deserved greater recognition. By the second century BC, during China's first Han Dynasty, his ideas became the foundation of the state ideology and were held in high respect until they were replaced by Chairman Mao's 'Little Red Book' and the Cultural Revolution. Confucius' grave and monument were desecrated by the Red Guards. Now they have been fully restored and in the new communist China, Confucian schools offer some of the best education in the country. There are well over three hundred and the number is growing. *(See Note 10, Confucius)*

G.K. Chesterton, in his study of St. Francis, points out that Jesus lived *before* Christianity, and that the world he encountered was largely pagan, apart from the relatively small Jewish community in which Jesus himself grew up. Now Christianity was slowly turning Jesus' teaching into a doctrine, a set of beliefs, developing a theology and a faith formulated by creeds. Over the centuries the creeds continued to be statements of what the church believed and it expected all Christians to adhere to them. It seems that this early theology was beginning to turn God into a problem to be solved rather than someone with whom you could enter into a personal relationship, and was in danger of losing sight of Jesus' passionate vision of the Kingdom of

God. Properly understood, the word 'theology' means the study of God's word to us, not our words about God. *(See Note 11, G.K. Chesterton, Life of St. Francis)*

Theology is the systematic and rational study of concepts of God, and the word comes from the Greek words (Θεός) meaning God and (λογία) meaning word. Put more simply, it is exploring the word of God. When I first began to study theology I got totally lost! I have now come to believe that you cannot really begin to study theology without relating it to your experience of God as you travel the road of life, and developing a deeper and growing understanding of the word of God as it was understood by the earliest disciples of Jesus. On its own, theology can be barren; it has to be clothed with the humanity of the life Jesus himself lived, and of human life in all its extreme variety. To make sense it must jump from the pages on which it is written into everyday life.

No wonder I got lost when I was in my early twenties! I had hardly begun my journey of faith. While attending lectures on eucharistic theology (the study of the communion service) among all the arguments as to when God became present I recorded this comment in my student notebook: "No account whatever has been taken of the people kneeling at the altar rail; the family of the faithful with all their uncertainties, doubts and devotion is the very stuff of which the church family has to be constructed and must never be ignored".

The Middle Ages

By the Middle Ages the church had become a well-established Institution, a very powerful force in the world, with the word of the Pope held as gospel truth, an authority which most ordinary Christians dared to challenge at their peril. We must remember that much of mediaeval life was still governed by superstition, and the main purpose of the church was then seen as rescuing souls from this wicked world. Only if you were a properly baptised, confirmed and communicant member of the church could you be absolutely assured of the salvation of your immortal soul and guaranteed entry into the Kingdom of Heaven. The church began to assume the image of a powerful global company, and saw itself as the custodian of the whole salvation industry and as guardian of the Catholic faith 'which unless a man believed faithfully he could never be saved'. Faith, from being a response to the inspiration that those early disciples felt when in Jesus' presence, and a way of life, a means of entering into a close and personal relationship with God, was now becoming more a matter of accepting creedal statements of belief, and the authority of the Church.

St. John tells us that perfect love casts out fear, but many of our mediaeval churches contained large scale mural paintings warning of what would happen if you refused to accept the teachings of the church. St. Thomas's church in Salisbury possesses a particularly well-preserved 1475 wall painting, the largest of its kind in the whole of England, and shows all the righteous being admitted to heaven and all the wicked literally being pitchforked into the sufferings of hell.

But the preaching of hellfire and damnation cannot be limited to the Catholic church of the Middle Ages. The famous John Wesley, formerly an Anglican priest and founder of the

Methodist church, preached hellfire with a vengeance. I possess an ancient copy of the *Church of England Magazine* printed in 1845, given me by a recluse who lived in a remote, dilapidated thatched cottage on the Isle of Wight; it includes many hour-long sermons on the same theme. He also gave me a 1741 copy of the Book of Common Prayer which includes a Thanksgiving service 'To be celebrated yearly on the 5th day of December for the deliverance of King James I and the Three E*ſ*tates of England from the mo*ſ*t bloody and intended Ma*ſſ*acre by Gunpowder.'

The Rev. Rob Bell, an evangelical megachurch pastor, has caused a stir with his take on hell in the best-seller *Love Wins*. He writes "In the biblical testimony, there is infrequent mention of hell, Gehenna, a place of retribution and a place of fire and torment. One thing that impresses me is how seldom it is mentioned. There is good reason to say that it is a possibility, but there is no reason to say it is a significant part of following Christ." He goes on to say that seventy-nine percent of mainline Protestants in the United States believe people not of their faith, including non-Christians, can go to heaven. The debate over who goes to hell stretches back to antiquity, when Christians were still a persecuted minority in the Roman Empire. Origen, a theologian who lived around AD 185-254, challenged the idea of eternal punishment. He taught that hell is real but its fire would serve more to purify sinners than to torment them. Ultimately, Origen argued, God will restore all. *(See Note 12, Robert Bell – Love Wins)*

The process of salvation itself became big business and was largely based on fear. By the sale of indulgences any devoted parishioner could pay money to the church in exchange for the forgiveness of sins. You could also pay for masses to be said for your soul after your death, which might also reduce your time in Purgatory. You even received a written receipt for your transaction! By offering a sacrifice in the Jewish temple called Corban, pious Jews could buy their way out of their duties to their aging parents and earned Jesus' anger. The church now seemed to be adopting the same principles. Jesus warned the Pharisees in strong language that they were setting aside the commandment of God in favour of their own laws.

Just as the Roman Emperor Titus had used the gold and wealth plundered from his destruction of the Jewish Temple in 70 AD to build the Colosseum, with the proceeds from the sale of indulgences Pope Julius II began the laborious project of reconstructing St. Peter's Basilica around 1505. He commissioned Michelangelo to paint the ceiling of the Sistine Chapel. It was only the arrival of the Reformation that finally put paid to indulgences and the sale of salvation. In *The God Delusion*, Richard Dawkins refers to the sale of indulgences and purgatory:

"The doctrine of Purgatory offers a preposterous revelation of the way the theological mind works. As late as 1903 Pope Pius X was still able to tabulate the numbers of days' remission from purgatory that each rank in the hierarchy was able to grant – cardinals 200 days, archbishops 100 days, bishops a mere fifty days."

This sort of absurdity does indeed bring religion into disrepute. If, and it is a big if, purgatory does exist, who are we to direct how God administers the length of a person's sentence and to whom did you present your certificate of remission on arrival?

This corrupt practice was challenged by Martin Luther, who believed that salvation was justified by faith alone. With the nailing of a copy of his 95 Theses to the door of the Wittenberg Castle church on October 31st 1517, he formally launched what became known as the Reformation. After this protest there followed a 'Sermon on Indulgences and Grace' published in colloquial German in Wittenberg in 1518. The pamphlet was an instant hit and was reprinted 14 times in 1518 alone, in print runs of at least 1,000 copies and spread all across Europe, reaching a wide audience. He was summoned to defend himself at the diet of Worms and eventually had to go into hiding. On May 4, 1521 Elector Friedrich the Wise allowed Luther to be brought to the Wartburg near Eisenach. The powerful Elector hoped that taking Luther out of the limelight would weaken the constant attacks against the Reformation. Luther lived incognito at the Wartburg; he called himself Junker Jörg (Knight George) and grew his hair and a beard, occupying himself by translating the Bible into German. So began a popular revolt against the establishment of the mediaeval church – a Mediaeval 'Brexit' – when large sections of the Church's European Union triggered Article 50 and disconnected themselves!

Even when I was ordained in the mid-1950s, we were still somewhat preoccupied with the idea of spiritual salvation. As in the Middle Ages, there still lingered the residual thought that ensuring the passage of a person's soul to heaven was the chief purpose of the church and of our life here on Earth. The Church in those days was much more inward looking than it is today, though there were of course many exceptions. I believe that we are at last beginning to realise the full thrust of Jesus' vision of the Kingdom of God as being equally concerned with both our earthly as well as our heavenly destiny, something that we should all strive to build here on Earth. There is now much more focus on the needs of the poor and the underprivileged and the way in which we organise human society, though in the secular world the pendulum may have swung too far in this direction, with little or no thought given to one's eternal destiny and our own personal salvation. In reality Earth and Heaven are two sides of the same coin. People have prayed for 2000 years for 'God's Kingdom to come and his will to be done, on Earth as it is in Heaven.' We have no excuse!

Pilgrimages to shrines also earned enormous wealth for the church. Its loss when Henry VIII finally abandoned his allegiance to the Pope and disestablished the monasteries must have been a severe blow to those whose livelihood depended upon it; just as disastrous for them as the 'credit crunch' and the threat that terrorism has become to tourism in places like Tunisia and Iraq.

The Church had also kept the Bible (the Word of God), and the liturgy (worship), firmly chained in the original Greek and Latin, shackles which only the invention of the printing press was able to dislodge. William Tyndale was eventually burned at the stake for daring to translate the bible into his native English, an English that is still enshrined in much of the King James Bible. The New Testament contains Jesus' teaching about the Kingdom of God, which is revolutionary, and their fear was that making it available in the local language might lead to the people rising up against the authority of the church, which of course they eventually did.

But long before the Middle Ages King Alfred authorised many Anglo-Saxon translations from the Vulgate – the principal Latin version of the Bible, prepared mainly by St. Jerome in the late 4th century and adopted as the official text for the Roman Catholic Church. Old English literature is remarkable for containing a number of incomplete Bible translations that were meant to be circulated independently. King Alfred around 900 had a number of passages of the Bible circulated in the vernacular. These included passages from the Ten Commandments and the Pentateuch (first five books of the Bible), to which he prefixed a code of laws he promulgated around that time. Alfred is also said to have directed the Book of Psalms to be translated into Old English. Between 950 and 970 Aldred, his scribe, worked on a translation in Old English of the Lindisfarne Gospels into the Northumbrian dialect. In approximately 990, a full freestanding version of the four Gospels in idiomatic Old English appeared in the West Saxon dialect; these are known as the Wessex Gospels. Seven manuscript copies of this translation have survived.

Through many of those early centuries, right from the time of Constantine, the Christian hierarchy was often primarily interested in preserving both its religious and its political power. It was also keen to protect its financial privileges, and it gradually became dangerously similar to the sort of institution led by the High Priest and the Scribes and the Pharisees in Jerusalem, which Jesus himself challenged so fiercely, and which led to his arrest and crucifixion. As we have seen, the mediaeval church set out to 'monopolise' salvation by making it totally dependent on the acceptance of ecclesiastical dogma, creeds and the authority of the Church. This was accompanied by much corruption. Many of the later popes developed lavish lifestyles, and sexual immorality was often rife.

During the ninth century Rome was in decline. This period was perhaps the darkest in the history of the Papacy. After the death of Pope Formosus in 896, there were sixteen Popes within fifty years. It is known or suspected that fifteen of them were murdered – the only one who was not was Leo VII, said to have died of a heart attack while having sex! The papal throne was being controlled by the local political players of Rome, who were often ready to do anything to have their man as Pope.

The papacy at one time was even governed by a woman, named Marozia. Born between 890 and 892, she was the daughter of the Roman consul Theophylact, Count of Tusculum, and Theodora. This couple rose to dominate Roman politics. When Sergius III became Pope in 904 Theophylact and Theodora made sure that their teenage daughter was introduced to the Pontiff. Soon Pope Sergius and Marozia were lovers and she became pregnant and bore him a son, who was named John. For the Pope to have any children was a serious embarrassment. The House of Theophylact continued to dominate Roman politics and the papacy into the 920s, when Marozia's parents and husband died, leaving her to assume total leadership. John, her nephew, was appointed Pope John XIII.

These were not the only popes to betray their office. The Second World War Pope Pius XII established a concordat with Adolf Hitler to safeguard the status of the church. Before the War the Catholic Church was a force to be reckoned with and a bold denunciation of Nazism, while dangerous, might even have altered the course of history. Even Hitler might have found it hard to eliminate the Pope of a worldwide Catholic Church. He soon broke the terms of the concordat and many Catholic youth organisations became fodder for the Hitler Youth programme. Peter, the first Bishop of Rome, was crucified defending the Faith. However when Hitler began his elimination of the Jews, the Pope's voice was never raised in protest. Instead a picture of birthday greetings to the Führer hosted by the bishops of Germany would become an annual tradition until the war's end.

Considering all that has happened in the church throughout the history of the two millennia that have passed since Jesus' death, perhaps the greatest miracle is that so much of Jesus' original vision of the Kingdom of God has managed to survive at all. I have often wondered how different today's world would have been, and the world of all the previous twenty centuries, if the church as a whole had been more possessed of Jesus' own vision instead of trying to work out who He was, and directing so much of its efforts to maintaining its own power and authority. Would the church have become 'established' in quite the same way? Would the Crusades have ever taken place with their battle cry 'God wills it?' One commentator wrote: "Many peasants and knights plunged into battle yelling the battle cry of the Christians!" This is perhaps a timely reminder that Crusaders once charged into battle in much the same way as fundamentalist Moslems shout 'Allahu Akbar' – God is great.

The Crusades

The Crusades began with a declaration by Pope Urban II at

the Council of Clermont in 1095: "Most beloved brethren urged by necessity I, Urban, by the permission of God chief bishop and prelate over the whole world.... do urge you to root out corruption in the church. I also, or rather the Lord, beseech you as Christ's heralds to persuade all people of whatever rank, foot-soldiers and knights, poor and rich, to carry aid promptly to those Christians and to destroy that vile race of Infidels from the lands of our friends. Moreover, Christ commands it. All who die by the way, whether by land or by sea, or in battle against the pagans, shall have immediate remission of sins. This I grant them through the power of God with which I am invested." (This is a brief summary of a lengthy document.)

Modern scholarship now queries much of our earlier understanding of the Crusades. Those leading them were totally misinformed about conditions in Jerusalem. Before their arrival the Moslem rulers had tolerated both Jews and Christians and respected their churches and synagogues. On arrival in Jerusalem the Crusaders praised Christ as they slaughtered the inhabitants till the city ran with rivers of blood. *(See Note 13, Malcolm Billings, The Cross and the Crescent)*

However another statement made at that time claimed that "Jews, Moslems and Christians all believe in the same God, making the struggle of the Crusaders worthless". This needs a great deal of clarification. We certainly do not all believe in God in the same way. The religions of the 'Book', as they have been called, have all at times made the mistake of trying to enforce their beliefs – either by force of arms, fear or the enforcement of religious rules and regulations. One of the chief differences between the Moslem and

Christian faiths is that the Moslem faith concentrates more on *submission* to God (the word Moslem itself means surrender or submission) whereas Jesus draws people to faith by inviting them to *respond* to God's love, and to grow into a personal relationship with God.

The Middle East, then as now, was full of warring tribes seizing each other's territory. The prophet Mohammed, like Jesus, was also born into this uneasy world and at first encountered great opposition to his teaching from those in power; the wealthy traders in Mecca forced him to flee to Medina, where he gathered many more followers. But Mohammed, unlike Jesus, called his followers to fight for God, and in AD 624 he personally led an expedition of some three hundred men in battle to intercept a rich caravan returning from Gaza to Mecca. Later, when established in Medina, he built himself a house with a large courtyard, with apartments for his dozen or more wives and concubines. This stands in marked contrast to the early life of Jesus and his home in Nazareth. Nor did Jesus to our knowledge ever handle a sword. On the contrary he said to Peter in the Garden of Gethsemane, "Put your sword back into its place, for all those who take up the sword shall perish by the sword." Both Christians and Moslems at times have betrayed God's call to show mercy. *(See Note 14, Montgomery Watt, History of Islam)*

As we think of all the violence that still persists in the Middle East, the cradle of our Christian Faith, this is a somewhat sad note as we begin to conclude this section, but beyond the monolithic control that the church once exercised over much of Christendom there was much more that was positive. The Monasteries laid the foundations of our educational system, which became the nucleus that generated all our ancient Universities. They were also pioneers in medicine and provided the nearest equivalent to today's NHS. Among the hospitals they helped found is the world-famous Bart's Hospital in London, established in 1123 by Rahere, a monk in the nearby Priory Church of St. Bartholomew the Great, a favourite courtier of King Henry I. Much later, at the time of the Dissolution of the Monasteries, the priory church was preserved and the hospital was refounded by King Henry VIII in December 1546 by the signing of an agreement granting the hospital to the Corporation of London.

Through all the centuries there were many who did their best to imitate the teaching of our Lord, people like St. Francis and Chaucer's 'poore parson of the towne' "Who taught the lore of Christ and his Apostles twelve and firste followed it himself," whereas the Pardoner made more money in a day than the parson earned in two months by selling 'pigges bones' as relics!

There was also fierce criticism of the established church in William Langland's 'Piers Plowman' of the early 14th century: "I found there friars of all the four orders, preaching to the people for profit to themselves; explaining the Gospel just as they liked. To get clothes for themselves they construed it as they would." This poem was adopted by those who took part in the Peasant's Revolt. The poem, part theological allegory and part social satire concerns the narrator's intense quest for the true Christian life.

Despite all their weaknesses the churches have preserved much of Jesus' teaching, even though they sometimes have not always 'followed it themselves'. Despite all their mistakes, without the leadership of all those who have served the Church over the centuries the Gospel message might never have reached across the world, and Jesus' teaching and his revelation of God's love for all mankind might have been lost altogether.

The Role of Religion in Today's World

In these pages we have drawn a distinction between faith and religion. We must now examine the role that religion has played in the growth and the nurturing of faith. If Jesus' teaching was to survive at all, there had to be a community or structure of some sort to bind their fellowship together. Christians would have found it very difficult to maintain their faith in the pagan world all on their own.

Without central organisation, the early Christians could have made little impact. This is true in all walks of life. A great debt is owed to the early 'Bishops' of Rome and the early Christian congregations who faced great dangers and in some cases suffered martyrdom. Their bodies still lie buried in the catacombs where the tombs of the bishops carry the inscription 'Papa' (father), though the title Pope was not adopted until the time of Pope Leo I in the fifth century. In the sixth century Pope Gregory the Great established Christianity in England.

Without some form of organisation and without the fellowship of the church, much of Jesus' teaching might never have been preserved. Religion has to play its proper role in this task, providing the ground in which faith can be nurtured. The Church above all is the structure within which Jesus' vision of the Kingdom of God has to be passed on to succeeding generations, and in a way that is relevant to the needs and challenges of every new generation.

From the time of Constantine onward, the organisation of the church was shared by Rome in the West and Constantinople in the East, co-existing until the eleventh century. They broke apart in 1054, in what became known as the East–West Schism, between what are now the Eastern Orthodox and Roman Catholic churches, which has lasted since the 11th century.

A succession of ecclesiastical differences and theological disputes between the Greek East and Latin West predated the formal rupture. Prominent among these were the issues of the source of the Holy Spirit, whether leavened or unleavened bread should be used in the Eucharist, and the Bishop of Rome's claim to universal jurisdiction over Constantinople, the Orthodox equivalent of the position that Rome occupied in the West

In 1053, the first step was taken in the process which led to formal schism. The Greek churches in southern Italy were forced either to close or to conform to Latin practices. In retaliation the Ecumenical Patriarch of Constantinople, Michael I Cerularius, ordered the closure of all Latin churches in Constantinople, burning up energy that should have been directed towards those outside the Christian community.

Sadly the two churches are still divided, but thankfully they now co-operate fully with each other and both the Orthodox and Anglican churches are at the forefront of organising relief aid among the thousands of refugees stranded in Athens. Both Greece and Italy have borne the brunt of the thousands of refugees who have risked life and limb crossing the Mediterranean Sea, a much more positive note on which to end this chapter.

Before examining the spiritual needs of the 21st Century, we must now look at all the changes that have overtaken science, religion and morality in the centuries following the birth of Christianity and have led to a deeper understanding of both the universe and the spiritual reality of what it means to be truly human.

CHAPTER EIGHT

RELIGION AND SCIENCE

The night sky has always held an irresistible fascination, and it has taken the roadmap of my faith on more distant travels. When my younger brother first saw the stars, he exclaimed "Daddy, look at all the holes in the sky!" As mankind has gazed up at the heavens, every culture has asked questions about their origin, wondering how the universe came into being and about our own place in the scheme of things. In the figurative account of creation in the book of Genesis as they pursued these questions they add this little half verse, almost as an afterthought – "and he created the stars also" – as if they were so many hundreds and thousands scattered on the cake of our earthly existence.

From our perspective, creating 'the stars also' is a far more stupendous feat than all the rest of their story put together. Just looking at the stars inevitably stretches the horizon of our thinking. Without having studied astronomy, most people have barely an inkling of the enormous extent of the observable universe and its myriads of galaxies such as our own. A study in 2013 indicated that there are 225 billion galaxies in the observable universe. More amazing still is the astounding fact that with the aid of a telescope the stars can be observed through the tiny speck of creation that is each one of us through the lens of our own eyes.

When you feel insignificant on the world scene, or when watching the vast crowds at Heathrow Airport and wondering how we can ever convey God's love to all mankind, remember that not even Jesus himself could have reached everyone personally. In his parable about salt he reminds us that a few grains of salt can flavour a lot of bread. Likewise, if we plant a few grains of faith there is no limit to where it can spread. Remember also the words of the psalmist: "No man can make agreement to God for another man's soul; he must let that alone forever". He got it right. All any of us can do is to be alongside those whom we meet day by day, remembering that everyone is known to God who wants to surround them with his love.

Those early writers, with their very limited scientific knowledge, saw the universe in a vastly different way from the way we do today. Most information was still passed on from generation to generation by telling stories. Later these stories were written down and assumed the form of myth which then became recorded in legend; over time legend was then often mistakenly assumed to be factual truth. The

Genesis creation stories took their place alongside the multitude of many similar creation myths that sprang up among cultures all over the world. The only tool they had was their imagination, along with the belief that some powerful force must have been responsible for the creation of the Universe, a transcendent power above and beyond our understanding, which led to the concept we now call God.

Since those distant days the advances made in scientific exploration have changed our own perception of the Universe beyond all recognition. It was not that long ago that we still believed the Sun went around the Earth. Scientists lived with this Earth-centred Ptolemaic view of the Universe well into the Middle Ages. Even as late as the 1960s Fred Hoyle, a highly-respected astronomer, was wedded to the concept of a steady state universe which has existed, and will exist, forever. That theory has now been totally abandoned since the evidence for the Big Bang (ironically, a phrase Hoyle coined himself) has become overwhelming. Many early scientific hypotheses have been superseded as science has progressed. Science is always changing and is always learning. So must religion.

In our current quest to explore the reality of our Universe, and the meaning of our own existence, science cannot afford to ignore the realm of spiritual reality; and likewise religion cannot afford to take account of all the tremendous strides made in our scientific understanding of the Universe. Both disciplines must also explore the awareness of the very 'esse' of our consciousness; the very core of what makes each one of us a human being.

The Biblical Story of Creation
The First Creation Story

Let's begin by exploring the first Creation 'story' given in the book of Genesis in which the writers give their 'explanation' of the origin of the universe. That first book of the Bible starts with the well-known words 'In the beginning God created the Heavens and the Earth'. The work of creation is then divided into six 'days' and on the seventh day God takes a rather well-earned rest! As early as sixteen centuries ago, the Christian theologian and philosopher St. Augustine wrote, "What these days are is difficult or even impossible for us to imagine". He was already wrestling with this story, which later generations came to regard as the last word about creation since it was enshrined in the Bible, the inspired and unalterable word of God.

Significantly, some of the Genesis story was 'borrowed' by the Jews from the Babylonians, who possessed a much more sophisticated civilisation than the writers of the Old Testament; they were also highly skilled in mathematics. The Babylonian number system base 60 is still used to determine the number of degrees in a circle; hours have sixty minutes, and a minute has sixty seconds; lines of longitude are also based on this system.

The Babylonian creation epic, the Enuma Elish, describes pre-creation as a time "When above the heavens had not been named, and below the earth had not been called by name." The original Hebrew narrative is also different from later translations and reads as follows: "In the beginning of God's creating the skies and the earth, when the earth had been shapeless and formless, and darkness was upon the face of the deep, and God's spirit was hovering on the face of the water, God said, 'Let there be light'". In both Enuma Elish and the earlier Hebrew narrative, creation is an act of divine speech. In Genesis each act of divine creation is introduced with the formula "And God said, let there be..." The sequence of creation is identical – light, firmament, dry land, luminaries and man. In both, the source of creation is light, without which life cannot exist.

Light lies at the heart of both the scientific story of Creation and the heart of the New Testament. John also starts his Gospel by saying "In the beginning." In the beginning was the Word, and the word was God. In him was life, and the life was the LIGHT of men, the light that gives light to every man coming into the world." Jesus is also frequently described as the Light of the World, without which we human beings cannot progress to a full understanding of the meaning of our own humanity, or of the world around us. What happens when men and women turn away from the light that radiates from God's love and compassion for all mankind is plain for all to see as we look at the horror of terrorism and the death, violence and destruction that has been inflicted on so many innocent people all over our planet from generation to generation.

Light is fundamental to all scientific exploration; we now measure astronomical distance in light years. Without light astronomical time could not be measured, but the writers of those early creation stories looked at time in a very different way. There were no digital clocks ticking away the seconds and the hours. Time for them was measured by the seasons. In Psalm 90 we have these words: "Lord, thou hast been our dwelling place in all generations. For a thousand years in thy sight are but as yesterday." I believe those early writers would have been horrified to think that we could ever have thought that in their creation 'story' they were talking about six days of twenty-four hours. They were far more intelligent than that! That time capsule is infinitely small in comparison to the universe, and only reflects the time it takes for our tiny planet to spin once on its own axis. The 'six days of creation' was a poetic device to tell the 'story' of God's continuous work of creation over the ages. Their enormous contribution was to attribute what they saw to some powerful force to which religion has given the name God; and also the recognition that morality has an important role to play in the way in which we handle the gift of life.

The Second Creation Story

The second Creation Story is rather different and is the one most people remember. It is set in the Garden of Eden. It is still unrivalled in its perception of human behaviour. God tells Adam and Eve not to eat the fruit of the tree of the knowledge of Good and Evil. Eve looks at the lovely apples and says to herself. "Shall I? Shan't I? They look so good! Why not?" Eve pauses, remembering that they are forbidden fruit. "Go on, take one" says the voice of the serpent hidden inside her brain. "It won't do any harm." (All our brains are sometimes home to unwelcome 'talking' serpents.) The serpent continues "Your husband's not around. No one will see you. It's OK. No one will suffer." So she took the apple in much the same way that I sometimes sneak a slice of cheese when my wife is not around, doing my best to make it look untouched!

Then God takes a walk in the garden in the cool of the day and sees an apple core beneath the tree, just as my father once found a forbidden strawberry hull hiding in one of my young brother's trouser pockets, which had stained his little underpants pink! God first challenges Adam, "I think you've been eating apples my lad, when I told you not to." "Well no, it...it...it wasn't me – not really, it was that wretched woman you gave me, all her fault it was! She took one and g...gave it to me." God then turns to Eve. "Well Eve, what have you got to say for yourself?" "It...it wasn't really me either. Truly it wasn't. It was that serpent who t... tempted me. Not my fault really." What describes human nature better than that? You seldom hear politicians apologise. With the help of their professional spinners they invent yarn upon yarn to excuse themselves. When possible we all pass the buck to someone else and they then pass the buck on till it's got nowhere else to go. It even gets passed back to God himself at times! The Adam and Eve story is a very well-spun yarn.

In the story God now drives Adam and his wife from their home in the Garden and places a security guard around the Tree of Life. For a long time this story was misused to explain the origin of death, even by one of my lecturers as late as the early nineteen-fifties. Death was seen by the church for a long time as God's punishment for Adam's disobedience. In fact physical death has nothing whatever to do with Adam being a bad boy. Observation shows that all of creation is subject to death, and has been from the very beginning. Plants, trees, animals and birds all die just as we do, and stars and planets also. Death was part of the structure of the universe long before the first scientists and religious writers ever existed. Physical death is simply amoral. It's just the way the universe works. In fact without death it would implode.

This biblical story does however contain one very important and intrinsic truth; we really do die spiritually when we recklessly override all moral laws and set aside all the social conventions by which human life is made rich and rewarding; or as a religious person might put it, when we disobey the word of God, or when we commit 'sin', a very unpopular word to modern ears. Whichever way we put it, human disobedience to God's will still remains the root cause of all the 9/11s, the struggles in Afghanistan, Iraq and Syria, and all the genocide that has ever taken place throughout history; all are marked by our failure to understand and respect God's love for the whole of his creation.

The Scientific Story of Creation

With no scientific training I have wandered alongside Stephen Hawking in his *Brief History of Time* and mastered, or sort of mastered, a layman's understanding of singularities and black holes, black matter and the Big Bang theory. The modern thinking is that the universe began 13 billion years ago in a gigantic explosion which has become known as the Big Bang, a blinding flash of LIGHT. We mustn't think of the Big Bang as a gigantic volcanic explosion thrusting stars into space as we falsely sing in some of our hymns, but more as a blinding flash of Light releasing gigantic clouds of cosmic dust and gas from which the growing force of gravity eventually forced matter to coalesce to form the stars and the building blocks of creation from which all life has eventually emerged, including our own. Tremendous strides in our understanding of black holes have been made since the publication of Stephen Hawking's Brief History of Time, and our knowledge increases with every passing year. *(Note 15, Stephen Hawking, A Brief History of Time)*

In 2016, spectacular observations of the events taking place surrounding the black hole at the centre of our own galaxy, the Milky Way, mark the fruition of years of work by Professor Donald Lynden Bell. Black holes, once thought to be the most destructive structures of the Universe, are now known to be the power houses that drive both the recycling and creative processes of every galaxy, exuding powerful radiation that preserves the intricate balance that prevents galaxies from becoming overcrowded.

At this very moment scientists through the aid of advanced radio telescopes are eagerly monitoring the gas cloud being drawn by gravity to the entrance of our own black hole, where it may either be spectacularly gobbled up or nibbled away bit by bit. Quasars, some of the brightest observable objects in the Universe, are believed to be powered by accretion of material into supermassive black holes in the nuclei of distant galaxies, so some black holes in fact appear to be blindingly white! All this new knowledge stems from the pursuit of maths and the complicated algebra worked out by astronomical scientists. But there are limits to our powers of observation, and we may never be capable of exploring the interior of a black hole. That remains a mystery, a barrier we cannot cross, any more than we can explain the mystery of God's own being, beyond our experience of his reality and the revelation of his love given by Jesus.

Over the last ten years astronomers have even begun asking what preceded the Big Bang, some now dismissing that idea altogether, while others are trying to accommodate it in new attempts to explain the origin of the Universe. As fast as one keeps abreast of modern science, the goalposts keep moving. All this reminds us that there are limits to our understanding. Sometimes we try to think otherwise, but we would do well in all our attempts to understand the Universe to leave room for mystery. Both disciplines reveal wonder; science all the wonders of the Universe, and faith the miracle of how our lives can be transformed when irradiated with the light of God's love.

This particular 'Faith-head', a phrase coined for believers by Richard Dawkins, has also begun to get his head around a tiny smattering of quantum mechanics. The debates between Albert Einstein and Niels Bohr represent one of the highest points of scientific research in the first half of the twentieth century because they called attention to an element of quantum theory, quantum non-locality, which is absolutely central to our modern understanding of the physical world. Another advance of the last century was the discovery that light first thought of as travelling only in waves is also made up of particles, a discovery only recently confirmed by observation. Particle physicists are now re-examining the nature of the atom, thought for so long to be the smallest unit of matter, and are delving deeply into the exact meaning of what we label space-time. The search for the ultimate truth about the reality of our physical world continues to be an ongoing scientific pursuit.

Quantum mechanics was used in a recent documentary to describe how European robins pilot themselves hundreds of miles from the Arctic to warmer climes in the south. How do they do it? Each of a robin's eyes has a receptor, one located on the left-hand side of the brain, the other on the right. The receptors follow a wave of the Earth's magnetic field, which acts as a sort of Ordnance Survey map for the bird's flight. If it strays too far to the left, the right receptor pulls it back to the wavelength; too far to the right, then the left receptor drags it back. It is the same principle that enables some modern cars to park themselves. Its flight is governed by a sort of automatic pilot. In an experiment it was demonstrated beyond all doubt that a robin which is blind in one eye could never complete the journey. What impressed me most was the concluding remark made by the scientist presenting the programme: "Though I have seen the experiments with my own eyes, I still find it hard to believe." In matters of faith, when we finally discover how faith works by putting it to the test, if we are honest, it still remains a bit of a mystery, and there are people of faith who still at times find it hard to believe.

Returning to the Big Bang theory, let's think of it in another way. Let's go from the infinitely large to the infinitely small. I grew up in a garden and have handled seeds all my life long, attracted by the mystery of their growth. Take a poppy or a foxglove seed; they are among the smallest of seeds, except perhaps for the dust of the begonia. But wrapped up within every single seed is the genetic programme for that seed's growth and development. First moist nutrients from the soil assist its growth as it bursts through its outer casing. Sufficient warmth allows chemical messages to direct the hidden root growth that precedes the emergence of the first two seedling leaves. Those messages always then move towards the furthest point of the growing seedling, causing it to branch and develop side stems. Other chemical messages direct the formation of the flower bud, its form and colour. The sun then plays its continuing role, finally drawing the bud open. The very first explosion of all that growth is not unlike our present understanding of the Big Bang. And let's remember that we ourselves were once tiny specks before we 'exploded' into life; all parents know only too well how explosive their children can sometimes become!

I neither studied science or maths, beyond learning some of the basic formulae, like that used to solve quadratic equations. I learned it by rote, but I never quite understood what it was for! My wife however, a mathematics graduate, describes maths as the Queen of Sciences. In a way it is also a philosophy. Though to me the hieroglyphics of maths are a foreign country, one can see that the whole universe is governed by conformity to mathematical rules. Every structure possesses mathematical qualities. Maths is both the key and the tool that helps unlock the secrets of how it all works, and provides scientists with the means to solve those equations and the development of formulae which lead to new knowledge. When applied with assiduity, plus the occasional odd hunch of brilliance, it then provides the key that opens the door to the intricacy by which our world and the whole universe is so delicately held in being.

The great advances made in our growing understanding of the universe in the last century have been driven by the remarkable development of modern technology and machinery. With the aid of increasingly fast computers, scientists have been enabled to substantiate their theories much more speedily by submitting them to ever more detailed experiment and observation. Faith also needs to be tested by the same sort of discipline. Roger Bacon, a thirteenth-century English philosopher, placed considerable emphasis on the need to study nature through empirical methods, and set much store on maths. He called mathematics the gate and key of all the sciences and wrote "The Devil found it most convenient when people ignored maths since that made both theology and philosophy useless." He also wrote that experiment was fundamental; it was the right way to test a mathematical result, *and even a revelation from God,* and all arguments should be tested by experience. Jim Al-Khalili is a British-Iraqi theoretical physicist, author and broadcaster and currently Professor of Theoretical Physics at Surrey University in a recent broadcast stated "Without experiment, theory remains arid and worthless". This is profoundly true for both physics and faith. Faith is a response to Jesus' Vision of the Kingdom of God for life here on earth, but can only be 'proved' to work by the experiment of putting it into practice in our daily lives.

Stephen Hawking, however, has been driven to say that there is no God. *"When people ask me if a god created the universe, I tell them that the question itself makes no sense. Time didn't exist before the Big Bang, so there is no time for God to make the universe in. It's like asking for directions to the edge of the earth; the Earth is a sphere; it doesn't have an edge, so looking for it is a futile exercise. We are each free to believe what we want, and it's my view that the simplest explanation is; there is no god. No one created our universe, and no one directs our fate. This leads me to a profound realisation; there is probably no heaven and no afterlife either. We have this one life to appreciate the grand design of the universe, and for that I am extremely grateful."*

To think of God as being limited by time is just as futile as asking for directions to the edge of the Earth. And who knows if the reality of God may not run parallel to, as well outside space-time altogether? There is no way this can be proved by scientific enquiry, just as science cannot prove the existence of our soul. Our soul, though unseen, is the most intimate and closest reality that we all experience, the experience of being ME and no one else. It can only be viewed through a lens directed towards the spiritual dimension of our life, but can be observed and tested by the reality of our spiritual experience.

The whole world holds Stephen Hawking in great affection with his inimitable, cheeky wrinkled smile. When interviewed once by Dara O Briain, he was asked to define a black hole; after a pause Stephen muttered "A black sock with a hole in it!" Above all else his life is a visual parable of perseverance in the face of extreme adversity, which should encourage us all. I feel regret that his enquiring mind can't just take one more step and think of God not as having had no time to make the Universe, but rather as existing both before, beyond and alongside time. The use that Stephen has made of his gift of God-given life seems to me to be one more witness to faith, and I would like to believe that there is a place for him in the Kingdom of Heaven.

Scientists have set themselves the task of 'shrinking time' by building the Large Hadron Collider, the world's most powerful particle accelerator; by compressing time they are attempting to take us back to the initial moment of the Big Bang when time were created. Descartes in his famous statement 'Cogito ergo sum' (I think therefore I am) goes on to argue that although the concept of infinity and of an infinite being is beyond our grasp and understanding, it can be touched by our thoughts and by reason. Of course we may be free to think whatever we choose, but we are never entirely free to believe just what we want; false beliefs when held with fundamentalist conviction often result in disaster and heartbreak, just as mistaken mathematical formulae lead to wrong conclusions. *(Note 15, Stephen Hawking, A Brief History of Time)*

Knowledge and Faith

There is much more to life than the pursuit of knowledge; if scientists only ever used the language of science when talking to their wives, that would be no recipe for a happy marriage! That goes for theologians too. Scientific knowledge, religious knowledge, or any other form of knowledge, on its own, does not lead to a rounded personality. Francis Bacon, a philosopher of the late 16th century, wrote "Into the kingdom of knowledge as into the kingdom of heaven whoso would enter must become as a little child." Besides the intellectual side of our nature we all possess a spiritual side which requires nurturing with just the same sort of diligence as scientists apply to all their studies. The Spirit is the 'scientific' tool of faith that enables us to discover the depth of God's love revealed to us by Jesus, which then becomes the key, the 'mathematics' that opens the door for us to follow in his footsteps.

Fred, a South Sudanese priest and a former student at the All Nations College in Herefordshire, has been a regular visitor to our home. With some hesitation, I once asked if he would enjoy looking at a programme about the Earth's orbit around the Sun. At first he was a bit puzzled, then he spent the rest of the programme leaning further and further forwards, head in hand, watching with rapt attention. Afterwards he made this comment – "I've never known anything about how the world works and that has made God's work in creation even more wonderful." (Fred is now leading relief work among the refugee camps set up in north Uganda.) Charles Darwin makes a similar statement at the close of his *Origin of Species*: "There is a grandeur in this way of life, with its several powers having been breathed originally by the Creator, and that from so simple a beginning endless forms most beautiful and wonderful have been, and are being evolved". *(Note 16, Fred Taban)*

When we look at the universe through the eyes of science, that does indeed make the world more wonderful than just looking at what we see with our normal vision. But we need to look at the universe beyond both the 'burkas' of science and religion – to pick up a metaphor from the closing chapter of The God Delusion. Adding the spiritual dimension of God's infinite love makes our understanding of life and of the universe even more inspiring still. Without that love in our hearts, our vision remains much more limited than it need be.

The Spirit within each one of us may be invisible, but it

is just as real as the Universe around us. Faith enables our awareness of that spiritual reality, of a spiritual 'presence' beyond and above our sensual experience of the material Universe. Without the light of the Spirit we would still see the Universe, but only as a spectacular jungle of wonderful stuff. It is the Spirit that gives it value. All those searching for truth, whether scientist or theologian, or anyone with an enquiring mind, are in fact driven by an invisible spirit that lies hidden deep within the depths of our inner being, which is the very source of our humanity.

The Life of the Spirit

While scientific theories can be confirmed by observation, and the radio telescope can even help us draw a map of the Universe, faith has to be measured through a different type of lens, the lens of spirituality, of realising that the life of the Spirit is just as much part and parcel of our total experience of life as is knowledge of the way the world works. Faith has to be just as finely tuned to a spiritual wavelength as have scientific instruments. The first rule of experimental religious psychology is that spiritual truths must be spiritually discerned.

This is no easier a task than exploring the wavelengths directed to the Earth from outer space, and it requires just as much persistence. For much of the time our spiritual vision is often clouded. We often only 'see through a glass darkly'. Science also has had its own misty moments, but in the hard slog of scientific exploration someone just occasionally has a 'hunch', which after months, perhaps even years, of laboriously working out equations results in a spectacular breakthrough. Such moments also occur in our spiritual lives.

In his little book entitled *Sense and Non-sense*, Dean Alington from my schoolboy days argues that everything we experience in life is governed both by sense (sensual perception) and non-sense (spiritual perception) Quoting the letter to the Hebrews, he reminds us that faith is the 'evidence' of things unseen. The spiritual values of love, compassion, patience and kindness are perceived not only by our senses, but by our perception of other people whose faces reflect those qualities. Spiritual awareness is enhanced by observing other people's actions in the same way that theories of science are validated by observation and demonstration. Though mysteriously linked to our earthly bodies our soul, the source of spirituality, is governed by more than the mechanics of scientific reality. *(Note 17, Dean Alington, Sense and Non-sense, 1949)*

Immanuel Kant, the great German philosopher, has this to say: "Knowledge and intellect are only capable of interpreting what we observe by our senses. We have to go beyond knowledge to make room for faith, and though reason may be constricted by the conditions of this life it has the ability to put us in contact with the infinite, taking us beyond biology to grasp moral law and leads us to understand that every rational being is of infinite worth". He goes even further: "Faith puts us in touch with what we experience spiritually, and a destination that is not conditioned by the restrictions of this life but reaches to infinity."

Religious truth is superbly demonstrated in the well-known parable of the Good Samaritan, the parable so admirably brought up to date by my fellow student at Warminster. This well-known parable demonstrates a religious 'truth' that is eternally embedded in the story itself. We all instinctively know that the person who went to the aid of the man who had been mugged did the right thing. It doesn't matter to what specific religion he may have belonged, or none; in fact in the original story it was the despised Samaritan, an untouchable pagan half-Jew, who went to the injured man's aid. The word 'Samaritan' has now become synonymous with anyone who goes to the aid of a person in trouble, enshrined forever in the charity that bears that name founded in 1953 by Chad Varah, a vicar in the Church of England Diocese of London.

What matters is that we recognise this truth. The Christian Faith was first known simply as The Way; following the way by which Jesus lived his life is the key to discovering religious truth. Jesus said to his disciples "I am the Way, the Truth and the Life". The proof of the pudding of Christian Faith lies not in verbal discussion but in the eating, and is observed not through the lens of a microscope, but demonstrated by the way we conduct our day-to-day lives. The greatest school of all is provided by one's journeying along the road of life. Faith is a living experience, nourished by all the people you meet on your life's journey. It is forever growing deeper, just as scientific knowledge has broadened almost beyond imagination even in one lifetime.

The place of religion and of the churches is never to dictate faith but to be the soil in which faith can germinate and grow to fruition, and as the writer of the letter to the Hebrews reminds us once more, faith also requires us to "Follow peace with all men, and holiness, without which no one shall see the Lord." Both science and faith share one thing in common, whatever you happen to believe. The more we discover and the deeper you travel, the more we all become aware that we are still only scratching the surface; life becomes a greater mystery than one could ever have imagined, an experience you cannot fully explain and before which the only proper response is reverence.

The Journey of Faith

However it is important for both scientist and theologian to realise that the vast majority of humankind rarely travel this deeply, often struggling just to manage their day-to-day affairs. In many parts of the world life is primarily a matter of survival amid poverty and violence and dangers mostly unknown to many in our more comfortable secular society; though even in our more affluent Western world there is still a great deal of poverty.

Jesus took upon himself the task of sharing the lives of ordinary people. To help them understand the simplicity of his vision of the Kingdom of God, he described that vision in parable after parable as he tramped the road of life beside us. The power that inspired his teaching was his personal experience of God and his passionate desire to reveal the nature of God's unbounded love to the whole world, and he invites each one of us to follow his example and make the sharing of that love the guiding principle of faith amid our daily lives.

This is a way of life open to all, tramp or millionaire, a ploughman, a tax collector, a housewife, an employer, a scientist or a theologian, whether you are comfortably off, or struggling to make ends meet. You don't need to master either complicated equations or creeds to set out on your journey of faith; above all else you need perseverance and love. Ponder these words of Jesus: "If anyone hears my words and does not believe, I do not judge him; for I did not come into the world to judge the world, but to save the world." We all yearn for peace in this troubled world, both among nations, among our family relationships, and deep down in the depths of our own soul. It is only as we respond to God's love and share it with each other that we can finally discover true peace.

This fundamental plank of Christian faith was recently illustrated in the much-loved and popular BBC programme *Call the Midwife*. Here are some gems culled from two of its concluding episodes: "Love always grows, changing its shape when required" and "There is nothing we can do without love. Love in all its fullness invisibly enfolds us in its embrace, precious fragile and enduring it cannot be bought. Love is a priceless gift offered in silence and richer than gold and makes all our lives worthwhile".

The God Delusion

Richard Dawkins, the highly-respected evolutionary biologist, in his book entitled *The God Delusion*, contends that a supernatural creator almost certainly does not exist and that religious faith is a delusion. Though an avowed atheist, his thinking seems at times to be to be pulled in many other directions; perhaps he can't quite escape his early associations with the Anglican Church! In recent interviews for *The Spectator* he admits that he would consider going into a church, and would miss 'aesthetic elements' such as church bells if they were gone; also that he is grateful to Anglicanism, which he claims has a benign tolerance, enabling people to enjoy its traditions without necessarily believing in them, and continues "I sort of suspect that many who profess Anglicanism probably don't believe any of it at all in any case, but vaguely enjoy the ethos it reflects, and as a cultural Anglican I see Evensong in a country church through much the same eyes as I see a village cricket match on the village green. I have a certain love for it." I suppose I also could describe myself as a 'cultural' Anglican, having been nurtured within the family of the Anglican Church from childhood. I can understand Richard Dawkins' position perfectly when he suspects that many who profess Anglicanism probably don't believe any of it at all, but with one significant correction, they by no means reject it all.

Much of what he rejects is in fact 'outdated religion', not living faith. Many thoughtful Christians also reject much of what he rejects, which is largely drawn from the inherited dogma of early centuries; dogma now long past its sell-by date, and which has outgrown its original purpose and usefulness. To the secular world it is like Mediaeval Latin, beyond their comprehension! There are many faithful Christians who also find it equally perplexing, among them many of today's most forward-thinking theologians, who are openly insisting that doctrines like those of the Trinity and the Atonement need radical re-statement.

In part one of his autobiography, *An Appetite for Wonder*, Richard Dawkins writes: "I have always been interested in the deep questions of existence, the questions that religion aspires (and fails) to answer, but I have been fortunate to live in a time when such questions are given a scientific answer rather than supernatural answers." This is absolutely right in one respect. Any supernatural answer that contradicts the laws of nature by which the whole universe is so delicately balanced must of necessity be false, but this in no way prevents the supernatural from working within and alongside those laws.

The dictionary definition of the word 'supernatural' is "a manifestation or event attributed to some force beyond scientific understanding or the laws of nature: or a supernatural being, or more figuratively, that which is said to exist above and beyond nature". Religion is simply not qualified to explain how the universe works – that is not its purpose – but it provides more reason for our existence than science has so far achieved.

Another quote from *The God Delusion*: 'Rivers of medieval ink, not to mention blood, have been squandered over the mystery of the Trinity'. I am inclined to agree, and as early as the second century an even greater amount of ink was consumed by the writings of the early 'church fathers' and those who drew up the creeds. The Athanasian Creed concludes: "The Catholic Faith is this, that we worship one God in Trinity... neither confounding the persons, nor dividing the substance ... Which except a man believe faithfully he cannot be saved." With all its earlier repetitions, that final statement leaves little or no hope of salvation for the vast majority of humankind. In reality we do not experience God as substance, but as a presence. There is much justification in what Richard says; intellectual argument about correct belief has indeed led to much turmoil and bloodshed, but so have secular and atheistic ideologies like Nazism and communism, all in complete contradiction to all that Jesus came to proclaim.

In *The God Delusion* he also says: "There are always paths not taken, but if a different path is taken, I think there is a magnetic pull; there is a sort of something that pulls you back to the pathway having taken a fork in the road, and that it is important for reasons of history if nothing else to have some working knowledge of the Bible." That sounds a bit like how robins migrate. *The God Delusion* concludes by bravely expressing the hope that it may lead religious leaders to embrace atheism. I am afraid that for this particular 'faith-head' the author has actually succeeded in becoming one of that great crowd of people who have helped grow and confirm my faith by forcing me to explore it more deeply. But elsewhere he also makes this statement: "Faith is evil because it seeks no justification and brooks no argument". I can forgive the label 'faith-head' and find it somewhat flattering, but to describe faith itself as being evil goes one step too far. I hope that what I have written may help a 'science-head' see that faith, far from being evil, can become a gateway for an enquiring mind.

There are many who find much of the mistaken religion singled out and rejected in *The God Delusion* rather refreshing, but that is no reason for a 'science-head' to condemn all religion. So perhaps I might be equally brave and dare to hope that by looking at "the paths they have not taken" he and other atheists may embrace a deeper understanding of faith that might respond to that magnetic pull, the sort of something that pulls you back to the pathway, having taken a fork in the road. Perhaps that 'sort of something' may even be akin to a 'sort of faith' which when fed by an 'Appetite for Wonder' and love of science, and freed from dogma and superstition and the restraint of any one single approach to truth, can lead us all to the richness of a mind wide open to a living and enquiring faith, a faith far removed from one that is set in stone or mediaeval ink. (*Note 18, Richard Dawkins, The God Delusion*)

Waking Moments

Waking moments arrived with alarming regularity every morning during the week before submitting my final manuscript for publication, sometimes even in the middle of the night. Stephen Hawking apparently experiences them while going to bed! One of those waking moments led me to transfer some comments of Richard Dawkins made in the Spectator from the Index as part of my final appraisal of *The God Delusion*. Richard wrote as follows: "Christianity may actually be our best defence against aberrant forms of religion that threaten the world... Christianity, unlike Islam, does not make use of violent methods to fulfil its teachings. There are no Christians, as far as I know, blowing up buildings. I am not aware of any Christian suicide bombers. I am not aware of any major Christian denomination that believes the penalty for apostasy is death". He also admits that he has "mixed feelings concerning the decline of Christianity, because this faith-based group might just be the best bulwark we have against something far worse.

What he is really saying is that the false ideology of

brutality, torture, wholesale destruction of cities and ethnic cleansing must be replaced by a new ideology. In fact Christianity, when inspired not by human construct but by Jesus' vision of the Kingdom of God and his revelation of God's love for all humanity, is a profoundly powerful ideology. Paul also put his finger on the truth when he described the fruits of the Spirit as 'kindness, goodness, patience, gentleness and self-control against such there is no law'. These qualities are by no means limited to those people who might call themselves 'religious'; they are far flung across the whole world and I have encountered them time and again amongst all sorts of people among the nearly sixty countries I have been privileged to visit. Jesus' ideology is so very simple. God's gift of love is entirely free, though it is challenging to put into practice, and at times can be very costly. It cost Jesus his life. In our increasingly secular world where belief in God has sometimes been completely set aside, Gregory Doran of the Royal Shakespeare Company was profoundly right when he concluded that Dimbleby lecture by saying "There are many who find a God-shaped hole in their consciousness".

When considering a title for this book I toyed with the idea of 'The God Solution'. As we have already discovered, the mediaeval church saw its main purpose as ensuring the safe passage of people's souls to the Kingdom of Heaven, to which our life here on Earth was only subsidiary. It almost demeaned our earthly existence as something from which we were all longing to escape. Our life on Earth was seen as a burden to the soul. The old funeral service was absurdly distressing and read like this: "Almighty God with whom do live the spirits of the departed after they are delivered from the burden of the flesh... we thank you that you have delivered your servant from the miseries of this sinful world..." What a miserable, gloomy, forbidding assessment of all the joy of our life here on Earth, despite all its pains and sorrows.

In reality it is within our life here on Earth that we need to find God most of all; among all our pains and anxieties, amid all the turmoil of the violent events taking place all over the world. This is just where Jesus revealed the power of God's healing power of love. He reached out to the vagrants, the untouchables, the prostitutes, the homeless, to all those who had lost their way in life, and he asks us His followers to do the same. His disciples once asked – "Lord, when did we see you a stranger and take you in? When did we see you hungry and feed you? When did we see you thirsty and give you a drink or see you naked and clothe you?" Jesus replied "In as much as you have done it to one of the least of my brothers and sisters you have done it to me", words so applicable to the desperate refugees tramping their road of life to they know not where. No use talking to them about getting their souls to heaven, even though that is still their ultimate destination. They need extra support in the here and now. They underwrite the need for us all to rediscover God as the 'Final Solution' of all the evil and the problems that we human beings make for one another and for ourselves in this troubled world.

CHAPTER NINE

ARMCHAIR MORALITY

"Most people pay lip service to a set of moral principles. We don't cause needless suffering, we believe in free speech, we don't do things to others we would not wish to have done to ourselves, we don't cheat, we don't' kill, we don't commit incest." This may be a reflection of the cosy armchair world of our highly-developed Western culture in which some of us are privileged to live, but even that society is by no means immune from violence and poverty.

This view of morality, taken from *The God Delusion*, is far removed from the reality experienced by vast swathes of humanity in places like Syria and Iraq, Somalia, Bangladesh, the Sudan and the Congo. On its own it lacks any real power to deal with the reality of evil, while too readily dismissing the contribution made by religion to many sectors of our so-called secular society. Religion can by no means claim a monopoly of morality, but many of the moral values of the Western secular world still lie deeply embedded in its early religious culture. Many of our most famous hospitals owe their origins to the infirmaries that were established by the monasteries. Education was almost entirely pioneered by religion, as were the early universities, and there remains a residual deposit of this heritage which has as its source an initial response to Jesus' Gospel of love, peace and forgiveness, and especially a care for others. This all lies buried deep down in our culture, and has evolved into the moral values which govern much of our modern secular society, and much of the UN and European Union charters of human rights.

There is some very direct evidence of this in research carried out by the presenter Jon Snow in the year 2004, when he conducted a national survey, inviting people to submit a new set of Ten Commandments. From all the submissions, the one that had most approval was to 'Care for others as you would care for yourself.' Some of the old Ten Commandments also still figured on the list – be honest, don't kill, respect your father and mother, and somewhat surprisingly don't commit adultery. No mention was made of God however! This is a significant omission as the most basic problem for all humanity is our control of evil thoughts and emotions that have their origin deep within the human psyche. This is where armchair morality completely breaks down. *(Note 19, Jon Snow)*

In a chapter of *Homo Deus* by Yuval Harari entitled 'A new Human Agenda' the author tracks the rise of humanism which sanctifies the power and happiness of humankind free from the restraints of any divine being. But he concludes that humanism contains the seeds of its own downfall, pointing out that if you start with a flawed ideal you often only appreciate its defects when the ideal comes close to realisation. This is also true of all scientific enquiry, and of all religion when based on a false premise. *The God Delusion* also depicts a rather incomplete picture of the life of the church today, and in particular of the Anglican Church, which still seems to hold a place of residual affection in the author's memory. It is not enough to quote fourth century creeds and recall past history, the Crusades and the failures of mediaeval Christendom; the Christian faith has moved on. Bishops and archdeacons no longer walk around in frock coats and spats! A true reflection of the Christian faith has to be observed in the lives of many of today's flourishing churches worldwide and their outreach to the local communities around them, of which little or no mention is made.

The Problem of Evil

How do we account for all the evil in the world, all the meaningless brutality of terrorism and the suffering of millions of refugees the world over from places like Syria, Somalia, South Sudan and the Yemen? The news bulletins flood into our sitting rooms daily, reminding us of all the horrors and evil in the world, and this prompts many people to ask how a loving God can allow such things to happen. Good news often seems to be very marginal and also does not sell newspapers; horror, violence and sexual misdemeanours do.

Think for a moment of an iceberg. A huge iceberg can appear very menacing but remember that what you see is only 10% of its total mass, the other 90% lies hidden beneath the waves. Among all our extensive travels worldwide my wife and I have only ever received human kindness and generous hospitality. In moments of tragedy people on the spot are remarkably resilient and respond very quickly by helping those in desperate need. When asking this question, remember that the part of the iceberg hidden from sight represents the vast majority of mankind, both religious and secular, who for the most part show kindness to one another.

Earlier in his life a renowned photographer once commissioned to take photos of Muhammad Ali was among those who had slaved to build the notorious Burma railway. He describes how amidst the degradation all around him he heard the call of wild elephants while observing a beautiful butterfly alight on the bare toe of a dead comrade. That moment, he said, gave him hope and the realisation that evil can never entirely blot out beauty and goodness.

War above all else is *the* moral outrage; it is both a crime against humanity and the sacredness of life, a misuse of the Earth's resources and a desecration of the planet on which we all live. It comes about when the 'origins' of evil in the world lie disregarded and unattended. Throughout history mankind has perpetually striven to eradicate war, but mostly by tackling its symptoms rather than by dealing with the root cause, which lies deep within humanity itself. The problem is not war but what lies within the hearts of those who decide to wage war. It is here that all the world's leaders face an enormous challenge. Thomas Payne, as we have already observed, declared in the late eighteenth century "The Proper study of Mankind is Man.' Human beings are ultimately the cause of war because of their failure to handle the problem of being truly human. While making giant strides in our understanding of the universe we have neglected the management of ourselves and our own inner existence, the art of learning how to BE.

The New Testament tells us that Jesus "knew what was in man" and taught his disciples to understand that sin and evil come from within a person, from within the heart, and that for these evils to be overcome there has to be above all else a change of heart. Jesus, addressing Nicodemus' question as to how this can be achieved, replied "Unless you are born again you cannot enter the Kingdom of God." Some fundamentalist Christians hijack this question for solely religious purposes when it properly applies to the whole of humanity. This is an observation also made by many commentators who understand that the bestiality of terrorism cannot ever be defeated by military might and diplomacy alone. The battle against evil has to be won by a change of heart and ideology among those whose minds are in danger of being taken over by false ideology and mistaken interpretations of religion based upon false dogma rather than faith and love.

At the heart of all conflict lie two major realities:

i. Greed and the abuse of power.

ii. The disparity between extreme wealth and extreme poverty.

History is littered with numerous examples of this. All the world's great empires have been built upon power and privilege; much of that power when corrupted has led to untold wealth among the ruling classes and extreme poverty and suffering among the poor. This is true among all sorts of organisations, even world football! The power and wealth of democracies has also at times been built upon the labours of the poor and upon slavery. Throughout recorded history these two factors have persistently contributed to the collapse of all of the world's great empires as those in abject poverty rise up in anger against those wielding power and living in luxury. The history of China, one of the world's oldest empires, provides a supreme example of this, with dynasty after dynasty falling from power from the Shang Dynasty (1600-1050 BC) to the Maoist people's revolution in 1949, followed by the Cultural Revolution in 1966. All have succumbed.

The real challenge now facing the modern world is based upon the way in which we manage the whole of the global economy. But for the skilful management of the banking crisis in 2008, there was a real danger that the whole system would implode. A simple analysis of the 'credit crunch' is that the banking system, instead of supporting industry, was concentrating on making money out of money – often other people's money – while at the same time offering almost limitless unsecured loans from money that really did not exist except in cyberspace. Even debts were being traded on the financial markets. According to Yuval Harari: "Coins and bank notes are a rare form of money these days. The sum total of money in the world is about 60 trillion dollars of which only 6 trillion dollars is held in coins or bank notes. The remaining 50 trillion Dollars shown in our accounts exists only on computer screens." *(See Note 6, Yuval Harari)*

Steve Hilton, in his book *More Human - Designing a World Where People Come First,* argues that the frustrations people have with government, politics and their economic circumstances are caused by deep structural problems within the systems that dominate our modern world. He also demonstrates, through compelling stories and case studies taken from across industry, politics, education and social action, that changing these systems to put people first is both possible and profitable. Steve Hilton's book is ultimately a manifesto, a call to change the whole way by which the global economy is presently managed with a more local, more accountable and more human way of living that will make us more productive, more fulfilled and ultimately happier. If our world leaders were to recover a deeper sense of what really matters most in life we would realise that together the governments of the world have access to enough wealth to eliminate poverty once and for all. The words of Thomas Jefferson, a US president of the eighteenth century, add a forceful message to the leaders of every national government: "The care of human life and happiness, and not their destruction, is the first and only object of good government." *(See Note 5, Steve Hilton)*

However formulating policies is insufficient on its own. It is one thing to say that we have become slaves to an unsustainable and ever-increasing policy of economic growth without offering an alternative. Kate Raworth, an Oxfam senior researcher, in her book entitled *Doughnut Economics*, asks "How on earth can we provide for the needs of seven billion people (and rising) sharing the limited resources of this one planet? Global economic growth, as we know it, isn't delivering; it's exacerbating inequalities while pushing the Earth beyond ecological limits." She argues that we need to rewrite the economic textbooks, making planetary boundaries and human rights the starting point of a new doughnut-shaped economics, leading us to question the nature and future of economic growth itself. While not ignoring people's economic needs, this involves researching the needs of real communities. The ultimate achievement would be the creation of a world order in which wealth was more evenly distributed and extreme poverty eliminated, so that all people could live a sustained and meaningful existence, with the eventual elimination of the conditions that promote strife and violence. *(Note 20, Kate Raworth, Doughnut Economics)*

This is not a pipe dream. The 1994 genocide in Rwanda was exacerbated by poverty and the fact that masses of young men were unemployed with no meaningful way of life. They had nothing to lose, so the offer of a machete or a rifle and some regular food was almost irresistible. Since the genocide, whatever the political ins and outs, and against severe odds, somehow a programme of reconciliation has managed to recreate a more stable and cohesive society in that country. 'Tribe' is no longer registered on identity documents. Rwanda has become the jewel of Africa. My wife and I have observed this process with our own eyes, and their goal is to eliminate extreme poverty by 2020.

Costa Rica, a small Central American republic, has eliminated its army, replanted much of the rain forest destroyed by logging, and is well on the way to building a carbon-free economy; it is also reported as being the happiest country in the world. We saw the horrendous effects of commercial banana growing, which leaves large belts of former jungle infertile, when we visited the country in the year 2000.

The events of the Syrian civil war fill us all with horror, and underline that there is something basically wrong with the way society is ordered. That human beings can spend billions and billions of dollars on the design and manufacture of modern weaponry and from the comfort of an armchair then watch while whole cities are laid waste by carpet bombing, accompanied by the indiscriminate carnage and slaughter of innocent civilians, lies beyond the understanding of most ordinary people. This all points to the fact that besides the mismanagement of world economics there is something inherently wrong with the way in which we human beings manage ourselves. There is a great need for change in our spiritual approach to life in a world preoccupied by economics. There is much more to life than just eating and drinking. Jesus put his finger on the problem when he said "God knows you need these things; but first seek the Kingdom of God and all these things will be added to you". (Learn to live as the human beings God wants you to become and you will be given all you need.

Fr. Richard Sihubwa, writing from Zambia, has this to say: "Salvation for me, and I believe for most people in Zambia, is well depicted by the image of being salvaged from the scrap heap, and put to better use by the Lord. However salvation does not end with spiritual transformation, it must also extend to the socio-economic situation in which we all find ourselves."

Coping With Evil

Turning to the New Testament, Richard Dawkins writes "Theologians are obsessed with SIN; the Christian focus is overwhelmingly sin, sin, sin, sin, and the church at times has been far too preoccupied with sin, and making people feel guilty." My father once attempted to write an impossible book on infant baptism all based on the 'doctrine' of original sin, and the teaching of the early church fathers. While he was writing his brother made two visits; on the first visit he wrote this comment in my parent's visitor's book: "Found my brother full of Original Sin!" A year later he made a second entry, "Found my brother still full of Original Sin". My mother must have been a very long-suffering victim.

Original sin has in the past been regarded by theologians as the major flaw in our human nature, a tendency towards evil deriving from Adam's disobedience of God in the Garden of Eden story, all fixated by the fig leaf factor. In reality eating from the fruit of the tree of the knowledge of both Good and *Evil* is the price we all pay for our freedom of choice that enables us to become human beings rather than mere automota; but we all need to handle that choice with great responsibility amid the many challenges facing our modern world.

More fuel supporting the church's preoccupation with sin can be found in the 1662 Prayer Book's introduction to the baptism service still in use in the 1950s. It began with the words "Seeing that all men are born and conceived in sin". The adult version was even worse: "That which is born of the flesh is flesh, and they that are in the flesh cannot please God, but live in sin, committing many actual transgressions" – enough to cause any potential God Delusionist to suffer paroxysms! From the very beginning, my vocation was to share God's love and help create an awareness of his presence. I could never bring myself to welcome a young couple, joyful at the birth of a child, with those words of the old 1662 Prayer Book; above all else we should have been proclaiming God's love and welcoming their child into the loving fellowship of the church. The marriage service was just as bad. When a couple asked for the 'old service 'in the 1662 Prayer Book they didn't really know what they were asking for. The preamble to the service was worded like this 'Marriage is not to be taken in hand unadvisedly, lightly or wantonly, to satisfy men's carnal lusts, like brute beasts that have no understanding... " Thankfully the language of the modern services is a vast improvement.

For much of its later history the church even believed the sexual act itself to be impure, and sex almost became synonymous with the word 'sin' itself, an insult to the Creator if ever there was. The word 'procreation' literally means creating on behalf of; understood in this way it means that human beings have a direct share in the act of Creation. God has entrusted to us the task of passing on the gift of life we have all received at his hands. What a risk, and what a responsibility.

The Creator has in fact ordered the whole structure of his Creation in such a way that the precious gift of life is passed on in this particular way by all species. Introducing the English sixth form to *Paradise Lost* by John Milton, our English master once quoted these lines about what happens when we misuse this precious gift: "The resemblance of the image of God is changed, and they and all their friends their native home forget, to roll with pleasure in a sensual sty". The Creator has for obvious reasons made the sexual act very pleasurable, but it only reaches the depths of spiritual satisfaction when accompanied by love and respect. Rape is the ultimate prostitution of this gift because above all it is *not* accompanied by love and respect for the victim. Maybe promiscuity is sinful, but the power of falling in love is difficult to resist, just as difficult as it is to resist God's love for us when we come to fully understand it. In *The God Delusion* falling in love is described as "an irrationality mechanism, a process built into the brain by chemical selection, and of which irrational religion is also a by-product".' He is absolutely right about the love bit, but far from being irrational it is also a deeply spiritual experience that an octogenarian who has celebrated a diamond wedding plus two still recalls as a very treasured and precious moment. I have advised every couple I have ever married to preserve an element of romance in their relationship. Surely the corporate failings of much of our global society, which often uproot the lives and social structure of so many indigenous communities in the pursuit of wealth, is a far more grievous sin than a roll in the bushes?

So how does Faith deal with the problem of evil? At the heart of the Christian Faith lies its teaching of the ATONEMENT, of Jesus laying down his life on the Cross for all mankind to help us all become 'at one' both with our Creator and with one another. In *The God Delusion,* the atonement is described as "Vicious, sado-masochistic and repellent, and to be dismissed as barking mad. Why can't God just forgive us our sins without having himself tortured?" That is all far too simplistic and quite misses the mark (one of the more accurate meanings of the word 'sin'.)

While studying theology I wrestled with all four of the

accepted scholarly theories of Atonement; those theories, if not quite mad, were certainly complicated. The particular theory of the Atonement to which Richard refers was sometimes known as the 'Substitution Theory', which states that Christ was punished for our sins to satisfy God's anger and displeasure. I nearly gave up on religion at that point. It seemed to have nothing at all to do with my experience of God's love. Thankfully today's theologians, though unknown to many, are now beginning to recognise that the classical doctrines of the Incarnation, Atonement and the Trinity and the Virgin Birth all need restatement. (*Note 8, Keith Ward – A Vision to Pursue*)

Among some reflections recorded in a personal notebook begun in 1953, I wrote these words: "In an age which seems more preoccupied with theorising, the Cross stands out as the supreme 'doing' of God, not just the culmination of an old sacrificial system, which now only slumbers in the modern mind, and which for many has never been born". The old first century idea of sacrifice based on the slaughter of animals and sprinkling the altar with their blood is indeed now dead. However people living today can immediately grasp the idea of sacrifice expressed in Jesus' own words to his disciples: "Greater love has no one than this that he lays down his life for his friends".

Far from being 'barking mad', the doctrine of the Atonement reveals the great depth of God's love for all mankind. Many people have laid down their lives for a cause in which they ardently believe. Jesus above all else was driven by his passion to reveal the depth of God's love for all mankind and the need for us all to live our lives in harmony with that love and with one another, a vision for which he was prepared to lay down his life. That vision was a revolutionary one for those days, and was rejected by those in authority, leading to his death on the Cross. Atonement is all about Jesus laying down his life for our sake, and is the language of love, not madness.

But what of the problems posed by those suffering from lingering terminal diseases, or the disabled, or those whose family relationships are volatile and threatening, and where there seems to be no permanent resolution? Can the atonement that Jesus achieved make any difference? Some people's circumstances can never be changed, but faith need not be defeated and can become the sustaining power that enables them to cope instead of giving way to despair. We have all encountered shining examples of this in many people's lives, of which the Paralympics are an outstanding parable. When it comes to human relationships the capacity to forgive also has enormous healing power, but it can be very costly, and must always be mutual. Above all else it frees us from harbouring continuing resentment and bitterness, which can become a canker slowly eating away at our inner self.

We must never make the mistake of reducing our understanding of the Atonement to a theory; it is part and parcel of the eternal nature of God himself. For Jesus himself it was an *experience*; "all arguments should be tested by experience", wrote Roger Bacon. Only after you have entered into that experience by faith and stood alongside Jesus in his suffering on the Cross, just as his first disciples did, can you begin to understand that Love is the only key to understanding the full significance of the Atonement, a powerful tool in our struggle with evil. Greater love has no man than this that he lay down his life for his friends. Jesus did just that.

Personality and Spirituality

However the primary response of the disciples to Jesus was not a 'religious' response, nor a response to his teaching, but their recognition of his personality, of the sort of person he was. Schooled as they were in their Jewish faith, they sometimes found it hard to understand his teaching but were irresistibly drawn to who he was. Besides being drawn to his personality, their own response was also very much a spiritual response. Being with him affected the way they were and awakened the spiritual reality within them. Personality and spirituality are far more than just an activity of the brain; they lie at the core of our very being. Our brain, with all its chemical and electrical components, is indeed a wonderful instrument that enables us to think and the engine that drives all our bodily functions, but left to itself it can make a bad master. However, when governed by love and compassion, it can become a wonderful servant.

During research scientists have to exercise great discipline and control over their brains, and we all have the power to direct and control our thoughts and where necessary reject some of them. This is a challenge and is much more easily done if we seek God's help. Brother Lawrence, writing in the 17th century, has this to say: "Useless thoughts spoil all, mischief begins here and we ought to reject them as soon as we see their impertinence to the matter in hand."

But let's close this chapter on a more light-hearted level

by thinking about falling in love. Though at times it may result in irrational or even bizarre behaviour it is also a deeply spiritual experience. In *The God Delusion* it is described as "an irrationality mechanism, a process built into the brain by chemical selection, and of which irrational religion is also a by-product". An even worse passage continues: 'The symptoms of an individual *infected by religion* may be startlingly reminiscent of those more ordinarily associated with sexual love, an extremely potent force in the brain and that it is not surprising that some 'viruses' have evolved to exploit it.'

But emotion is so much more than a response triggered by chemical reactions in your brain. Emotion registers itself in facial expression and is also a spiritual response, a response of the heart. Messages in Valentine cards are enclosed within the accepted symbol of a heart, not a brain! When I proposed to my wife, I didn't say "Darling I've just suffered an irrational chemical impulse in my brain directed towards you which is quite beyond my capacity to control"! True, we are strongly motivated by sexual impulse, but you don't fall in love with just anyone, and it has to be mutual. Falling in love goes far beyond sexual attraction and leads to a very personal relationship; falling in love with God establishes just as close a relationship, one which has the ability to endure all the challenges that life can throw in our way.

Art and music are also far more than just the production of brush strokes and decibels; the last night of the Proms has an atmosphere that transcends all scientific analysis; the thrill of riding a motorbike is greater than the functioning of all its constituent parts. To discern the whole truth we have to look at the whole of life through the discipline of both scientific and spiritual knowledge in tandem, never in isolation. In the final conclusion of their book entitled 'The Left Hand of Creation', Barrow and Silk have this to say 'We are limited to answering questions about the Universe only in terms of things we know and understand, but as yet we are from understanding all of physics. We might even wonder whether a complete knowledge of physics will ever be sufficient to explain and understand the universe.' *(Note 21, Barrow and Silk, The Left Hand of Creation)*

Of course religion, like anything else, can be invaded by viruses, fundamentalism being a case in point, but so can science. Morality can also be twisted and distorted to suit one's own motives, but beyond all our human failures the love of God remains just as constant as the fine-tuned balance by which our Universe is perpetually kept in motion. His energy, like that of the Universe, is unchanging. Love is the yardstick by which morality needs to be measured. Cosy armchair morality on its own is ill-equipped to deal with all the untold evil and suffering in the world. Charles Spurgeon, the famous preacher, wrote "Prayer girds human weakness with divine strength, turns human folly into heavenly wisdom, and gives to troubled mortals the gift of God's peace."

CHAPTER TEN

FAITH IN THE 21ST CENTURY

The time has now come to build a more coherent picture of how the Christian faith can be presented in a relevant and challenging way for the 21st century. However we read the text of the Bible, it is always subject to our own reflective thinking, but one fact remains absolutely certain above all others – the writers themselves thought they had an important message to convey. In the New Testament this was all wrapped up in the one word 'Gospel' - Good News. St. Mark begins his book with these words "The beginning of the Gospel of Jesus Christ", and all four Gospels strive to present Jesus' vision of the Kingdom of God as a way of life to be lived, not just a set of beliefs, or a table of rules to be followed to the letter.

This way of life was just as much a challenge to the pleasure-seeking consumer society of the first century as it is to our own. That society was as sexually orientated as much of our modern Western culture is today. But there was one major difference; it was a world in which religion was almost taken for granted. In pagan society there was a wide choice of religious activity; in contrast, among what was a rather harsh and often brutal society, the early Christians proclaimed that there was only one God and were renowned for not only caring for their own poor and needy but for the needs of all their neighbours. Tertullian, an early Carthaginian writer, noted how non-Christians would comment with astonishment, "See how these Christians love one another."

To present Christian faith to our Western secular and largely non-churchgoing society of the 21st century, the church may well have to abandon much of the outdated dogma and ecclesiastical 'talkspeak' of days gone by, which for most people has now become a foreign language. This is no more challenging a task than that which Jesus himself faced as he struggled to proclaim his vision of the Kingdom of God and his love for all mankind to the pagan world of his own day.

To do so we must reconsider how we use the Bible. There are those who believe that it has to be accepted in its entirety as the unchangeable Word of God. But we need to remember that it was written by the hands of men responding to the spiritual wisdom and inspiration of their day. The New Testament in particular was addressed to the contemporary society of the first century – not to us. Since those days our understanding of the Universe has changed beyond recognition; science, while building upon its early foundations, has had to reject many of its earlier errors. So must religion. The apostle Jude, writing when the early church was under attack, urges us to contend for the 'Faith once delivered to the Saints'. That is fine as a foundation, but not as the last word about faith. Both disciplines have grown and changed beyond all recognition since the first century.

Science no longer relies on early medical practices, though it was led on its way by what they first discovered. Doctors still take the Hippocratic Oath formulated by the renowned Greek scholar of medicine Hippocrates, but none of us would happily submit to 'state of the art' mediaeval surgery in the 21st century! William Harvey destroyed a thousand years of scientific dogma when he described the systemic circulation of blood being pumped to the brain and body by the heart. So as we ponder religious truth we have to realise that a great deal of some of the thinking upon which the faith of the early Christians was based has also been superseded. This particularly applies to the early Christians' expectation that Jesus would return to Earth in their own lifetimes, what the Church calls the doctrine of his 'Second Coming' and which still figures large on the horizon of many fundamentalist Christians. The first Christians really did believe that Christ would come back down to Earth in their own lifetime, but they were mistaken, it never happened.

Both politicians and royalty, as late as the nineteenth and early twentieth centuries, were still fascinated with this idea and saw Jerusalem as the likely scenario. Great Britain, France and Russia all sought to gain control of

Jerusalem, a subsidiary cause of the Crimean War. There were English and American evangelicals who believed that if they could take control of Jerusalem and convert the Jews this would hasten the second coming by creating the most propitious conditions for this event.

Sunday by Sunday we still proclaim that 'Christ will come again' as we recite the early 4th century Nicene Creed, the product of all the arguments that developed over who different groups of Christians thought Jesus was. That Creed was based on the Ptolemaic view of the Universe with the Earth firmly rooted in the centre. Heaven was definitely UP and Hell was definitely DOWN below; both were quite literally accepted as physical locations, and God dwelt above the firmament, beyond the stars; a scientific dogma which remained firmly entrenched until challenged during the late fifteenth and early seventeenth centuries by Copernicus and Galileo, both of whom were persecuted for daring to challenge the authority of the Christian church. See The Coleum Empireum Habitaculum Dei, the dwelling place of God in the Ptolemaic Diagram below. Much of Copernicus' thinking was fed by his research into the classical Islamic astronomy of the tenth century, which was already challenging the Ptolemaic view of the world. Their advanced observatories were revealing that the planets were rotating around the Sun. Copernicus included many of the diagrams and calculations worked out by Islamic scholars.

Richard Dawkins tells us that when a science book is wrong, someone eventually discovers the mistake and it is corrected in subsequent books; turning to religion he then claims that this doesn't happen with holy books. This is not quite true. Professor Keith Ward in his *Vision to Pursue* writes "We should admit that the early disciples were mistaken in their belief in the second coming; they got it wrong, it didn't happen. That the earliest Christians had some mistaken beliefs is neither very disturbing nor very surprising. Why should such people living in a pre-scientific culture not have believed many false things? We have to admit that the Bible is not infallible in every word. This is a view shared by many other modern theologians. Once we accept that some of the early Christian beliefs were wrong, stories like that of the virginal conception of Jesus (the doctrine of the 'virgin birth') begins to look like obviously mythological narrative expressing the uniqueness of the person of Jesus. Disputes will always continue, since we cannot go back to ancient history to check the facts."

I shall never forget the joy that invaded my soul when I first read this, and the great feeling of release I experienced when freed from the burden of having struggled to accept some of the perplexing dogma that is included in all of the creeds, and the false eschatological teaching of earlier centuries that still pervades much of our Christian thinking. *(Note 18, Richard Dawkins)*

The Second Coming of Jesus

The New Testament vision of Jesus coming back 'down' to earth on the clouds of heaven is a remarkably difficult concept for modern minds and hardly fits our present understanding of the Universe with its myriads of galaxies. It is this sort of idea that turns many thoughtful people away from religion. Those of us who have grown up within the church family don't fully realise how great a stumbling block this sort of language can be to those searching for a faith that can guide them through the challenges of life in today's world. We have got to learn to abandon dogmas that have been proved to be mistaken and out of date, even when included in the Bible, especially dogmas that either get in the way or prevent the modern world from accepting Jesus vision of the Kingdom of God. As far back as the early 19th century, Kierkegaard, the respected Danish philosopher and theologian, underlined the absurdity of certain religious 'truths' preventing us from reaching a closer relationship with God.

The Virgin Birth

Faith is, first and foremost, our response to God's love revealed by Jesus, whose last command to his disciples was to share that love with one another. It is a terrible tragedy for us ever to allow doctrine or dogma to become a barrier to our finding a faith which paves the way to a personal and living relationship with God. All we really need to know about Jesus' birth is that he was born of Mary. In chapter two of the birth narrative of Matthew's gospel the writer quotes these words of the Old Testament prophet Isaiah: "All this was done that it might be fulfilled which was spoken by the Lord through the prophet, saying 'Behold, a virgin shall be with child, and bear a Son, and they shall call His name Immanuel'", which when translated is "God with us". In the Hebrew language the word 'Almah' is used, which we wrongly translate as virgin. Almah means a young woman or girl, a young or unmarried woman and derives from the words yonek or yanak (קֵנוֹי) which means suckle.

St. Luke writes: "The Angel Gabriel was sent from God to a city of Galilee named Nazareth to a young 'woman' betrothed to Joseph descended from King David whose name was Mary". Don't be put off by the conventional picture of an angel! God still sends messages to people today, as I know only too well (see Chapter Eight). She is told by the 'angel' that she has been much blessed. Mary becomes very troubled. The angel continues "Don't worry, you have found favour with God, you have conceived in your womb and will bear a son whom you will call Jesus. He will be great and will be called the Son of the Most High, and will become the Saviour of the World." Mary is dumbstruck – who wouldn't have been? – but responds with her song of praise known as the Magnificat – "My soul rejoices in God, my Saviour who has regarded the lowliness of his handmaiden".

Quite properly Jesus' birth is shrouded in mystery, just as is our own birth. Far better to stand in awe and wonder at Jesus' birth than to indulge ourselves in an endless, fruitless argument which we can never prove.

Moving in a world of likelihood and uncertainty entails that no secure doctrinal system can ever be built upon the interpretation of scriptural texts, and in particular just the two birth narratives in Luke and Matthew, especially Matthew, whose very first chapter begins with a long genealogy of Jesus to prove his descent from Kind David, and who was driven by the desire to gradually win over the Jewish community for which it was largely written. We have to remember that the Gospels only took their present form probably somewhere between the years 80 to 90 AD, some forty years or more after Jesus was put to death. Up to that time there would have been hundreds of 'stories' of Jesus passed by word of mouth. In turning these into written text the Gospel writers may have included additions to the true story added by their repeated telling, and may also have lost important facts on the way; recall the story told to me at that Camberley coffee morning about a bishop who had coughed out his false teeth while preaching in Durham

Cathedral, which I was only able to correct because I was actually there – no one can know the exact truth. But behind every story there usually lies one significant fact that launched it on its way in the first place, in this case that Mary gave birth to Jesus. This said, there is also a great deal recorded in the New Testament that we truly can believe.

Bishop Nigel McCulloch writes "The Holy Spirit doesn't hide in a book, not even when that book is the Bible." Nor does He hide in early fourth-century creeds, nor in all of the psalms, though from among the creeds and the psalms and within much of the Bible there are many priceless sources of spiritual inspiration. The Bible is also a rich repository of poetry, of history and of the religion and faith of the people who inhabit it, and also a valuable means of communicating the word of God; but unless those words jump from its pages into the way of life that Jesus revealed to the world they remain just words, merely ink on paper. They have to be translated into life and tested by experience.

John Midelo, a priest working in a poor parish in Tanzania, with whom I constantly keep in touch by email, wrote in his Christmas Greetings of 2015: "What we do in this four weeks of Advent is compassion to others, love, sustainability of peace within the community and out of community, the practical theology is to collect all closes (clothes) and food from the believers among my parish. It's 100% successful, and we send to orphans and elderly who don't have."

After worship on a Sunday over a cup of coffee I normally tell one of my large stock of stories to three elderly ladies whom we ferry to church. I once asked them if they understood the old traditional service. One answered "No, not really, it's all a bit complicated, I do trust in God and I enjoy the hymns, but the thing I value most is the company". It often took Jesus a great deal of hard work to explain his vision of the Kingdom of God, and even when he spoke in parables taken from their everyday lives they still sometimes found it hard to understand, and he never ever used creeds.

When you consider the situation in Syria and the Middle East the need is not for religion - there is more than enough in that part of the world - but for a totally robust presentation of the way in which Jesus calls us all to live. We need a Brian Cox of the 'Science of Theology' to combat the cynicism of a large proportion of the people in our so called Western secular culture, where many are searching for some sort of faith, but a faith freed from the burdens of the more unlikely dogmas and fundamentalism that have travelled with us down the ages.

I know this to be true from the conversations I have had with many people from all walks of life; people who service gas boilers, builders and other tradesmen, and in particular many of the staff and patients during my eighteen days spent in hospital after my heart operation in 2010, most of whom had seldom darkened a church door. In conversation we discussed Jesus' vision of the Kingdom of God and his way of life, and of our need for help to follow his example. One of the staff responded with these words: "I might even consider coming to church if that's the church's message for the world, but so much of what takes place there is in a language we don't understand."

The Resurrection

And what about the Resurrection? When Paul spoke about it to the intellectual Greeks they pooh-poohed the idea, and many still do so today. After some of the events and experiences in my own life I can have no doubt at all that the disciples experienced the risen Jesus in some sort of way, and that he made himself known to them in a deeply spiritual way, as he still does.

After Jesus was crucified the disciples bolted the door of the upper room where they were assembled for fear of being themselves arrested. There was no knock on the door, but suddenly they were aware of Jesus' presence among them as he gave the traditional Jewish greeting – 'Shalom – Peace be with you.' How do we interpret this and the other recorded accounts of Jesus' resurrection appearances? More words from Professor Keith Ward: "Most New Testament scholars now believe that what the first disciples experienced after his death was a series of visionary manifestations the interpretation of which was left to them, and that they felt the presence of Jesus in the same way as many Christians do today." St. Paul tells us in his letter to the Church in Corinth that just as we have possessed an earthly body in the resurrection we shall possess a spiritual body, and remember that he himself had experienced the risen Jesus. It is the body that defines our individual identity. Identity is so important. Jesus appeared to them in a recognisable form. *(Note 8, Keith Ward)*

Take the experience of the two disciples walking to the village of Emmaus. I can imagine those two disciples walking along the road talking to themselves about the crucifixion and feeling very downhearted. A stranger joined them and began commenting on what had happened and how it had all been foretold by the prophets. They invited him to supper, and the moment he broke the bread they recognised him and in that moment of recognition he disappeared from their sight. So they rushed back to Jerusalem to tell the other disciples that they had seen the Lord.

In 1970 I had a very similar experience. For a whole month after major spinal surgery I had to lie flat on my back on a plaster cast without even a pillow. I asked some men from my Birmingham parish to visit me the Sunday following my operation so I could celebrate the Communion Service from my hospital bed, not an easy task in that position. Beforehand, while rehearsing the words used by Jesus at the Last Supper, "Take, eat, this is my body which is given for you, do this in remembrance of me", words I know by heart, I suddenly became aware of much the same sort of experience as that shared by those two disciples at Emmaus when Jesus blessed and broke bread with them. Whether my eyes were open or shut I have no idea, but for a brief moment I 'saw' the most wonderful face of love looking down at me, and just like them in that moment of recognition that face vanished from my 'sight'. I was both shattered and filled with joy.

As a young man I thought that Jesus could not be known personally, just that he had come into this world to reveal God's love and invite us to follow his way of life. I now see that He is the precious link, the go-between between us and God our Creator. I recorded the following words immediately in my little 'black book' of reflections, in which are stored all sorts of quotes and experiences.

I knew instinctively that this new given certainty would make the leadenness of much of our ordinary life even more leaden, and that the battle to convey the truth revealed to us by Jesus would be just as challenging a task as it was before, perhaps even more so. But I also knew that for me as an individual argument or 'apology', or the need to convince myself of the truths of the Christian faith was no longer necessary... But oh for the grace to enshrine them in the business of the day-to-day affairs by which we are all burdened.

During the modern communion service the priest says "The Lord is here" and the people reply "His Spirit is with us." On just a few occasions I have had a whole congregation say "There was something very special about that service, wasn't there Vicar?" Once in the parish where I worship in Devizes the congregation had just made the response "His Spirit is with us" when my mobile phone's ringing tone echoed round the church. The Vicar very quick-wittedly intervened "That proves it!"

CHAPTER ELEVEN

THE CORE OF CHRISTIAN FAITH

So in this 21st Century, what is the essential core of the Christian message to the world? Above all else it is a call to faith, a faith centred upon God and his love for all mankind as it continues to be revealed to the world through the life and teaching of Jesus; a faith that links us to his presence, a faith that besides meeting our own personal needs is a faith that demands community and the strength of fellowship and reaches out to people worldwide.

Our twenty-first century faith, while built upon the foundations laid by all those who have gone before and to whom we owe a great debt, even to their mistakes, must be continually guided by the inspiration of the Spirit. We possess a rich heritage. Cathedrals and places of worship are a great capital asset, steeped in prayer and worship over the centuries; used imaginatively, they can lead people to an awareness of God and deepen or even be the springboard for faith.

Within the freedom of what the Anglican Church calls Common Worship, it is entirely possible to create a form of worship that is intelligible to anyone entering a church building for the first time. Some churches have already achieved this, marrying some of the simpler, older traditional prayers with some of the wonderful new ones, and selecting readings from the Bible that include a contemporary and meaningful message for the society in which we all have to live. The use of both good traditional hymns and the best of the modern songs can unite the older, more traditional worshippers with the younger generation, whose experience of life in our modern age is totally different from that of those who grew up, like myself, with the old 1662 Prayer Book. The church has indeed moved on since I first became a priest and I rejoice that over the sixty-two years that I have been a clergyman, it has become much more open to the needs of the whole of the community than it was when I first started work.

Over the centuries, despite all their shortcomings, all the Christian churches have helped preserve Jesus' vision of the Kingdom of God, even when it got lost among dogma and insensitive theology. The Bible tells us that God sent Jesus to reveal his love not just to the Church but to the world. I personally owe a tremendous debt to the whole Anglican Communion and the experience of Christian fellowship that has nurtured me from childhood and continues to lead me on my way. We all need a growing faith that not only speaks to today's world but equips each one of us to meet the particular challenges that we all encounter in our moments of personal stress, perplexity and sorrow as we progress along the road map of our own life's journey; we also need the inspiration of the Holy Spirit to proclaim Jesus' vision for all humanity with power and confidence in a language that all can understand.

The God-Shaped Hole in Secular Society

In St. John's Gospel Jesus, speaking to his disciples, spoke these words: "You say there are yet four months until the harvest? Look, I tell you, lift up your eyes and see the fields, they are white for harvest already. I believe that the fields of our largely secular Western world are equally ripe to Harvest, and that there really is a God-hole out there waiting to be filled.

The problem with the secular word is not that it is bad but that it is incomplete. We abuse our material achievements striving to find happiness in the amount of goods we possess; urged on by the pursuit of profit by those who urge us to consume, consume, consume we are in danger of failing to meet the inner needs of the soul. Wealth does not guarantee happiness or deep spiritual peace, but neither does condemning people to live in abject poverty. We can only experience all the blessings of Faith by allowing it to become part of a Way of Life that reaches out to all people. *(Note 22, Alison Morgan, The Wild Gospel)*

I can't resist one more true story. Travelling by train recently, I found myself locked inside an electronically-controlled loo. The release buttons were nowhere near the door; they were behind me beneath the washbasin! Returning through the standard class section of a first-class carriage, I was then accosted by a man shouting in a loud voice "Are you the father of Robbie Williams?" I told him I had never heard of Robbie Williams! He then rolled out a list of many more famous pop stars. By now I was shouting a little myself and bawled that I was born in 1930. "That's a funny time of day to be born!" he roared. "The 24-hour clock hadn't been invented then" I responded, and to wind him up further I told him how I had got locked in the Loo. We were already centre stage and there were now thirty or more people roaring with laughter. Seizing the moment, I announced that I was a retired clergyman and that in my old age I had come to the conclusion that what mattered most was for us all to love one another and share that love with others; then, pointing to the sky, I added 'And we all need His help to do so'. Their response was a prolonged round of applause.

Recently, while I was on the island of Malta, a man in his early forties asked me where I came from and then what I had done in life. I told him my story of how those two young students at my old theological college had asked if I was one of the old monks who were going to invade their school swimming pool. Finally they asked if I had a message for them, if you remember, and I told them that this old monk believed that God had sent Jesus into our world to reveal God's love for all mankind. One or two other people were gathered beside me and my new-found Maltese friend replied, "That's a very profound message."

Today we are challenged to go out to a world where

religion has been largely put aside and in which even belief in God's very existence is often denied and where some people have even coined the phrase "God is dead". To say that God is dead is like denying global warming. The Polynesian islands in the South Pacific are already beginning to watch rising sea levels destroy their homes and livelihood. Their Bishop writes: "Denying climate change when it is happening all around us is like denying God – it is a denial of reality – God is in our midst and calls us to care for everyone, which means there can be no development without God at the centre."

Filling that God-shaped hole and struggling to keep the spirit of faith alive amid the violence that has afflicted the whole of recorded history is no new battle. Every generation requires a new presentation of the Christian Faith relevant to its own 'modern age', but all too soon time will relegate our modernity to the past. Nothing stays 'state of the art' forever, even less so in an age of ever-speedier technological change. With our ever-increasing knowledge of the Universe in an increasingly secular Western culture, where does this leave the proclamation of the Gospel, the Good News? How can our faith help us find a way through the maelstrom of events that seems to hit the news every day?

In our secular age, where two generations at least possess only the vaguest smattering of biblical knowledge, we need to convey Jesus' teaching by using modern parables. Take for example Jesus' parable of the wealthy farmer who said to himself "I know what I shall do with all my wealth. I will tear down my barns and build larger ones, and there I will store all my grain and my goods", and he said to himself, "Soul, you have many goods laid up for many years to come; take your ease, eat, drink and be merry." That parable can easily be updated. There was once a manager of a large company who said to himself "I know what I will do; I will build bigger and better branches, I will go global and extend my business all over the world and make more and more money, then I will retire and take my ease". He did not realise that he was soon to die of a heart attack.

A recent BBC documentary described the life of the 'Beast of Billingsgate,' a former ruthless boss trader in the famous London fish market, whose chief aim in life was to 'make a killing', to make more and more money. In Mexico City he didn't get a look in and made a loss; they were even more ruthless than he was! He next edged his way into the largest market in the world, in New Delhi. There he discovered a totally different ethos that allowed all traders, from the boss to the humblest porter, not to make a 'killing', but to make a sufficient profit to meet their respective needs. This form of trading caused the Beast of Billingsgate to re-evaluate the way he had lived, and led by his in-between visits to the local Hindu temple, he began to look at his life in an entirely new light.

Both stories are in essence modern parables about the ruthless trading world in which we live today. They may not be very well received by the business and financial markets, but nor was Jesus' original parable, which concluded with these words: "God said to the wealthy farmer, 'you fool! This very night your life will be demanded from you. Then who will get all that wealth what you have prepared for yourself? This is how it will be with those who store up treasures for themselves on earth, but are not rich toward God'." Our task in the 21st century is to help people build their faith in such a way that it enables them to meet the challenges of living in today's world. Jesus offers this sort of faith to all those prepared to put their trust in him by living richly towards God by sharing his love with all whom they meet.

We do well to remember Jesus' own words: "Come to me with all your burdens and I will refresh you. Take my yoke upon you and learn from me and you will find rest for your souls, my yoke is easy and the burden is light." Religion has at times turned that yoke into a ton of bricks!

Among the miracles based on the faith of the believer is the story of the centurion who sought healing for his servant, and to whom Jesus spoke these words "I have not found so great faith not in all Israel, not among the whole religious community". Can you imagine Jesus saying to that centurion "This is the Catholic Faith, which unless you accept I cannot save you or your servant?" Jesus never spoke in formal creedal language; he always looked for a faith that stemmed from the heart. To the Samaritan woman at Jacob's well, Jesus said "A time is coming and has now come when the true worshippers will worship the Father in Spirit and in truth, for they are the kind of worshippers the Father seeks." His whole mission was to draw people to faith in God, to a personal relationship with God, a task he commits to all who strive to follow his way of life. For that relationship to grow and deepen we need all the help we can lay our hands on, including prayer.

Prayer

Most people resort to prayer when in distress, but more

informed prayer as part of our daily experience can help us meet the challenges we all encounter with increased strength. In moments of extreme stress, to know that you are being prayed for can also strengthen your own weakness. Where we find difficulties, we need to ask questions. We need the companionship of studying and worshipping together. We need to be thankful for the gift of life that we have all received and for the faith of all those who have travelled the road of faith before us. In our own private lives, when we get stuck it is sometimes helpful to use a little book of more formal printed prayers. Or you might find this adaptation of one of our lovely new prayers helpful.

Lord when we were still far off
you brought us home.
Both by his life and by his death
Jesus declared your love,
Gave us grace, and
opened the gate of glory.
May we walk in his ways and
share his love with others;
May the light of his Spirit
shine throughout the world.
Keep us firm in the hope you
have set before us,
So that we and all your children
shall be free, and the whole earth
Live to praise your holy name. AMEN.

One of the problems with prayer is that many people never

outgrow the first prayers of childhood; God bless Daddy, Mummy and the cat and Auntie Vee!

We just go on adding to them but don't progress much further. Prayer is not always easy, especially as we become weighed down by all the pressures of our daily lives, which in many ways have become much more burdensome in the troubled and sometimes frenetic world in which we all have to live.

Prayer has to grow continually as we continue to tread the winding road of faith, and faith is so much more than the recitation of what we believe; belief has to be transformed by faith, which like prayer can lead us to a living relationship with God. Some of us are simply drawn to God directly, but for many Christians this takes the form of first finding a personal relationship with Jesus, whose main mission is to lead us to God, and help us to understand his love for all mankind.

SILENCE

There are also times when we should simply tell God what is in our heart in our own words, even when we are angry with Him – that may well help to release you from some of your anger which is seldom constructive. We need to talk to God in ordinary conversation, and maybe most of all to be silent and to listen to what he may be trying to say to us when He can get a word in!

This song from Taize can be very helpful.

O Lord, hear my prayer
O Lord, hear my prayer

When I call, answer me
O Lord, hear my prayer
O Lord, hear my prayer
Come and listen to me.

Sometimes words cannot cope. One morning this short poem flooded into my mind and virtually wrote itself on a scrap of paper. I gave it the title of Eternity.

ETERNITY

What is the moment we call 'Now'
but the future pushing its way
into the present of our little lives;
Relentlessly, unerringly,
constantly rasping the shingle
of our life's rough shore.

Moment by moment,
amid silence and clamour
our tomorrows become our yesterdays
Sometimes hastened by the force
of a tsunami wave
Sometimes quietly passing us by
in the silence of sleep.

No soul on traffic duty can stay tomorrow,
no mind undo the past
As all these moments we call 'Now'
are swallowed by the tide of life
Into the eternity of our mortality.

We need a faith that widens our horizons to the 'Intimations of Immortality' and speaks of God's Kingdom both here on Earth but also in Heaven; A faith that fills the 'God hole' people don't always recognise in our secular society. Such faith should also fill us with joy and hope for the future "as all these moments we call 'Now' are swallowed by the tide of life into the eternity of our mortality".

The Mystery of Time

When you stop and think about it, time is a very strange thing. In our daily lives we are all slaves to time. We have to be at work on time. We expect trains and buses to run on time. We expect our electronic clocks magically to update themselves when a New Year arrives. However there are also other magic moments when time almost ceases to exist, or seems to stop.

All our lives long our brains are busily 'compressing' time into an almost seemingly solid state, in which all our memories are permanently enfolded as they are swallowed by the tide of life into that eternity of our mortality. Through the eye of faith and our experience of God we in a sense already experience a foretaste of eternal life, something far greater than life just going on forever; it is much more a quality of life that possesses eternal value. As we pass through time each one of us remains the ME that we were when we were born, and as we draw to the close of our lives that ME has become much more than we were out the outset. Our memories, besides being the sum of all that we have done and achieved, are also a reflection both of what we have been and of what we have become, the record of all our BEING.

Discovering how to BE lies at the very heart of being human. As Paul talked to those Greek philosophers who gathered on the Areopagus, he reminds us that it is in God that we live and move and have our Being. Was this a reference to the ideas taught by Socrates, who died four hundred years earlier on the very spot where Paul was talking? During our lifetime on this Earth we are bound by the dimensions of space and time, though there are indeed moments when we nudge the infinite, an idea first explored by the philosopher Descartes.

In childhood it seemed an eternity from one birthday to another. Time was a straight line. In older age the next birthday arrives almost before the previous one. Time becomes a circle. Imagine your memory as a gigantic reservoir from which an ever-flowing river heads for the top of a large waterfall. As some of your memories reach the top of that waterfall they dissolve into little droplets; in calm weather you can even trace the fall of a single drop of a waterfall.

If I delve deep into my computerised memory and dial 'Find', little droplets of memory become places and the places become occupied with people and surrounded by activity and just occasionally visual pictures. I see all the thousands of flowers that I have nursed into growth in garden upon garden, just where they used to grow in all their glory, giant tree parsnips, and further a field dwarf irises nestling on a hillside in Andalusia, tiny single marigolds among the cracks of an old Roman street in Tunisia. Those memories lead me to all those who have walked beside me on my life's journey, all miniature videos of all that has made up my life, as they are swallowed by the tide of life into eternity.

Every generation still asks the question that my nineteen-year-old barrow boy asked while I was in the army: "What's going to happen to me when I die?" We all face the challenge of making sense of our being alive in this world. In the next chapter we shall explore our need for faith, and some of the dangers that at times have clouded Jesus' vision of the Kingdom of God as we try to find some assurance of where the roadmap of each of our personal lives may lead.

CHAPTER TWELVE

GROWING IN FAITH

My Bishop in Guildford described himself as a 'Theologian of the Road', the road of life. As I travel the remaining years of my earthly pilgrimage, I ask myself, how has my faith grown? Where have I been led by all the people and all the experiences I have shared and all the books I have read? What is my own personal 'theology'? How has it grown to fruition? The answer to all those questions comes through my own experience of God's love revealed along every step of that journey. It has taken me all of my 86 years to grasp even a little of the depth of God's love, which is more than sufficient to overflow all of life's sorrows and tragedies in this troubled world.

In Scripture I treasure one particular verse from the twelfth chapter of the letter to the Hebrews to which I have previously referred: "Seeing we are surrounded by so great a cloud of witnesses, let us lay aside every weight and the sin (the burdens) that so easily beset us, and run with patience the race that lies before us, looking to Jesus, the author and perfector of our faith." Throughout my life my own personal faith has been stimulated, if not by thousands, then at least by hundreds of witnesses, all of whom have helped ensure its continual growth. Everyone's faith has to grow continually and to be perfected by our ongoing experience of life and God's love.

As a priest you are, or should be, more conscious of your failures than any successes. I know too that without the faith and the example of all the people I have met along the roadmap of my life's journey, my faith would be nowhere near what it is become today. Faith is built through fellowship, never just on one's own. Bishop Desmond has this to say in his book entitled *In God's Hands*: "In our part of the world we have something called '*ubuntu*'- the essence of being human. We say a person (*umuntu*) becomes human (*ubuntu*) through other persons. "Being in fellowship is the very essence of being human, of being 'ubuntu'. *(Note 23, Bishop Desmond Tutu)*

As I have tramped the road of life, my mind has often returned to where it all began, to my very own personal Garden of Eden, and to the love with which my parents and my family surrounded me from the moment I was born. By doing so I also return to my early awareness of God's presence and the love which began to grow in that garden of my childhood, the memory of which remains as real and crystal clear today as ever it has.

Over the years I have revisited that Garden whenever

our journeying has taken us in that direction. During the last century that Georgian vicarage, like many others, became an 'Old Vicarage'. At one stage it was abandoned and fell into serious decay, but then by some miracle a builder saw its potential and restored it to its former glory. On one visit his wife was kind enough to show us all over the house and much appreciated some of the extra history I was able to provide, especially the location of the old water pumps.

The garden is now mostly down to grass, though the holly and yew hedges survive all neatly trimmed. The Tree of Life has long since passed away; after all it was already 'dead' in my childhood! 'Heaven' is still there. Some of the trees in the orchard are also still around and I think among them is the Tree of the Knowledge of Good and Evil. Shutting my eyes I am able to return that garden almost immediately to its former glory and with them open, mark the spots where all the plants I knew once used to grow. I remember it all so very vividly.

Nor can I forget the sense of God's calling me to share that love with others that led me to the priesthood. At that time my understanding of the fullness of his love was still rather undeveloped. It had not been tested by many of the challenges of life, or by moments of doubt and uncertainty, and the times when I even questioned God's very existence. I had yet to fully understand how the message of the Cross helps us cope with those moments and all the evil in this world, especially the plight and suffering of so many innocent people.

Above all else all our very existence is a God-given gift – one that we are all meant to share. To do so we need faith, and my faith has led me to the personal conviction that the God-given gift of Love is the only answer, not only to our own personal problems, but to all the problems of this often broken but still wonderful world. Faith can never be reduced to argument; more properly it is a response. This conviction was deepened in a very special way by a succession of wonderful experiences that followed my recovery from major heart surgery in the Bristol Royal Infirmary during the Holy Week of 2010.

CHAPTER THIRTEEN

THE HEART OF
THE MATTER

Holy Week in Hospital

An extensive tour of East Africa early in 2010 went without mishap, no broken femurs this time round. After visiting many of the churches we know so well in Uganda and Tanzania, there followed a few days 'human safari' in Botswana organised by a company specialising in short visits to African homes. One of these was a cattle station where the family honoured us by spreading the floor of our apartment with newly-laid dung! Outside, a non-flushing Western-style had been place on top of the pit latrine besides which her hen had built her nest and was

288

busily nursing her young chicks! Later we tramped eleven kilometres along a trail used by David Livingstone before returning to the capital, Gaborone.

On the Sunday we shared in the exhilarating worship of the new cathedral. Amid lively singing and dancing while exchanging the Peace – a traditional form of greeting – a lady deacon invited me to join the clergy in the sanctuary. The celebrant and I first blessed a large number of children and then a man suffering from cancer as he knelt at the altar rail, after which I helped administer the chalice to the large congregation. There are no words to describe the warmth of welcome, the joy and the vibrancy of that church family and their music. They didn't even know we were coming. I was just a white stranger wearing a 'dog collar'. Jill had to leave early to collect our driver and our belongings from our guest house before returning to the Cathedral. When she entered she got a big round of applause and after thanking them invited everyone to sing *All People That On Earth Do Dwell*. It was picked up by the organist and soon that large congregation joined in singing to the Lord 'with cheerful voice'. Little did I imagine when I first turned my collar round that I would one day lead worship in African cathedrals and in chaplaincies across the world.

Just over a month after our return home I was admitted to Swindon Hospital with a suspected slight heart attack. Two consultants asked what I had been doing during the last few months. I told them about our African trip, which included visits to numerous churches, lots of preaching and talking and being bounced about in four by fours over rough country roads to isolated church communities. Their comment was "Someone must have been looking after you, you shouldn't be here!" I had been running around with one fully-blocked artery, two that were just trickles, and one that was trying to do the work of all the others.

After four days I was transferred to Bristol Royal Infirmary to prepare for major heart surgery. Post-anaesthesia problems are a common enough experience, especially when one's body is still being pumped full of drugs of one sort or another. While I was first recovering there were moments at night when I saw daffodils continuously walking across the door lintel. I also thought the bare plaster walls were wallpapered with flowers all taking afternoon strolls. Naturally my family became very worried. This all eventually came to an end, but there are those who might attribute much, if not all of what follows to that state of post-anaesthesia. Maybe drugs do put the brain into top gear, but there is a world of difference between mistaking the mop heads of lady cleaners viewed through a clouded glass window for the black bushy microphones of a TV crew and my experience of God's love.

After leaving intensive care I was on my own for much of the day, but from time to time a nurse or a member of the cleaning staff would arrive; many were from overseas and I got into the habit of asking them their names and the countries from which they came. One morning I was feeling very down in the dumps when a cheerful young African came to empty the waste bin. I asked him how he was. "Fine" he replied. "I am Samuel and I am a member of the Anglican Church of Namirembe in Kampala in Uganda." I was stunned and told him that only six weeks ago I had been a guest in the Namirembe Guest House, had been introduced to his Bishop, and had worshipped in his cathedral. For some moments we were both silent and gazed at each other in utter amazement, and at the ceiling. I don't believe in the sort of angels with unlikely-looking wings, the sort that inhabit stained glass windows, but I do believe that Samuel was a very special angel sent to me by God that morning. I didn't jump straight to the top of the ladder, but this experience took me a few steps from the bottom rung. He too had been feeling homesick and found comfort by sharing so close a personal a link with his home city.

More 'angels' arrived on the Good Friday morning. At 6 am a young Turkish nurse came to take my blood pressure. She started talking about her country and how Ataturk had made it a wonderful place and how the militancy of the terrorists was now spoiling their Moslem faith. Putting her hand on her heart, she said "It hurts me here." I told her that I was a Christian priest, and touching my newly 'repaired' heart I said "It hurts me here too". She, a young Moslem girl, then took my hand in hers and we both prayed silently together for some time before she took my blood pressure. Here is a parable for our distracted world to ponder. People of all faiths who acknowledge God's care for this world should be joining hands to bear witness to his love for all mankind. If there is a *Jihad* (struggle) to be waged it should never be between people of faith. People of faith should be working together to share God's love with those who have little or no knowledge of that love.

Shortly afterwards a bright young Chinese girl arrived with the morning tea trolley, asking if I would like a cake. I was a bit dubious about eating cake at six o'clock in the morning and asked what it was. She held up a hot cross bun.

I immediately thought of our close friend Bishop Jackson in Uganda. He just adores hot cross buns, or 'Good Friday' buns as he calls them. My mind quickly travelled to Africa, where I knew there were not just hundreds but possibly thousands of people praying for me. That was so encouraging. That Good Friday bun suddenly became very special; it became a sacrament of all those prayers.

Then along came my third angel, an ordinary hard-working girl from one of the poorer Bristol housing estates, who informed me that she was a Christian. I asked her if she belonged to any church. "Oh, I don't go to any church," she replied, "I just do my cleaning job and try to help people and cheer them up." This echoes the words of one of George Herbert's well-known hymns – "A servant with this clause makes drudgery divine, who sweeps a room, as for thy laws, makes that and the action fine." Was ever a young girl following Jesus' last wishes that we should all love one another more than her? It must surely rejoice his heart that despite many of the failures of his Church over the years there are thousands, no millions, of so-called secular people who often quite unconsciously have grasped the true meaning of his message of love and compassion. There might even be an atheist or two among them!

To me, that Good Friday morning, all three were literally heaven-sent angels, real angels, and they lifted my spirits no end. Above all else, an angel is a messenger from God. Sleep comes very hard in hospital, and all of the previous night I had prayed for the relief that sleep brings. None came. I then remembered that Jesus had had no sleep at all that first Maundy Thursday night, and like Peter I felt rather ashamed; the angels sent to me that Good Friday morning were a far greater gift. Later yet another nurse came to attend to me, Lise Kauraisa; she announced she was a member of the Anglican Church in Namibia! In conversation we discovered that Jill and I had visited her local supermarket and bought petrol at the adjoining filling station near her home. We prayed together and she gave me her address. I wrote to Lisa some days after I returned home and received a reply telling me how she had been feeling very down that Good Friday morning and how the prayers we shared had made all the difference. *(Note 24, Lise Kauraisa's letter)*

Some time before Good Friday I had a totally different type of experience, comparable in some ways to that of Jon Snow when he recently volunteered with two other prominent people to take part in a laboratory-controlled cannabis experiment; the three of them were given doses of either 'skunk', cannabis resin or a placebo. None of them knew which they personally had received. John was given the skunk in vapour form and described his experience as follows: "I lost all control, it was devastating and the paranoia was overwhelming. You hear me describe that my soul had been wrenched from my body. It was as if I had been robbed of Me." That must have been a truly devastating experience.

I turn now to my own experience of the blackness into which Jon descended after taking part in that drugs experiment. My experience was just as traumatic and distinctly similar to Jon's, but with one major difference; I had not taken skunk and was still very much 'myself' and aware of all that was going on around me, but the ME I know was slowly being stripped bare.

That particular night I encountered a feeling of utter and total despair; I felt as if all the things I treasured in life were falling away from me one by one, then in an increasing surge, till I was utterly naked. It was like watching a roof being stripped of every last tile. Everything became black, bleak and desolate. I felt that God had totally forsaken me. In sheer desperation I picked up my mobile phone, trying to contact my brother – anyone whose phone number my numbed brain could recollect, even Bishop Jackson in Uganda. Unbeknown to me I even dialled the police! I asked the staff repeatedly to call my wife, only to be told I must wait till the normal visiting time the next day. I spent a whole night in utter desperation.

After my night of black agony, the morning staff relented and allowed my wife to come early. The moment she arrived and touched the tips of my fingers with hers, all the tiles of my life of which I had been so totally stripped bare suddenly jumped back into place one after the other, in exactly the same way as by the wonders of modern computer technology old ruins can be totally restored; stone after stone and tile after tile fluttering quickly back into place till the ruins become the wonderful buildings they were in their prime.

Long after writing this I found the notes I scribbled while lying on my hospital bed tucked away in an odd corner of my study; it is so easy to enlarge and embroider this sort of experience by hindsight. My memory was confirmed in every single detail.

Later, looking back, I believe that for the very first time amid that bleakness and utter blackness I drew very close to understanding the full depth of Jesus' agonising cry of despair on the Cross – "My God, my God why have you forsaken me?" – which does not just reveal his own sorrow but mirrors the anguish and the deep sorrow experienced by God's heart of love which is continuously being bruised by all the evil that human beings so often inflict on one another; his pain was so much more than the pain of just his own physical suffering.

The more you ponder that cry – My God, my God, why have you forsaken me? – you begin to understand that it needs no theological explanation. It was much more than Jesus quoting the opening verse of Psalm 22; it was a very heartfelt human cry from the very depth of his being, a cry that identifies him with our frail humanity and the personal desolation we ourselves sometimes experience. It is also a cry amid the silence of an even deeper sorrow, a cry of deep anguish that the world was so blind to his Gospel of love and peace and compassion, and cannot see how humanity, transformed by love, could complement the beauty of the natural world if only we devoted all our energies to living our lives in harmony with our Creator.

And that cry still speaks to us over all the centuries since it was first spoken, centuries during which there has been so much cruelty and violence. Every time a suicide bomber presses his or her button of destruction and every terrorist act is a crime against God's love; even more so when the perpetrators dare to commit these acts in his name. Far from entering Paradise, their hands will forever remain stained with innocent blood; and far from obtaining the crown of Martyrdom, it is their victims who become the true martyrs. St. Paul tells us that our bodies are temples of the Holy Spirit. Every human being is a divine miracle and modern technology reveals the enormous intricacy of our human bodies and the delicate balance by which our life is sustained. The purposeful destruction of one's own body, especially when it also leads to the wholesale destruction of many others of God's children, is not only a crime against humanity, but an insult to God from whom we all receive the gift of life.

Whether those who perpetrate these crimes can ever be forgiven is not for us to decide. Judgement rests in God's hands and is never ours to administer. Significantly, these thoughts are found both in the Bible and the Koran. But God's power to reconcile and forgive goes far beyond anything we can imagine. Only when such people experience a complete change of heart can the evil they commit finally be overcome. Peter once asked Jesus how many times he should forgive his brother, suggesting he might just about manage seven times, to which Jesus replied, "Not seven times, Peter, but seventy times seven," in other words till it becomes a habit.

Corrie Boom in her book *Tramp for the Lord* describes a very moving encounter she experienced in a German church in 1947, after speaking to a German congregation about the love of God, and how He can forgive even our worst sins. "In fact" she declared, "God takes our sins and casts them into the deepest ocean". After the service, as people were leaving the church, she noticed a balding, heavy-set man in a grey overcoat making his way towards her. As he drew closer, her blood ran cold. She recognised him as a former Ravensbruck camp guard who had been among the cruellest and most inhumane of her persecutors. This guard now stood before her with an outstretched hand pleading for forgiveness.

Reluctant at first, she prayed for the courage to do so and writes: "For a long moment we grasped each other's hands, the former guard and the former prisoner. I had never before known God's love so intensely as I did then." *(Note 25 Corrie Boom, Tramp for the Lord)*

Later in a small recovery ward I had another totally different experience. Whether this happened before or after the one I have just described I cannot now remember; when you are in hospital for some time days run into each other, especially when you have had very little sleep. The night nurse had checked all four of us before finally dimming the lights. About an hour or so later the ward was suddenly swathed in an unaccustomed brightness and I felt myself transported to the shore of a vast and beautifully calm lake and heard a voice speaking these words: "I have given you a great deal of love. There is far more than you need for yourself. You must share the rest with others." There followed a moment of profound silence. Just that, no more. Then I was back with a bump on my hospital bed in the dimly-lit ward. I have later described that lake to myself as 'the Ocean of God's love.' Like Paul on the road to Damascus, I was stunned. I looked across at the other three people in the ward and instinctively prayed for them.

My immediate response the following morning was to hobble round the other bays of the ward with my stick talking to people, following the example of that lovely Bristol girl. I heard a lady quietly singing hymns to herself in a little side ward. I told her I was a priest and asked if I might join her. She was waiting to go home and told me she had been longing for someone like me to come. We sang together, talked and prayed and I gave her a blessing.

Returning to my ward I met a Moslem lady sweeping the corridor. In my own cheerful way I greeted her by offering her my outstretched hand. She quickly withdrew hers into her robes. I asked her if she never felt the need to get alongside people. "Of course I do," she replied. I then offered her the handle of my stick. She took it in her hand and there was a moment of very precious communication.

Back in my room I searched for the story Paul told of his experience on the Damascus road; my Bible almost opened itself at the twelfth chapter of his second letter to the Christians in Corinth. Of course I knew where to search, but it opened at the very page where Paul writes "I know a man in Christ who fourteen years ago, whether in the body, or out of the body I don't know – God knows – a man who was caught up to heaven and heard inexpressible words..."

I felt myself terribly humbled by all these experiences and asked myself "Why me of all people?" Knowing myself as I do, and as we all know the real truth about ourselves, I felt so unworthy, but like Paul I cannot possibly deny that this happened.

There were many more experiences that I encountered during that particular Holy Week which enriched my personal understanding of the depths of our Lord's suffering and passion in a way that I had never before experienced. I thought of that moment when as a young boy I first heard the story of the Crucifixion while walking the few yards from the church to the beauty of my father's garden and had found it so hard to believe how anyone could have inflicted such pain and cruelty on the Lord Jesus, and quietly sobbed my heart out. Holy Week is one of the most sacred weeks of the Christian year, a time when all Christians ponder Jesus' passion and crucifixion, and one could argue that one was already alert to these sorts of ideas; but many of those experiences went far beyond pondering. Maybe my son was nearer the mark when he commented, "You can't expect a priest to be in hospital in Holy Week and nothing to happen!"

Simon and his wife brought Jill to fetch me home on the Saturday before Easter Day, the feast of the Resurrection. The moment they sat me in my own chair Ruth told me my face visibly changed colour. I felt as if my whole life was being resurrected. The clergy of our local church brought me the sacrament on Easter Day. I was somewhat overwhelmed. My son was profoundly right; a great deal had happened to this particular priest in hospital during that particular Holy Week, and it has profoundly affected my faith ever since, and deepened it yet further in ways I could never ever have imagined.

Part of the extreme desolation Jesus experienced on the Cross was the rejection of his vision of the Kingdom of God. We must now turn our thoughts in a completely new direction and ask what Jesus himself believed, which is far more important. What was his own personal theology? And how did he grow into his understanding of that vision.

CHAPTER FOURTEEN

JESUS' VISION FOR HUMANITY

Childhood – the missing years

Jesus grew up in Nazareth. If he was fully human he must have done so in much the same way as do we all, looking at the world and asking questions, just as every child does. Some of the questions children ask are not easy to answer, as every parent knows; I find myself asking what Jesus thought about the world as he grew up. What did he himself believe? What did he think of the religion in which he was nurtured? What did he think about God? What was his theology?

These are difficult questions which one asks with some temerity – questions that cannot be answered with any certainty – but there are many clues scattered throughout the Gospels. It may surprise you to know that the word 'Trinity' does not occur in the Bible at all, not even in the New Testament. The Trinity is a theological concept and never passed Jesus' lips even though he devoted his whole life to God. But that devotion was to a rather different concept of God from that with which he had grown up within the Jewish religion. Above all else the foundation on which Jesus built his life was his personal trust in God, and his personal awareness of his presence from his earliest childhood.

Secondly, he never ever tried to *explain* God, but simply addressed God as his Father. Desmond Tutu writes: "When we try to speak about God we have to use language in a very figurative way so we speak of God as Father, the source of life and existence, and not in the sense in which a human father is a father." Jesus himself may once have thought like that, but he also speaks of God as someone with whom he had a very personal and intimate relationship; when his disciples asked him how to pray he taught them simply to say "Our Father, who art in Heaven." The God he revealed to his followers and in his teaching was above all else a God of love and compassion, a God who loved all humanity, a forgiving God. This picture of God was at the heart of the Gospel he proclaimed. For Jesus God was an *experience*, never an argument.

Thirdly, Jesus ardently believed in the Holy Spirit. St. John, one of his closest disciples, describes the Spirit as the true light that lights everyone coming into the world.

Scripture forces us to acknowledge that in Jesus the light of the Holy Spirit shone more brightly and in a way beyond all our imagining. *(Note 23, Desmond Tutu)*

So the core of Jesus' own personal faith, his own theology – his own word about God – was not really comparable to the creeds of later centuries. It was built upon his trust in God, as both Father and Creator, and the personal relationship he shared with him through the Holy Spirit, his own very personal Trinity. It was his ever-deeper experience of the Spirit that empowered his growing vision of The Kingdom of God, the spirit with which he later promised his disciples they would also be endowed, and who in turn would carry his vision to the whole world. Jesus simply lived the Trinity and invites us to follow in his footsteps. That is the only yardstick by which we can measure our attempts to describe the mystery of God and his love and compassion that Jesus has revealed to all mankind. The Trinity is much more than just a doctrine. To try to explain it is a vain pursuit. If we must have a creed we need the simplicity of those gradually replacing the old fourth century creeds, creeds like the following.

We believe in God the Father
From whom every family in heaven
And on earth is named.
We believe in God the Son
Who redeems us and all mankind
We believe in God the Holy Spirit
Who strengthens us with power from on High
We believe in one God, who is
Father, Son and Holy Spirit. Amen

To the Christians at Ephesus, Paul writes "The mystery of God's grace was given to me by revelation", and as you read on you see how his whole life was driven by his experience on the Damascus road. For those of us whose faith, like Paul's, is also anchored in personal revelation, the Trinity is best understood as mystery and experience; you find it just impossible to distinguish one 'person' of the Trinity from another. You are simply aware of being invaded by God's presence, from whichever direction it comes. Psalm 139 describes this in a wonderful way:

I am fearfully and wonderfully made; marvelous are your works as my soul knows very well. Lord you search me out and know me; you understand my thoughts long before. You spy out all my ways. How can I flee from your presence? If I take the wings of the morning, and lose myself in the uttermost parts of the sea, even there your hand shall lead me. If I say let the darkness cover me you turn my night into day. The darkness and the light to you are both alike.

This is an abridged version; why not read the whole psalm?

In between times however, you have to live as normal a life as anyone else, enjoying your family, bringing a sense of purpose to your daily work, or if retired tending your garden, planning your next holiday, checking your bank account and in my case putting our unmade bed in order while my wife makes my night-time cocoa. I then take a last-minute look at any incoming emails. If not you would run the risk of becoming a spiritual bore or a religious bigot. But in all your daily activities you see the world in a different way. You look out on life through God's eyes of love, compassion and mercy, revealed by Jesus marvelling at the wonder of the whole creation with reverence and a desire to bring God's love wherever you go to try and help relieve the pains and sorrows of what at times can seem to be a very broken and tragic world.

The Kingdom of God
(Jesus' call to proclaim the Kingdom)

Throughout all the Gospels Jesus talks about the Kingdom of God and uses parable after parable to describe it; he compares it to a grain of mustard seed, a woman baking bread, workers in the market place waiting to be hired like the dock labourers of the early twentieth century, to a shepherd looking for a lost sheep. So the next question we need to ask is how that vision began to take shape, and to see if we can trace the way in which it came to maturity. I believe we can. If Jesus was human, in the full sense of that word, his understanding had to grow just like ours.

Jesus was brought up in a devoutly religious home. We hear in Luke's Gospel how he used to go regularly to the synagogue and how his parents went to Jerusalem every year. When Jewish boys reached the age of twelve they were expected to recite the Mishna, the oral recitation of the basic tenets of Judaism, including the law. Luke specifically tells us that when Jesus was twelve his parents took him to the Temple in Jerusalem.

The Mishna must in some ways have resembled the Madrassa in which Moslem children are taught to recite the Koran. The Bar Mitzvah later superseded the Mishna and is still part of a young Jewish boy's admission to adulthood. We often underestimate young people's spiritual vision. No wonder that the boy Jesus with his religious background grew up with an awareness of God. Many children do. But it seems that he was no ordinary pupil. When he arrived at the temple, apparently recitation alone was not enough; he stayed behind for three days without even telling his parents! After searching for him they eventually found him in the temple, sitting with the teachers, not only listening to them, but more significantly *asking them questions.*

This was the Jesus who in later years would challenge the learned Sadducees, telling them to their faces that they didn't understand their own scriptures; that's a bit like a thirty-year-old curate telling his bishop that he's got it all wrong! The Scribes and Pharisees also felt threatened by his teaching and later sought to have him arrested. But for now the young Jesus was taken back to the family home in Nazareth, where Luke tells us he was subject to his parents and increased in wisdom and in stature. Then follow what are often called the 'missing years' spent in Samaria and Jerusalem.

Like ourselves, Jesus would have had to construct a working map of the district around his home. Perhaps during those missing years he also spent a great deal of time on his own as his vision of the Kingdom of God grew to maturity. We can never know for certain, but with all the research that has been made into the life of a 1st century Jewish home we can use our imagination. We can think of Jesus' daily family life with his parents and brothers and sisters; their walking to the synagogue on the Sabbath day where they would also have taken part in the rites and numerous religious feasts of Judaism. They would have made the annual pilgrimage to the temple in Jerusalem;

their life would have been identical in many ways to that of any good practising Jewish family of that time.

During this period of his life, like all of us, Jesus would have been acquiring more and more skills and knowledge. From knocking up a rough toy or two from his father's offcuts, as did my sons, he would have become a skilful carpenter and maybe learned to fashion farming implements. Perhaps he may also have wandered around the nearby hills taking silent refuge there, as he was often to do in later life. Amid the silence of those hills his childhood awareness of God's presence must have grown ever deeper and deeper until it developed into that full personal relationship with God revealed in the Gospels, where he always describes God as his Father.

Nazareth in those days may have been a small village, but it was by no means a backwater; it lay on the trade routes to the Roman town of Sepphoris, a major Roman city that served as the capital and administrative centre of the Galilee province. It was only five kilometres from Nazareth and was still under construction; it included a network of colonnaded paved streets, markets, residential houses, public buildings, bathhouses, a theatre and several synagogues. As a young man Jesus may well have travelled there to obtain wood and other necessities for his father's carpentry.

The Nazareth of the first century was a largely gentile community; then as now, Jews were already pioneering settlements there. In the first chapter of John's gospel we hear how Jesus gathered together his first disciples, and how one of them invited Nathaniel to meet Jesus. Nathaniel, reflecting the Jewish sentiment of his day, retorted "Can anything good come out of Nazareth?" At this time a lay movement sprang up in the villages called the Haberim, groups of like-minded men who met to discuss their faith, the Prophets, and the Jewish law and its application to contemporary life. Kenneth Bailey, a lecturer in Middle-Eastern studies, writes "We can be confident that Jesus took part in such a group because his teaching reflects the Rabbinic style of debate which they nurtured." Students of Socrates will note how questions were often answered by questions in Socratic debate, a technique Jesus himself frequently employed, highlighted especially when the Pharisees tried to entangle Him in His talk. Tell us, what do you think? Is it lawful to pay taxes to Caesar, or not? But Jesus, perceiving their wickedness, said "Why do you test me, you hypocrites? Show me the tax money." So they brought Him a denarius. He said to them, "Whose image and inscription is this?" They replied, "Caesar's." To which he responded by saying "Render therefore to Caesar the things that are Caesar's, and to God the things that are God's." When they had heard these words, they marvelled, and left Him.

Maybe the Haberim were also influenced by Socrates, who himself challenged the reality of the ancient Greek Gods and the democratic government of Athens. So after eighteen years of 'theological study' Jesus was well prepared to begin his public ministry, and was often given the title of Rabbi *(Note 26, Kenneth E. Bailey)*.

The city of Jerusalem, from its earliest days right up to the present moment, has been the scene of violent struggle, suffering siege upon siege, and has been destroyed and rebuilt on numerous occasions. At times it was part of the Egyptian, Assyrian and Hittite empires and the scene of immense violence and slaughter both among local tribes, and then later both by Christians and by Moslems. When people's faith in God is sometimes shattered by all the events occurring in that part of the world today, we do well to remember that the Middle East has always been victim to this sort of strife; this was all part of the world into which Jesus was born. He was no stranger to brutality and violence.

In his lifetime Jerusalem was part of the Roman Empire, whose Governors did their best to maintain law and order, but often in a brutal way. As a young man Jesus may well have passed many crucified bodies. Luke tells us that some people came to Jesus asking about the Galileans whose blood Pilate had mingled with their sacrifices. The Romans never quite came to terms with the Jews. They allowed all other pagan religions to continue to worship their own gods provided they included the Emperor among them. To the pagans, the more gods the merrier! The Jews refused. The Romans found Jewish worship totally confusing. They only had one god, and they didn't even have an image of him in their temple.

Though they believed in one God, their idea of God and the sacrificial worship practised by the temple priests was in some ways not totally dissimilar to that of the pagan worship of their Gods. Elijah's sacrifice and that of the Prophets of Baal were carried out in exactly the same sort of way. The priests who ordered the sacrificial worship of the temple, the Pharisees responsible for teaching, and the Scribes who enforced the keeping of the religious laws (all 600 off them and more), were all looking for a Messiah who would restore the Kingdom to Israel and sit on King David's throne; a Saviour who would free them from Roman authority.

Alongside the priestly system there were the Prophets, who vehemently criticised the temple worship and the idea of Yahweh as a warrior god fighting on their behalf. Isaiah in his very first chapter rails against sacrifice portraying God as sick to death of animal sacrifices, describing them as a 'stench in his nostrils' and concluding 'What does the Lord God require of you but to do justly and to walk humbly with your God?' Jesus himself grew up within this prophetic tradition. Standing on the Mount of Olives he wept over the city, saying "O Jerusalem, Jerusalem, you who kill the prophets and stone those sent to you, how often have I longed to gather your children together as a hen does her chickens, but you have refused to understand the things that belong to your peace. *(Note 27, the poem Jesus Wept)*

So as we look back over those missing years, Jesus' relationship with God as 'Father' must have grown ever deeper and deeper as he discovered more of the power of the Holy Spirit, which we ourselves also experience, though never so overwhelmingly as he did. So just like his first Apostles and all the Christian priests whom they ordained, and every priest or minister who has since served his church, and the whole company of all those who have followed in Jesus' footsteps over the centuries, Jesus must have grown into his calling, his vocation, which blossomed into his vision of the 'Kingdom of God.' It was now that his public ministry began.

The Synagogue in Nazareth

The Gospels tell us that Jesus began to preach in many of the synagogues in Galilee; maybe even Sepphoris was among them. Then came the day when he was invited to preach in his home town of Nazareth. "He came to Nazareth where he had been brought up and went to the synagogue as was his custom. He was handed the scroll of the Prophet Isaiah and invited to speak; unrolling the scroll he found the place where it was written the Spirit of the Lord is upon me, he has anointed me to preach the Gospel to the poor, to heal the broken hearted, to preach deliverance to the captives, the recovering of sight to the blind, and to set at liberty those who are imprisoned."

He handed back the scroll and sat down, and all eyes were fixed upon him. What was he going to say? "Today is this Scripture fulfilled in your hearing," he began. As they listened to him expounding those verses of the Prophet, I suspect that he would have developed that text suggesting that Isaiah wasn't only talking about the physically blind, but the spiritually blind, and those whose minds were imprisoned, locked up in a world entirely of their own making, and held captive by a religion set in stone.

He went on to illustrate this by drawing attention to a man called Naaman. "There were also many lepers in Israel in the time of the prophet Elisha, and none of them was cleansed except Naaman the Syrian." He was pointing out that Naaman, a gentile, an untouchable, had revealed a deeper faith than the Jewish lepers ever showed. He then reminded them that the widow who cared for the prophet Elijah came from Serepta, a city near Sidon in the Lebanon, an Arab city. He was confronting them with the thought that among their forefathers it was often people outside the Jewish community who took notice of the Prophets. Whoops! What was this arrogant young man going to say next? He was thrown out, and they tried to pelt him with stones and throw him over a nearby cliff.

At the temple, much later in his ministry, he challenged the whole system of sacrificial worship and threw out the money changers, turning their tables upside down. In taking this action he was upsetting a whole applecart of ideas, and the apples he upset started to roll everywhere, including a challenge to the Levitic Priesthood of Aaron, which was hereditary, and which monopolised the privileges of priesthood. But Jesus went further. The Gospels tells us that he also criticised the Scribes and the Pharisees, who organised the religious laws and all the beliefs and the worship within the Jewish religious hierarchy.

Jesus opposed them, often virulently – "Woe to you Scribes and Pharisees, you hypocrites! You shut the door of the kingdom of heaven in people's faces; you neither enter yourselves, nor allow those who are entering to go in. You permit a man to avoid his duties to his aging parents by saying 'Corban' [by making a gift to the temple] so making void the word of God by your tradition, and many such like things you do. Well did Isaiah prophesy of you hypocrites saying this people honours me with their lips but their heart is far from me. In vain do you worship me; teaching as doctrines the precepts of men you leave the commandment of God, and hold fast the tradition of men." And the Church itself over the centuries has at times added all sorts of dogma and traditions to the simple faith that Jesus taught, and to which the faithful have been exhorted to hold fast.

Little wonder that Jesus' teaching encountered strong opposition from the establishment, with all their perks and privileges and vested interests in keeping the system going.

Over four centuries earlier Socrates had made an almost identical challenge against the democratic government of Athens, a challenge that led to his own trial and eventual death.

In 2014 Archbishop Justin Welby, in his Easter Day sermon in Canterbury Cathedral, described Jesus as the most controversial person in history, and his Gospel, when fully understood, is just as controversial today as ever it was. His vision for humanity was centuries ahead of the days in which he lived on Earth, and though not acknowledged, it forms the basis of both the United Nations declaration and the European Convention of Human Rights. The Lord must be horrified by the poverty gap between the rich and the poor, and might well have spoken to many of today's institutional establishments in much the same sort of way as he did to the Scribes and the Pharisees. *(Note 28, Socrates)*

As a consequence he became persona non grata among the religious hierarchy. So what did he do next? He preached to all the 'ordinary' people, people like you and me, not in the synagogue or the temple but in people's homes, at the supper table of some of the Pharisees, and of those to whom the Romans farmed out the task of collecting their taxes, and to the large crowds who began to assemble wherever he went. He took his message of the Kingdom of God which had slowly been maturing during those hidden years well beyond the boundaries of organised religion. He reached out to the pagan world, just as the church of today must reach out to our secular society to help fill the God-hole in a world which for the most part has relegated God to the sidelines.

Matthew tells us that the thing that most struck all those who heard Jesus teaching was that he spoke as one having authority, and not like the Scribes. When the Scribes were asked questions I can picture them searching their pocket books of the law, or saying we'll have to look it up. There were too many laws to remember! Jesus by contrast spoke from the heart. Can you possibly imagine Jesus pausing every two or three minutes to look at his sermon notes?

As Jesus met more and more people he realised that his main vocation was the need to reveal God's love to them and to encourage them to share it with everyone with whom they came into contact. He saw them as sheep without a shepherd. The gospels reveal a tireless programme of preaching and teaching. He also realised the special need to pass on his vision of the Kingdom of God to a close group of followers, those who would become his disciples, and later the Apostles; revealing his gospel of love to the whole world was not something he could do all on his own. He needed their help. He desperately wanted them to understand his vision, but even among them this proved to be a bit of an uphill task. Like the leaders of the synagogue they too had grown up embedded in the law and within the culture of the Jewish faith, avoiding gentiles, who could not even be touched without making yourself ritually unclean. Like Jesus himself, the disciples also had to learn to escape their heritage. To break away from their old traditions required a quantum leap of faith.

That was not easy. They didn't always get it. He often had to explain even the simplest of his parables. He once turned to one of them, Philip, and said "Have you been with me all this time and you still don't understand?" One day looking across the fields while walking with his disciples, Jesus said to them "Don't you have a saying it's still four months until harvest? I tell you, open your eyes and look at the fields. They are already ripe for harvest." In his Gospel, Luke adds "The harvest is great, but the workers are few. So pray to the Lord who is in charge of the harvest; ask him to send more workers into his fields." I believe that today many people outside the Church are searching for a faith that can give more meaning to human existence than the hectic round of so much of what passes for life in our modern world, with all its uncertainties and dangers.

Jesus sent his disciples into a largely hostile, religious pagan world, worshipping many gods and surrounded by superstition. Most people had little real understanding of the universe. Those disciples faced a tremendous challenge, not unlike the challenge facing Christian disciples today and the challenge they face in presenting faith to a mostly secular world. Jesus' vision for humanity has been around for a long time now and reaches across the whole world, but because we have at times disguised it by 'teaching as doctrines the precepts of men' and clouded it by our own theology, instead of being governed by his theology, a lot of the world still does not get it, and not just the secular world; but many of his own disciples still have a lot to learn, as do we all to our dying day.

The Winding Road of Faith

Along the road of our life's journey, some awake to an early awareness of God's presence in childhood. Others, like many of the millions of refugees, find faith while tramping through the desolation of an arid desert; many are challenged by the barrier of a mountain of doubts; still more get lost in the dense fog of despondency and despair. Finding faith is always a challenge in our troubled world.

Faith, above all else, is learning to put our trust in Jesus and his revelation of God's love for all mankind. One can't offer any blueprint for finding faith; no one size of faith ever fits each individual soul. It can come about in so many different ways; through our family and friends, or sometime by a chance encounter with a complete stranger. I first thought of Jesus only as a supremely good man offering the perfect example of how to live a Christian life. But as you progress in faith, eventually you discover that Jesus is leading you into a personal relationship with God, which is what he came to Earth to do. I believe most of us first discover Jesus' humanity long before we grasp any understanding of his divinity. After all, Jesus' first disciples experienced Jesus as a man with whom they formed a close personal relationship in their ordinary day-to-day lives. Gradually he led them to call God their Father, as he did himself. He talked to them about fishing, plucked ears of corn with them as they strayed through the fields, and taught them how to pray. That is how faith works, right among the normality of our daily lives. Over the years our early grasp of faith grows deeper and deeper, before we finally discover that we also are gradually growing into that same wonderful relationship with Jesus as did the disciples themselves.

Jesus revealed God's love, not by giving lectures, using correct orders of worship and insisting on certain beliefs and keeping religious laws, but by living a life of service and ministering to the needs of all people, especially the poor, the sick, the vulnerable, and those who could not help themselves; he calls us all each and every day to follow his example. Jesus also describes the Kingdom of God as being at hand – all around us when we have eyes to see – something which we can all enter right now, something of which I became dimly aware from the moment I first woke up to life in my own personal Garden of Eden.

He also said to his disciples, "The Kingdom of God, the Kingdom of Heaven, is within you." It is how you are within your deepest self, within your thinking, within your heart, but above all within your **soul**. Only a very thin line separates God's Kingdom here on Earth from his Kingdom in Heaven, the line we all one day will have to cross. For very many millions of people, that precious unity of God's Kingdom here on earth with his kingdom in Heaven is frequently shattered by the evil of man's inhumanity to man. That inhumanity brings about not just hell but an *absolute* hell of human suffering here on Earth; the tragedy of wholesale destruction and terrorism and the cruelty inflicted on approximately fifty million refugees, many of whom have seen their loved ones brutally killed and who have lost everything they once called home and find themselves tramping the world with no real certainty of where life is leading them.

All that evil can so easily snuff out the hope that faith can bring to their lives, and often to many of ours as well, leading many to query the very existence of a loving God. Only Faith alone has the spiritual power to triumph over evil, which of itself is transient and possesses no eternal value whatsoever, whereas the heartbroken love that God showers on all humanity revealed to the world by Jesus is eternal. Desmond Tutu, in his book *Made for Goodness*, has this to say: "Whenever you feel victim to all the evil in the world, remember that God is with us in all our perplexity. All that is evil passes away, whereas love is eternal. Whoever would have predicted the end of Apartheid and the dawn of democracy led by a black President?" *(Note 23, Desmond Tutu)*

I have experienced this truth throughout the whole of my life, beginning with the destruction of Nazism at the close of the Second World War, though its ideology still tries to linger. All our East European friends eventually became guests in our home with the demise of the former Soviet Union. The Pol Pot regime was overthrown in Cambodia, as were the evils perpetrated by Idi Amin in Uganda, and here in the UK we now have a Ugandan Archbishop of York. Today's terrorist groups will one day disappear into history, while their victims will be held in eternal memory. Evil possesses no positive value and is transient whereas God is never absent; he is always alongside us sharing in all our perplexity and our pain.

When our faith becomes mature enough for us to enter into the full depth of our Lord's own pain, and the agony of his sorrow at our failure to grasp the simplicity of his vision for humanity, we begin to discover the truth of St. Paul's words that there is absolutely nothing in this world or the world to come, nor in life nor death that can ever separate us from the healing power of God's love.

Amid all the terrible suffering of our world, there are many, like those held prisoner in the Nazi concentration camps during the Second World War, the fearless firemen who perished rescuing people from the Twin Towers, those who volunteer for service in the nation's lifeboats and many more – all of whom were prepared to lay down their lives, not just for their friends, but often for total strangers, just as Jesus himself did when he was crucified. Handel's great Oratorio reminds us that our Redeemer lives, and he underlines this truth in the magnificent music of his Hallelujah Chorus, a melody that lingers in many more heads than just mine. It begins with the triumphant shout of Hallelujah and continues "For the Lord God omnipotent reigneth, and shall reign for ever and ever, King of Kings, and Lord of Lords". It began as musical notes scratched on to a stave before being transformed by orchestras and choirs into the most sublime and awe-inspiring music ever written, music that has reached the whole world. But our shouts of Hallelujah ring hollow if we don't recall how Handel also reminds us that the Lord has borne our griefs, and carried our sorrows; that he was bruised for our iniquities and wounded for our transgressions.

Standing as we all do on the threshold of eternity, the thin line which divides our earthly existence in God's Kingdom here on Earth from our final entry into his Kingdom in Heaven, we must all stand back in awe, wonder and reverence at the privilege of having been given the gift of living in a world which is so full of wonder, though at times also victim to so much evil. By entering God's Kingdom here on Earth we in a sense are already experiencing a foretaste of what faith means when we talk about eternal life; something of far greater value than life going on forever as we know it now.

We can no more imagine what that life will be like than we were able to understand our present existence before we began taking the first faltering steps along the roadmap of our earthly lives. Jesus, by tramping the road of life beside us and living the life of a human being, has the power to restore a sense of purposefulness to all our lives' journeys.

In this chapter we have tried to imagine how Jesus may have grown into his vision of the Kingdom of God, the vision that was to become the driving force behind his public ministry during the last three years of his life on Earth; a vision that was launched when he was first handed the scroll of the prophet Isaiah in the synagogue of his home town of Nazareth. It is important that our last reflections are rooted in scripture, so in conclusion we now turn to a new way of looking at St. John's Gospel. This Gospel, more than any other, enshrines the full depth of God's love revealed by the life and teaching of Jesus as he pursued that vision.

CHAPTER FIFTEEN

SEE THAT YOU LOVE
ONE ANOTHER

A Reflection on St. John's Gospel

Like everyone else, I still wonder what may lie beyond the boundaries of this mortal life. My mind often returns to that young soldier in 1950 who asked "What's going to happen ter me when I dies?" QI, one of my favourite TV programmes, is full of laughs and fun and also more serious information; at this point I have to play one of Stephen Fry's 'Nobody Knows' cards. The honest answer to that young man's question is that we do not know.

But faith can take us a step further. St. John, in the first of his letters in the New Testament, says somewhat cautiously "See what great love the Father has given us. He calls us his children; up to now it's not clear what we shall become, but we know that when he appears we shall be like Him, because we shall see him as He is."

St. John's Gospel is different from all the others. Matthew begins with a long genealogy of unpronounceable biblical names, and is directed towards the Jews. Mark dives straight in – the beginning of the Gospel of Jesus Christ. Luke, the physician and scholar, starts by saying, "There are many people who have tried to write about the things we believe as they received them from those who were eyewitnesses of the words that Jesus spoke; having had perfect understanding from the beginning, it seemed good to me also to set them in order." He does just that, outlining the astonishing activity of Jesus and his disciples, with Jesus continually addressing large crowds and speaking in the synagogues.

John on the other hand writes as an eyewitness. His first letter begins "That which was from the beginning, which we have heard, and seen with our eyes, which we have looked at, and our hands have handled, this we proclaim concerning the word of life." John is telling us that Jesus and his teaching were part of his own experience. He had spent time talking with him, had touched him, travelled with him, listened to him speaking to the crowds, shared meals and fellowship with his family and friends. John's Gospel is a very personal record of Jesus, but hidden within it there also lies a biography of many of the events that formed part of his own life.

In older age you become reflective. You tend to look back as you take walks around the gardens of your remembrance;

you think of the countless number of people whom you have met along your life's journey. John lived to a very old age, perhaps into his eighties. I expect he must have looked back in just the same way. Added to his own personal memories he would have also had access to many of the oral traditions of Jesus' life then in circulation, among them those of Papias, later to become the Bishop of Heiropolis in Asia Minor (Turkey).

Papias is considered to be one of John's disciples, perhaps even his scribe. The tradition that he was his scribe may have come from the fact that Papias was a compiler of the sayings and teachings of Jesus which made up his 'Expositions of the sayings of the Lord'. Unfortunately only fragments of this work have survived. Few as they are, these fragments provide a glimpse into the material then in circulation.

Early church traditions state that John spent the last years of his life at Ephesus, a very sophisticated city in Roman times; a busy trading port and a town of some consequence. Ephesus was the home of the great Temple of Artemis, the Goddess Diana, whom the whole world worshipped according to Demetrius, the silversmith. It drew pilgrims from many countries who bought silver replicas of her to take home as mementos of their visit. Demetrius was afraid his business of selling silver replicas of the goddess was about to be destroyed by Paul's proclaiming that her statue wasn't a god but a mere idol. Paul became involved in a riot. Just like Demetrius, our own cathedral shops still sell all sorts of religious artefacts. Approaching the shrine of the Black Madonna of Czestohova in Poland you are greeted with table upon table of not silver, but plastic Madonnas, crucifixes and Christmas cribs. One can understand the silversmith's anxiety.

In John's day the Temple of Artemis would still have been a fully functional pagan temple. Tourists still flock to Ephesus in their thousands. It is quite an experience to stand among the ruins of that ancient Temple. Artsinoe, Cleopatra's sister and a former ruler of Egypt, nearly defeated the Romans. Later however she was captured and paraded through the streets of Rome. Due to be beheaded, she was given a reprieve and found sanctuary in the Temple of Diana. Later, when Cleopatra became Pharaoh, she had Artsinoe dragged from the sanctuary and murdered on the temple steps.

Tramping the streets of the old city, you can visit the tomb where John is believed to be buried under the dome of what was the Basilica of St. John, and also the church dedicated to Mary, who, the earliest traditions believe, accompanied John to Ephesus. Of course you can't be certain of all these things, but you do know that John and Paul must have often walked the self-same streets as you do, tramping the paving stones leading to Harbour Street.

So now let's take a look at the gospel John wrote; not in the usual scholarly way, comparing text with text and examining other contemporary sources, but in an imaginative way, trying to clothe the skeleton of the Gospel record with the flesh of the everyday life with which its writing would have been surrounded. What we are searching for is not textual correctness, though that has its own importance, but for the message that John's Gospel contains; what it was that prompted John to write his

Gospel in the first place, and of equal importance, the message that it still has for us today.

*****

My desk is frequently littered with notes of waking moments, all scribbled on the backs of envelopes and mixed up with packets of must-sow seeds. I can picture John seated at a table, head in his hands, looking back over his long life and starting to scribble down reflections of his first meeting with Jesus on scraps of papyrus, the equivalent of those 'backs of an envelope', recalling his parables and his tramping with him from village to village. For the wedding in Cana a one-word reminder was sufficient; he was there. He thinks of the meals they shared together, but above all of the Last Supper before Jesus was arrested, beaten and crucified. Pausing, he may have thought of the deep despair the disciples all suffered during Jesus' dying moments and after his crucifixion. It was all just so vivid. His head goes back into his hands for a while. But where to begin? How should he begin the story he has to tell? "How am I to start?"

I have belonged to a writers' club for many years. When starting a new book you look for an arresting first paragraph (or two) that will immediately grasp the reader's attention. That is so important; otherwise the reader will put the book down and pass it by. So John searches, throwing away many false starts. Sometimes he may have got up in the middle of the night to jot down another long-forgotten memory as it flashed into his mind before lapsing forever into the hidden recess from which it had so quickly sprung. Then suddenly one morning in a waking moment another thought flashes into John's head; I know from experience that's often when one's most inspired thoughts arise. He knew his scriptures well. He awakes wondering why on earth he is thinking about the first verse of the Book of Genesis. 'In the beginning God created the Heavens and the Earth...' Then in another blinding flash it comes to him – In the beginning, that's how to start! "In the Beginning was the Word!" That's it. Eureka!

Quill in hand, he begins to write furiously. Word after word just arrives – an experience all writers share, and you write and write till you stop. "In the Beginning was the Word, and the Word was with God, and the Word was God... . and the Word became flesh, and we beheld his glory, the glory as of the only begotten of the Father, full of grace and truth" He had done it. Once he had completed those famous first fourteen verses, the In Principio, he was away, his quill began to flow; he knew just how to continue. That's precisely what happens to writers with a story to tell.

It is significant that the language in which John was writing his Gospel was Greek. At that time Greek was the 'English' of that part of the world, and the word John uses to describe God is 'ὁ λόγος', the very word that Greek philosophers used to describe the overarching reality that lies beyond and above the Earth and keeps the Universe in being. John takes this concept and expands it by saying "In the beginning was the Word, that the Word was with God, and more crucially, that the Word was God. He clothes that vague philosophical concept by describing 'The Word' as God. Amid the many pagan gods by which the Jewish Faith was then surrounded, only the Jews believed in just one God, and for John there was only one Word. Professor R.V.G Tasker used to say to us students in London, "God has many words for many worlds, but God's Word for this world is Jesus." In one of our carols we also sing "Love came down at Christmas, love all lovely love divine"; the Word was made flesh, a little bundle of fragile God-given life, who was to grow up to be the Saviour of the World, and to share the Words of God's love with us all. The birth of each one of us is equally surrounded by risk and mystery. It is a measure of God's great love for all mankind that he took the risk of entrusting the salvation of the world to the birth of a little child. Each of us, including all the world's leaders and statesmen responsible for the government of the nations, needs to remember that we were all once just 'little children'.

Of course language and words evolved long before Jesus was born, but no one as yet had ever revealed the true nature of God as a god of infinite power, love and compassion in quite the same way as Jesus was to do. For the most part men had created their own gods in the image they wanted them to possess; for many of the Jewish writers God was a mighty warrior, similar to Woden, the Viking god of battles; a god of vengeance, always victorious in battle, and always on their side. The Greeks trundled along with the idea of 'The Word' as a synonym for a creator god. Without words even God cannot speak to us, though there are moments in all of our more personal relationships when words are often unnecessary, or can even get in the way. Judas betrayed Jesus not with a word but with a kiss. The greatest wonder of all is that through the life of Jesus God speaks to us all in the only language that the whole world can understand – the language of our common humanity – revealing to us what it means to be truly human; or as St.

Thomas Aquinas, that great 13th century scholar, puts it in his masterpiece the *Summa Theologica*: "God became man so that mankind may become divine". In the life of Jesus we see the full measure of what it means to be truly human.

When politicians hide the truth, or the managers of global companies are caught fiddling their accounts, when we ourselves are caught shoplifting or even embezzling charitable funds – and it does happen – we often use the expression "Oh well they're only human after all". Using the word 'human' in this way as some sort of excuse is a total prostitution of its true meaning. To be fully human is to be caring, to have respect for others, to be like Christ. The brutality, greed and violence with which so much of our modern world is afflicted is essentially subhuman.

So when John began his Gospel by saying 'In the beginning was the WORD' he is describing God as the supreme Being whose creative power gives life to everything, and who above all else surrounds us with his love, and who has revealed his true nature as a god of infinite love and compassion through the life and teaching of Jesus. We once asked our elder son what he used to do at school on Sunday afternoons. His reply stunned us. "I just Be." I believe that the secret of our life in this world, and maybe for Eternity, is above all else to learn how to BE. It is significant that we always describe ourselves as 'human beings', never as 'human doings.' Being is what gives meaning to life. Without being we would not exist.

*****

We must now put philosophising to one side. In his gospel

after his introduction, John moves straight to John the Baptist, who came to prepare the way for Jesus. John the Baptist was Jesus' cousin. Perhaps in their earlier years the two young boys had played together, and they may well have kept in touch as they grew up. Jesus was well aware of John's own ministry beside the river Jordan, where John was confronting all the errors of the Jewish nation and their elders, and inviting his hearers to change their way of life and make a new beginning. The authorities in Jerusalem felt threatened and sent some of their teachers and lawyers to see what he was up to. They challenged him and asked by what authority he was baptising.

Some time later Jesus visits his cousin and presents himself for baptism. John tells everyone that he is unworthy even to unloose his sandals and proclaims Jesus as the Messiah. The whole Jewish nation was looking for a 'saviour', someone to deliver them from the tyranny of Roman rule. Having completed his description of Jesus' baptism, John's second chapter is of all things about a wedding. "And the third day there was a marriage in Cana of Galilee." Why does a wedding feature so early on in his Gospel story? It must have been a wedding of very special significance.

Thinking about all this one morning in one of those waking moments I have already described, an outrageous idea flew into my mind. Why was it so important to put a wedding at the very beginning of his second chapter? How did John know so much about this particular wedding, which only appears in his Gospel and nowhere else, and in so much detail? Could it have been the wedding of a close family member or, an even more outrageous thought, could it even perhaps have been his own wedding? That may be a step too far, but we know that Peter was married, as were some of the other disciples; marriage in the Jewish society of those days was the norm. But of one thing we can be certain: it was a real family affair. Jesus and his mother and his disciples were all there.

As the reception wears on the wine begins to run out. The master of ceremonies, the 'best man,' is desperate and approaches Jesus' mother.

"Mary, please ask your son if he can help," she tells Jesus.

"What's that got to do with you, woman?" he replies gruffly, almost a rebuke.

Mary says to the MC, "Don't take any notice of him. I know my son. He's like that sometimes. Just do whatever he says."

Jesus orders the servants to fill some stone water pots to the brim and take some to the MC. Then perhaps he could have gone to him and said "Sorry to hear there's no wine, but you've all had more than enough to drink already. Look at you all! Let's make do with water." A recent BBC documentary on St. John showed the water visibly *changing colour* while being poured. That beggars belief. Of course, nobody knows what actually happened; I don't believe for one moment that John's belief in God's love was founded on a 'sign' that would seem to override the natural laws that govern the universe, and a temptation that Jesus himself had earlier rejected in the wilderness. John's faith, above all else, was based on his personal experience of Jesus, and the beginning of his understanding of his vision of the

Kingdom of God, and of the power of the Holy Spirit revealed by Jesus in the life he lived.

It doesn't really matter whether we believe Jesus changed water into wine or not, or are simply agnostic, that part of the story may even have been a later embellishment. The leading Jewish teachers of the day were always asking Jesus for 'a sign from Heaven' to confirm his authority, and all the pagan religions based a lot of their beliefs on magic and signs. What we do know is that this was a family wedding in Cana, and that there must have been something very special about it for John to have included it in his Gospel so early on. This is a very personal story, so personal as to be a part of John's own life story, his own biography.

Just before his account of the wedding, we hear how John was talking to two of his own disciples. Those two men in all probability had already been baptised by him and were later to become part of Jesus' specially chosen group of twelve disciples. As Jesus approached, John said to them "Here comes the Messiah." They listened to what Jesus had to say and then as he left they followed him at a distance. Jesus, aware of their presence, turned around and asked them what they wanted.

"Master, where do you live?" they asked.

"Come and see," Jesus replied, and invited them to his lodgings.

They stayed the night with him because it was getting late, the 'tenth hour', the writer of the Gospel says. Then he continues "One of the two who followed him was Andrew, who the next day went to tell his brother Peter." But the writer never tells us who 'the other' disciple was. I can only believe that it was John himself; he is once more deliberately hiding his own identity so that Jesus remains the main character in the Gospel story. Who else could have remembered the precise time at which they arrived?

It all fits together as John continues to record more and more details of his own life within his telling of the Gospel. Towards the end of his Gospel story there are two more events that confirm this. At the Last Supper Jesus announces that one of them is going to betray him. The disciples were troubled, wondering who it might be. The writer then tells us that 'the disciple whom Jesus loved' was leaning his head on Jesus' shoulder; Peter reclining next to him whispers "Ask him who it is." He did and Jesus whispered in reply "It's the one to whom I shall give this piece of bread." He then dips the bread in the broth and passes it to Judas.

None of the others knew what was going on; they thought Judas was being sent to buy food for the Passover Feast. Only the 'disciple whom Jesus loved' knew what was happening, and perhaps Peter. All scholars agree that the 'disciple whom Jesus loved' was John, but once more he does not mention himself by name. This was one of his closest memories of Jesus, like my memory of Christine on her hospital bed who asked me how I was, and who died the very next day. It stayed with him all his life long.

Then perhaps most significant of all is the moment when Jesus is arrested and taken away to Annas, and then Caiaphas the High Priest. Simon Peter followed Jesus and so did another disciple who was known to the High Priest. He spoke a word in the ear of the girl who kept the door and brought in Peter. They both must have heard the accusations against Jesus. Who else could have been 'the other disciple' who gave so intimate an account of the proceedings against Jesus? It could once more only have been John himself.

Jesus is eventually condemned to death. The next morning he is led out to Golgotha to be crucified. Among the words from the cross as he lay dying there was a last request. "Now there stood by the cross of Jesus his mother, his mother's sister, Mary the wife of Cleopas, and Mary Magdalene. When Jesus saw his mother with 'the disciple whom he loved' standing beside her, he said to his mother, "Behold your son." Turning to the disciple he said, "Behold your mother". From that moment John took Mary into his own home.

Mary's whole life must have been haunted by the danger in which Jesus often placed himself. Her presence at the foot of the cross is the supreme example of motherly devotion. Amidst all his physical pain, his sense of abandonment and his spiritual trauma, he found time to speak to his mother and commend her to John's care. If ever there was a moment when his divine mission and his total humanity were joined together it was those precious words from the Cross. Those poignant words of Jesus are only recorded by St. John; the most significant proof of all of the very personal relationship that existed between John and Jesus.

Then after the Sabbath is over, Mary Magdalene goes to the tomb where Joseph and Nicodemus had taken Jesus' body after his crucifixion. Horror stricken, she finds it empty and runs to tell Peter and the other disciple whom Jesus loved. They run to the tomb together and 'the other disciple' gets there first and finds it is just as Mary had said. But it is Peter who then enters the tomb.

In this Gospel we also have an account of Jesus' conversation with Pilate. How did that become known and recorded in John's Gospel? Not everyone had access to Pilate. We read that after Jesus had died Joseph of Arimathea went to Pilate to ask for Jesus' body. Both he and Nicodemus were respected members of the Sanhedrin, the Rabbinical Court, before which Jesus was brought for trial, and were sympathetic towards Jesus. Joseph was a wealthy man and must have had access to Pilate. It is not too far-fetched to think that when Joseph asked permission to take Jesus' body for burial the two men talked for some time about the events that had just taken place. We read in John that Pilate, hard man that he was, became agitated, and wanted to release him. He had found no fault in him. Perhaps to make himself feel more comfortable with what he had allowed to happen Pilate unburdens himself to Joseph? Under Roman law Jesus should have gone free. He had given way and broken the law because he was afraid for his position should yet another Jewish riot ensue. So later Joseph passes on the account of his meeting with Pilate to John. It all becomes so real. How else could John have recorded what he writes about Pilate?

John closes this chapter with these words, the reason that prompted him to write his Gospel in the first place: "Jesus did many other signs in the presence of his disciples which are not written in this book, but what I have written has been done so that you might believe that Jesus is the Christ and that believing in him you might have life through his name." This is the natural conclusion, but the last chapter, thought to be a later addition, contains these words: "There are many other things that Jesus did which if they were written one by one I suppose even the world itself would not be able to contain the books that should be written." Imagine how you would have felt had you lived through all those events. As you read this particular Gospel you feel that John is there sharing his own story, as well as the story of Jesus' life. This is not true of the other three Gospels. They are written more in reporters' language. John writes as an eyewitness, and with deep spiritual insight.

There are all sorts of scholarly arguments about the authorship of the Gospel that bears John's name. I cannot lay claim to such levels of scholarship, but however the final text came into its present form one instinctively feels that the story told in this Gospel has at its core the observations and experiences of someone who was very close to Jesus. Perhaps more important still is its message of hope for those of us living in today's troubled and hectic world, the hope that prompted its writing in the first place – Jesus' vision that all mankind might grow into the fullness of our humanity as we grow in our knowledge of God's great love and compassion.

Probably some time later, towards the very end of his life, John puts pen to parchment again to write his letters, the first of which leads us towards his final 'theology'. In chapter four John writes "Beloved, let us love one another, because love is of God", emphasising that love is God's most important gift to all mankind. He then reminds us that this love is revealed most clearly in the life of Jesus, whose last commandment to his disciples was that they should love one another. What he says here differs from how he began his Gospel; there he was trying to piece together the philosophy of it all. Having watched all his fellow disciples die, others suffering persecution and some becoming martyrs, among them his own brother, John comes to the conclusion that beyond all knowledge and understanding, sharing Jesus' message of love and compassion with all those whom we meet as we tramp the road of our life's journey is much more important; a message today's world needs to grasp over and over again.

There is an early tradition that when John could no longer walk to church he was carried there, and that when he could no longer preach he just greeted everyone, saying "Little children, love one another." This is the final message of an old man who had 'handled the Word of Life', and a conclusion with which another old man is in total agreement!

Throughout my life I have been supported by that vast cloud of witnesses who have travelled the road of life beside me, and my vocation to share God's love has been confirmed over and over again, sometimes during the bleakest moments of my journeying. Finally the wheel of my vocation came full circle on that one particular night when recovering from major heart surgery I was transported to the shores of a vast ocean and heard a voice saying to me "I have given you a great deal of love; there is far more than you need for yourself. You must share the rest with others."

Whatever stage you may have reached on your life's journey, whether you are a bit like my Birmingham painter wondering quite what to believe, or perhaps with no belief, or more like our young Russian friend who pulled a Bible out of his pocket to declare his faith in God, I hope that the stories of some of the countless number of people who have led me on my way and deepened my faith may also lead you to a deeper understanding of the depth of God's great love for all humanity.

Jesus called his disciples his friends and promised them life in all its full abundance, an abundance we can all experience as we learn to live richly towards God and share that love with all those whom we meet as we continue to tramp the road of our earthly pilgrimage.

NOTES AND APPENDICES

Note 1: I was actually born at 27 Blackfriars Road, Salford at 1.30 am on December 7th 1930. The house still stands. My father was in charge of St. Saviour's church, which today has an outreach programme to those with learning problems. The walls of the north side of the church are covered in one massive War Memorial, where there may be upwards of well over a hundred names of young unemployed men who were drafted into the army during the Great War.

Note 2: John Naylor died in September 2015. On our very last visit we prayed together and for the first time for many weeks he joined in the whole of the Lord's Prayer, saying the closing petitions without any guidance.

Note 3: Bishop Barnes, *The Rise of Christianity*, 1947. Bishop Ernest Barnes was born in Altrincham on April 1st,

All Fool's Day, some would say appropriately! He was a "son" of Birmingham. In 1892 he entered King Edward VI Grammar School as a foundation scholar, winning a scholarship for mathematics to Trinity College, Cambridge. While at Trinity he was President of the Union and excelled at mathematics. He published no less than 28 academic journal articles between 1897 and 1910. main research area was with the theory of functions. He was ordained deacon by the Bishop of London, Winnington-Ingram, on 25 May 1902. As Barnes was a Cambridge don, he was able to present himself for ordination without any theological study. In 1915 he became the Master of the Temple, the incumbent of the Temple Church, before being appointed a Canon of Westminster. On October 2nd 1924 he became Bishop of Birmingham. In his controversial book *The Rise of Christianity*, his thinking was aimed at the remodelling of Christian theology by taking account of all his scientific knowledge. Far from being foolish, it still makes very interesting reading to this day.

Note 4: Michael Pye - *The Edge of the World*. A conventional view of history has the Dark Ages beginning with the decline of Rome in the 400s and the lights not coming back on until the Renaissance a millennium later. But Michael Pye questions this, and in the 'Gospel according to Heliand' describes how an early Saxon chief made the gospel story contemporary to convert his subject to the Christian Faith

Note 5: Steve Hilton (Former advisor to David Cameron) *Designing a World Where People come First*. An interesting example of purple prose! "Inhibiting globalisation would mean closing ourselves off and moving backwards: less connected, less empathetic, less human. Emotionally I sometimes feel like yelling: 'Enough! Let's stop these out-of-control global corporations and faceless money-shuffling plutocrats gambling with everyone else's savings in a luxury casino called the financial markets and go back to a blissful prelapsarian state where we all just grow our own produce and trade with each other in a charming local economy!' But it's not really possible. It is not rational. It would do more harm than good." See also Children and Technology.

Note 6: *Sapiens, A Brief History of Mankind*, by Yuval Noah Harari. Yuval Harari lectures at the Hebrew university in Jerusalem and traces the history of Homo Sapiens from the earliest hunter gatherers, through the farming 'revolution' and the industrial revolution showing how each group struggled against the other to obtain supremacy, before leading to the technical revolution of which we are a continuing part today. He points out that the normally invisible electro-magnetic waves are present in all our modern gadgetry like televisions, digital cameras, cellphones and computers. In *Homo Deus*, Yuval Harari's sequel to *Sapiens*, Yuval argues that man is progressing so fast that he will soon have so much control over the planet that one day death itself will be eliminated. Under the heading *The Last Days of Death*, he writes: 'In the 21st Century humans are likely to make a serious bid for immortality.' Later he admits that this may be a long way off, but tested by his own logic such an argument falls down completely.

Note 7: David Eagleman, neuro scientist, writer and presenter of the six-hour television series entitled 'The Brain'.

Note 8: Professor Keith Ward, Author of *A Vision to Pursue*, Regius Professor of Divinity at the University of Oxford, 1991 to 2004, writes: "We have now begun to live in the Third Stage of religious thought and practice. After the First Stage of local and limited religions came the Second Stage, bringing the great scriptural traditions, with their holy texts which claimed final and universal truth. But the rise of the historical consciousness and the findings of science have brought a crisis for those traditions, and beyond the crisis the Third Stage is on its way, transcending the second as the second transcended the first".

Note 9: Josephus, Jewish historian. He initially fought against the Romans as head of Jewish forces in Galilee, until surrendering in 67 CE to Roman forces led by Vespasian. Vespasian decided to keep Josephus as a slave and interpreter. After Vespasian became Emperor in 69 CE, he granted Josephus his freedom, at which time Josephus assumed the Emperor's family name of Flavius and he was granted Roman citizenship. He became an advisor and friend of Vespasian's son Titus, serving as his translator. Titus led the Siege of Jerusalem, which resulted in the city's destruction and the looting and destruction of Herod's Temple. Josephus recorded Jewish history, with special emphasis on the first century CE. Though he recounts the history of the world from a Jewish perspective his works provide valuable insight into first century Judaism and the background of Early Christianity.

Note 10: Confucius was a Chinese teacher, editor, politician, and philosopher of the Spring and Autumn period of Chinese history. The philosophy of Confucius emphasized personal and governmental morality, correctness of social relationships, justice and sincerity. His followers competed successfully with many other schools during the Hundred Schools of Thought era, only to be suppressed in favour of the Legalists during the Qin Dynasty. Following the victory of Han over Chu after the collapse of Qin, Confucius's thoughts received official sanction and were further developed into a system known in the West as Neo-Confucianism.

Note 11: G.K. Chesterton, an English writer, poet, philosopher, dramatist, journalist, orator, lay theologian, biographer, and literary and art critic. *Life of St. Francis.*

Note 12: Robert Bell, *Love Wins.* Robert Holmes "Rob" Bell Jr. (born August 23, 1970) is an American author, speaker and former pastor. Bell was the founder of Mars Hill Bible Church located in Grandville, Michigan, which he pastored until 2012. Under his leadership Mars Hill was one of the fastest-growing churches in America.

Note 13: Malcolm Billings, *The Cross and the Crescent,* A highly respected scholar in both Moslem and Christian circles.

Note 14: *History of Islam* by Montgomery Watt. William Montgomery Watt (14 March 1909 – 24 October 2006) was a Scottish historian, an Emeritus Professor in Arabic and

Islamic studies at the University of Edinburgh. Watt was one of the foremost non-Muslim interpreters of Islam in the West, and an enormously influential scholar in the field of Islamic studies, a much-revered name for many Muslims all over the world. Watt's comprehensive biography of the Islamic prophet Muhammad, *Muhammad at Mecca* (1953) and *Muhammad at Medina* (1956), are considered to be classics in the field.

Note 15: Stephen Hawking is the former Lucasian Professor of Mathematics at the University of Cambridge and author of the international bestseller *A Brief History of Time*.

Note 16: Fred Taban is a South Sudanese priest and a former student at the All Nations College in Herefordshire.

Note 17: *Sense and Non-sense*, Cyril Argentine Alington, 1949. Dean Alington argues that everything we experience in life is governed both by sense (sensual perception) and non-sense (spiritual perception) These thoughts are reflected by Immanuel Kant, the famous German philosopher who expresses them in more philosophical language.

Note 18: *The God Delusion* by Richard Dawkins challenges traditional Christianity and calls on all Christians to re-examine their own faith. Since completing my response to *The God Delusion*, ideas are now circulating stating Richard's admission that "Christianity is much better than Islam". He even concedes that Christianity may actually be our best defence against aberrant forms of religion that threaten the world.

Note 19: Jon Snow is an English journalist and television presenter, currently employed by ITN. He is best known as the longest-running presenter of Channel 4 News, which he has presented since 1989.

Note 20: Kate Raworth is an Oxfam senior researcher, author of *Doughnut Economics*, and a Senior Visiting Research Associate and lecturer at Oxford University's Environmental Change Institute.

Note 21: Barrow and Silk, *The Left Hand of Creation*. A philosophy of creation.

Note 22: Alison Morgan, *The Wild Gospel*. The Revd Dr Alison Morgan is a well-known author and speaker. Alison has a PhD from Cambridge University and prior to her ordination into the Church of England in 1996 worked as a university lecturer.

Note 23: Desmond Tutu - *In God's Hands*. Desmond Tutu, a very familiar face on television, was the first black Archbishop of Cape Town and Bishop of the Church of the Province of Southern Africa (now the Anglican Church of Southern Africa). Tutu's admirers see him as a great man who, since the demise of apartheid, has been active in the defence of human rights and uses his high profile to campaign for the oppressed.

Note 24: Lise Kauraisa, hospital nurse – see letter at end

Note 25: Corrie Boom, Author of *Tramp for the Lord*, was a Dutch watchmaker and Christian who, along with her father and family members, helped many Jews escape the Nazi Holocaust during World War II by hiding them in her closet. She was imprisoned in a concentration camp for her actions.

Note 26: Kenneth E. Bailey, author of *Jesus Through Middle Eastern Eyes*. This scholar of the Middle East provides a detailed background to Jesus address to the members of the Nazareth synagogue, quoting contemporary sources he points out that even in those days Israel was trying to expand its settlements in the Gentile town of Nazareth.

Note 27: *Jesus Wept (p.345)*, a poem by the author portraying Jesus looking out over the city of Jerusalem from the Mount of Olives. Drawn from the N. Testament it also reflects what he sees today.

Note 28: The Ancient Greeks triumphed in bodily perfection, whereas Socrates proclaimed that the mind was more beautiful than that of the body. (He himself apparently was rather ugly!) For him the soul, the essence of our Being, was the greatest treasure we all possess. Anything that damaged our soul was to be rejected. It was better to suffer evil than to inflict it which left a stain on your own soul. He posed a threat to traditional religious knowledge, and to the form of Greek democracy of his day, where the final judgment of those convicted of offences was determined by a jury of 500 ordinary citizens chosen at random, the system that condemned him to death. He claimed that Democracy doesn't work unless organised by educated people. His teaching was widely known during the time of Christ and Jesus may himself have been influenced by the Socratic tradition, which in places bears considerable similarity.

JESUS WEPT
By Francis Chadwick

He stood silently on the Mount of Olives,
chickens scratching among the fallen fruit
He looked over the city and wept
His eyes wandered to the temple,
a priest scurried among the money changers
pigeons scattered in flight.

He saw Moses dashing his tablets of stone to the ground
Jeremiah was crying from the depth of a hidden well
A Roman soldier brutally pushed aside some children
Further afield his gaze fell on Golgotha
and the corpses recently crucified
retching his heart of love.

If only men would understand
the things that belong to their peace.
Father ,why are they so blind?

No pain sears more cruelly
than that of unrequited love
His spurned vision is torn, leaving gaping wounds
jagged wounds
clogging the pounding arteries of a broken heart.

O Jerusalem, Jerusalem, if only you understood
the things that belong to your peace
But no! You stone your prophets
You rob the poor....

A chick brushed his sandal
His eyes turned downwards
his gaze fell upon little bundles of life
exploring their mothers scratching
He looked at them with love
and once again looked back towards the city

He wept
Deep pulsating tears
Bitter tears of anger
mingled with the myrrh of love
How many times
I would have gathered your children together
as a hen gathers her brood under her wings
But you refuse the things that belong to your peace

He still weeps over the city of Jerusalem
The Temple he knew is no more
An ugly new wall strains his searching eyes
He retreads his path of pain
along the Via Dolorosa.

But now his gaze moves further away
To Auschwitz
To the killing fields of Cambodia

To the legless corpse of a child in the city of Baghdad
the face still racked in pain
To the ravaged forests of the Amazon
To the collapsing towers of the Trade Centre
To the bloodied hand of the prisoner
languishing in guilt in a Rwandan jail
To the desert sand baking spilt blood
amid the rape of Darfur
To those dispossessed
by the blindness of market forces and unfair trade.

He is silent amid the silence of the olives
He weeps
If only you understood the things that belong to your peace!
He weeps
Deep pulsating tears
bitter tears of anger
mingled with the myrrh of love.

Then his gaze fell on me
Piercing, questioning, but full of that same love.

I wept.

Lise Kauraisa's letter
Bristol, 21 April 2010

Dear Francis,

Thank you the letter and it is really good to hear from you. I wanted to wish all the best before I left that Saturday, but the nursing staff were busy.

Thank you for your blessing that morning. As I didn't tell you I was very stressed that morning of things happening to my life. My young sister tells me I should work on my faith and God will be with me in sad and good days. In so many ways your blessings put a smile on my face.

I am happy you are doing well and there is someone caring for you at home as you just had a big operation and again I wish you a full recovery.

I am so glad you enjoy your stay in Namibia. Yes I do know Abdul Azeez. Here is his email
address...

Sorry for the poor English and grammar. I hope you will understand the letter.

Take good care of yourself and greeting to your wife Jill.

From: Lise Kauraisa